THE MIGRATION OF WORKERS
IN THE UNITED KINGDOM
AND THE EUROPEAN COMMUNITY

The Migration of Workers in the United Kingdom and the European Community

W. R. BÖHNING

Published for the
Institute of Race Relations, London
by
OXFORD UNIVERSITY PRESS
LONDON   NEW YORK   TORONTO
1972

Oxford University Press, Ely House, London W.1.

GLASGOW NEW YORK TORONTO MELBOURNE WELLINGTON
CAPE TOWN SALISBURY IBADAN NAIROBI LUSAKA ADDIS ABABA
DELHI CALCUTTA MADRAS KARACHI LAHORE DACCA
KUALA LUMPUR SINGAPORE HONG KONG TOKYO

ISBN 0 19 218403 2

© Institute of Race Relations, 1972

Printed in Great Britain by
Willmer Brothers Limited, Birkenhead

To
David Stephen

Foreword

The ceremony at Brussels in which Britain with other candidate-countries acceded to the European Economic Community represents a most significant step into a new era. Although so much has been agreed in detail, it is in many ways 'a Leap in the Dark'. Probably nothing has been less evaluated and quantified than the changes which will occur in the movement of peoples. The EEC has witnessed an unprecedented demand for labour within its boundaries. It has evolved a code of regulations which lay down common practices for the recruitment and employment of industrial labour. So far, in almost nineteenth-century styles, the whole emphasis has been upon the needs of the employers. Carlyle's 'cash nexus' has been the tie that binds together German or Dutch industrialists and Italian, Turkish, and North African workers. The so-called guest workers have been treated—and often well treated—as units of production, to be brought in, and moved out, according to the curve of production.

Britain, with all its failings, has regarded people from overseas seeking work in our island as immigrants (we have thousands of temporary European workers in our midst, but for most purposes we ignore them). Because these immigrants have been characterized as a 'problem', and a great deal of political mileage has been made out of this problem, our European neighbours—soon to be our supranational partners—believe that there is a disease in Britain which may infect them when we come in. Fantasies are not wholly confined to the British Isles, and the vision of a horde of Sikhs and Pakistanis disembarking at Calais and the Hook of Holland, waving their British passports, has already been created in many

European minds. Equally (as shown in the following pages), the British are almost as confused about the prospect of Italians flooding our sagging labour markets.

Roger Böhning's book will set the record straight. Few other volumes of comparable size have placed so much information within a framework of detailed analysis. Its first contribution is to introduce West Europeans and British to each other, as it were, through a careful examination of comparative practices and procedures. Between the European Commission and the member countries there is a tension, as yet not fully realized because not fully tested. As yet, the member countries retain the capacity to hold back the Commission to the limits which they, individually, are prepared to go. The addition of Britain as a major 'host' country along with France and Germany can only add to the difficulty of operating a kind of 'highest common factor' European policy. And the social and political implications of millions of people from the Third World living in Western Europe as an 'under class' have not yet even been recognized.

Roger Böhning takes us up to the starting-line of entry into Europe, and looks beyond. He does not attempt to assess all the implications of the unfolding situation, but he definitely does provide the essential start-line for any investigation into the formation of a 'Europe of Peoples'.

The Institute is indebted to Roger Böhning for carrying out this study at a time when he had many commitments, and for delivering it at such an opportune moment. We are also grateful to the study group, under the chairmanship of Lord Trevelyan, which first got to grips with many aspects of migration and settlement in Europe. The Institute is interested in sponsoring other studies of the causes and consequences of migration from the Third World into Europe.

Institute of Race Relations   Hugh Tinker
    January 1972

Contents

PART TWO
THE FUTURE DEVELOPMENT OF THE EEC
FREE MOVEMENT OF LABOUR SYSTEM AND
THE SUPPLY AND DEMAND SITUATION
IN THE MAIN COUNTRIES

PART THREE
BRITAIN'S ACCESSION TO THE EEC SYSTEM
OF FREEDOM OF MOVEMENT AND THE
FUTURE OF LABOUR MIGRATION
ACROSS THE CHANNEL

List of Tables

NOTE: The tables in this book have all been reproduced from working documents

Acknowledgements

In spring 1970 a study group was convened by Professor H. Tinker at the Institute of Race Relations with the aim of examining migratory patterns in the EEC and the UK, policies and practices relating to immigration, and the probable repercussions of Britain's entry into the EEC on those patterns, policies, and practices. The study group comprised people from public life, journalists, managers, academics —and two migrant workers, Mrs. G. Castles and myself, who were members of the group in an academic capacity, and who could contribute little of the experience of typical immigrants in Europe as we were most atypical in respect of colour, status, etc. Under the chairmanship of Lord Trevelyan we steered through the murky waters of the housing and working conditions of immigrants in Europe and through the tricky waters of the immigration policies here and on the Continent. My thanks are due to all members of this study group for their various contributions. If some of the participants do not recognize their own contributions in this book, then it is due to the fact that Professor H. Tinker encouraged me to write it as an autonomous effort and not as a summary report. In fact, during the last eighteen months there have been a number of new developments—of which the Immigration Act 1971 is only one—which require the whole book to be written in a greatly enlarged context.

My special thanks go to Professor H. Tinker without whose encouragement I would never have put aside my other work to write this book.

I am likewise most grateful to Messrs. J. Geldens and J. Werquin of the Free Movement of Workers Division of the Brussels Commission, who generously gave of their time and intimate knowledge earlier this year when David Stephen and I went to Brussels to explore some of the lesser known aspects of the EEC's policy in this field as part of the preparations for this book.

This book is dedicated to David Stephen and the great work he does at the Runnymede Trust, especially as regards informing the British public, majority and minorities, about the facts and the prospects of Britain's entry into the EEC in the sphere of immigration.

Centre for Research in the Social Sciences   W. R. BÖHNING
   University of Kent at Canterbury
November 1971

Note on References

In this work, references to sources appear in an abbreviated form giving the name of the author or editor, or the title of the work, the date of publication, and page numbers in parenthesis. Readers are referred to the Bibliography for full references.

The following abbreviations are used:
   BEC = *Bulletin of the European Communities*
   CEC = Commission of the European Communities
   HC Deb. = House of Commons, Parliamentary Debates, Official
      Report
   HL Deb. = House of Lords, Parliamentary Debates, Official Report
   JOCE = *Journal Officiel des Communautés Européenes*
   KEG = Kommission der Europäischen Gemeinschaften

I

Introduction

This book is about the migration of workers in the European Economic Community (EEC) and in this country. In order not to diffuse the subject, I leave aside the migration of self-employed and professional people, the workings of the Communities in the social and labour sphere, and the Social Fund and vocational training policy of the EEC. Similarly, I am not concerned with the effects of Britain's entry on labour law or industrial relations. I want to examine the patterns of contemporary labour migration on the Continent and here, their political, economic, and social determinants, and their likely future developments on Britain's entrance into the Common Market.

One of the main objectives is simply to fill two gaps of information. Very little is known in this country about the continental countries' concept and experience of labour immigration. Even less is known about what the Treaty of Rome terms 'freedom of movement for workers'. The former is due to the pressing adjustment problems of coloured immigrants here and the seemingly easy comparability with the situation in the United States. The latter is quite inexplicable, not least for a Government which, when still in opposition and since coming into power, has done a fair amount of research into various other aspects of the EEC such as agriculture and finance. When one reads through the various stages of the Immigration Bill 1971, in which the possible repercussions of entry into the EEC are mentioned, one is astounded by the lack of information and the amount of wrong information, little of which can be attributed to tactical political designs. When David Stephen and I published our information pamphlet *The EEC and the Migration of Workers*[1] (Böhning and Stephen 1971a) we gained the impression that for one reason or another the Home Office, in particular, did not seem to have done its homework. The most likely reason for negligence is a misunderstanding of the real nature of the EEC system; and the reason for this becomes clear when one hears the Home Secretary say during the Committee Stage of the Immigration Bill that immigration is one thing and migration of workers another and that our *im*migration regime is not affected by *migration* of workers from EEC countries. Whether the difference was seen in legal or conceptual terms, it will become clear from this book that social reality does not make such a differentiation.

Lack of information or wrong information is, of course, not the privilege of governments. The Labour Party's background document on the Common Market for presentation to the annual conference in Brighton in September 1971 boldly states that free movement of labour is one of the 'firm aims of the Commission' and should be 'negotiated away'—when the author must have known that it is a very firm reality which cannot be negotiated away. Even such eager informants as *The Times* displayed at least partially wrong advertisements on hoardings in various parts of the country in the autumn of 1971, asking the rhetorical question: 'Do you know that the Associate Members of the Common Market—like Greece and Turkey—do not have the advantages of free movement of labour?'—when they must have known (a) that Greece would have enjoyed these advantages from 1974 onwards had not the EEC frozen its relations with Greece since the take-over by the Colonels, and (b) that Turkey will be drawn into the ambit of the free movement system in 1976.[2]

Therefore, this book starts with a description of the present EEC system of free movement of labour (Chapter 2) and later examines the more relevant aspects of its envisaged future development (6). Following the discussion of the constitutional aspect is a description of the history of labour immigration into and among the Six, some other European countries, and Britain since 1958, i.e. since the Treaty of Rome came into effect. In Chapter 3 the immigration of coloured workers into France and the Netherlands is considered in some detail as it constitutes the only comparable case to Britain's

[1] This is an annotated version of the pertinent EEC legislation.
[2] Incidentally, the Department of Employment *Gazette* of July 1971 (p. 609) carried the same unqualified statement as *The Times* advertisements.

'colour and citizenship' problem. A large number of absolute figures are included in tables, indicating the range of regular statistics available, so as to give future research a useful data basis and a basis for evaluation. This is followed by an excursus on the dynamics of migration streams from low-wage to high-wage economies which permits one to put into proper perspective some of the misconceptions about contemporary labour migration. Chapter 5 attempts to establish, on the basis of the data given in Chapter 3, whether the gradual freeing of movement has had a significant effect on the migratory pattern in the Community—this being the so-called free movement effect.

In Chapter 7 the socio-demographic background since 1950 and the projected development up to 1980 is examined for each of the five main Community countries and for Britain in order to locate likely imbalances of labour supply and demand within and among these countries which could give rise to future labour movements. This discussion is rounded off by a short evaluation of the economic prospects, in which Germany and Britain are focused upon as the two countries between which significant future labour movements seem likely.

In the final section the repercussions of Britain's entry into the EEC will be discussed in detail, firstly, as regards the legal and political problems unsolved at the time of writing, and secondly, as regards the likely size and direction of cross-Channel movements. The latter point, specifically the possibility of an increase in the number of EEC nationals coming to Britain, is of course a subject which has attracted much attention and emotion from every quarter: from left and right, informed and uninformed, men in the street and political leaders—with the exception, perhaps, of those pro-Marketeers who talk about it in rather apologetic terms and never without mentioning that 'even on the Continent' the volume of intra-Community movements has been declining. It is in order here to survey briefly Britain's official and popular attitude to the development of the EEC system of freedom of movement.

When Mr. Macmillan's Government first applied for membership, it only reserved its position on Northern Ireland as far as free movement of labour was concerned, a question then in its fairly innocuous infancy stage (see Chapter 2). But the TUC would have none of this. In a memorandum of the General Council submitted to the Lord Privy Seal in 1962, it declared that it was unable to accept the provisions of the Treaty, i.e. Articles 48 and 49, which set out the political and legal basis of free movement between member states.[3] It regarded the existing British system as reasonable and the possibility that EEC workers could have priority over Commonwealth workers as deplorable. Mr. Heath denied the latter possibility, referring to the Treaty of Rome, and saw no reason for doing away with Articles 48 and 49 because such provisions were

[3] Article 48

1. Freedom of movement for workers shall be secured within the Community by the end of the transitional period at the latest.

2. Such freedom of movement shall entail the abolition of any discrimination based on nationality between workers of the Member States as regards employment, remuneration and other conditions of work and employment.

3. It shall entail the right, subject to limitations justified on grounds of public policy, public security or public health:

(a) to accept offers of employment actually made;

(b) to move freely within the territory of Member States for this purpose;

(c) to stay in a Member State for the purpose of employment in accordance with the provisions governing the employment of nationals of that State laid down by law, regulation or administrative action;

(d) to remain in the territory of a Member State after having been employed in that State, subject to conditions which shall be embodied in implementing regulations to be drawn up by the Commission.

4. The provisions of this Article shall not apply to employment in the public service.

Article 49

As soon as this Treaty enters into force, the Council shall, acting on a proposal from the Commission and after consulting the Economic and Social Committee, issue directives or make regulations setting out the measures required to bring about, by progressive stages, freedom of movement for workers, as defined in Article 48, in particular:

(a) by ensuring close cooperation between national employment services;

(b) by systematically and progressively abolishing those administrative procedures and practices and those qualifying periods in respect of eligibility for available employment, whether resulting from national legislation or from agreements previously concluded between Member States, the maintenance of which would form an obstacle to liberalisation of the movement of workers;

(c) by systematically and progressively abolishing all such qualifying periods and other restrictions provided for either under national legislation or under agreements previously concluded between Member States as impose on workers of other Member States conditions regarding the free choice of employment other than those imposed on workers of the State concerned;

(d) by setting up appropriate machinery to bring offers of employment into touch with applications for employment and to facilitate the achievement of a balance between supply and demand in the employment market in such a way as to avoid serious threats to the standard of living and level of employment in the various regions and industries.

(Source: Treaty establishing the European Economic Community, Rome, 25 March 1957. This is the authentic English text published in Cmnd. 4864.)

useful economically even under conditions of full employment (Brown, 1963, pp. 184, 193; and General Council's Report to 1962 Congress and Supplementary Report B, para. 284-8).[4]

The TUC, no doubt, had the legitimate interests of its members at heart and could have pointed to a Gallup poll of September 1961 where 43% of the sample considered it a 'bad thing' (and 38% a 'good thing') that Britain should agree to 'inviting workers here from other member countries to take up jobs which cannot be filled by our own labour' (Gallup, 1969, p. 245). This was possibly a somewhat loaded question as far as the word 'inviting' is concerned and one might be tempted to trust more the *Readers' Digest* poll of two years later which found 51% of Britons in favour, and 33% against, the free movement of labour in the Common Market, figures which were significantly lower and higher, respectively, than for any of the populations questioned in the Six (Rose, 1969, p. 102). But the least biased question of a 1966 survey by Opinion Research Centre (ORC)—whether it would be a 'good thing' or 'bad thing' that 'Europeans would be much more free to come and work here'—found the same proportions as Gallup, namely, 43% 'bad' and 41% 'good' (Raison and Taylor, 1966, p. 7). And although both Gallup and *Readers' Digest* (see the report in *European Communities*, Aug.–Sept. 1970, pp. 16–17) re-established their previous proportions in 1969,[5] it is clear to any observer of the British scene that there is a special British opposition to free movement of labour which is scarcely tapped by set questions of the general opinion poll type, but which comes to the fore in, for example, the many-sided discussions on radio and TV where one can almost sense the fears of 'alien hordes pouring into this country' and the 'cheap labour which is undercutting our wages and taking away our jobs'. The prima facie impressions on such occasions confirm the ORC picture that unskilled workers, women, and anti-Marketeers are disproportionately 'against' and the middle class disproportionately for (50%) the freedom of movement (Raison and Taylor, 1966).

[4] In February 1971, on the other hand, Mr. Victor Feather found the completed system of free movement 'relatively uncontroversial' because, it seems, he saw 'no reason to expect that patterns of migration to and from the UK would change much with entry'. See Feather (1971), p. 56; and generally, see also Beever (1969).

[5] Gallup: 42% 'bad' and 34% 'good'; *Readers' Digest*: 58% 'for' and 27% 'against'.

At the time of the Labour application to join the Common Market, Mr. Harold Wilson made the most extensive and detailed official statement yet on the issue (HC Deb., 8 May 1967, col. 1084 ff.). His interpretation of the system of free movement was rather restrictive and looked back at the Treaty of Rome, whereas the intermediate stage of the EEC's development had already gone further than the Treaty in some respects. As far as the Commonwealth population was concerned, Mr. Wilson assumed that only those who were registered or born as citizens of the UK and Colonies would enjoy the benefits of free movement. The White Paper of February 1970 (Cmnd. 4289) did not touch upon the problem, a low-key approach very much in contrast to the concern of the public. After all, both in 1961 and 1969 Gallup had found that this issue was in public opinion the third most important argument against entry. The low-key approach could again be seen in the House of Commons debate on the Common Market in January 1971, when there were virtually no substantial references to it.[6]

Meanwhile the 'Great Debate' was beginning to warm up: and it quickly sank to the level of 'alien hordes' and 'cheap labour'. Even distinguished academics made some rather undistinguished contributions. James Meade, for instance, noticed a rapid growth of population in Southern Italy which, seemingly predestined, would flow into the UK and which the country could obviously not absorb at a time when there was also large-scale immigration from the Commonwealth. 'It would, therefore, seem inevitable that there should be a special arrangement by which the UK should be able to impose at least as severe controls over immigration from Europe (EEC) as over immigration from Commonwealth countries' (Meade, 1970, p. 69). Paul Einzig's patriotic pen squarely faced the issue:

> ... the removal of barriers to the immigration of continental labour might induce the worst type of foreign workers to come to Britain, because of the possibility of being paid a full day's pay without having to do a full day's work. ... To the idlers and spongers of Western Europe Britain might well appear as the country of their dreams. ... The multitude of devices of malingering ... are bound to attract the parasitic type of foreign workers (Einzig, 1971, pp. 75–6).

[6] It was only during the acceptance debate in October 1971 that Mr. R. Carr acknowledged that 'free movement is a matter which causes concern, especially outside the House'. (HC Deb., 25 Oct. 1971, col. 1369.)

This line of reasoning quickly found its way into the anti-Marketeers' campaign. For example, a week before Einzig's book was published, the *New Statesman* carried an advertisement by the 'Referendum before Common Market Committee' in its Nicholas Kaldor issue of 12 March 1971, which ran in part as follows:

> Under the Treaty of Rome every inhabitant of the Common Market Area, from Sicily to the Baltic, including also labour from the French West Indies and Guiana, could come to Britain without permit or entry-visa, and many would do so for the sake of social-security benefits which would give them even while unemployed a standard of living higher than they could achieve at home.

Leaving aside the demagogy,[7] it is of course virtually impossible to talk to such people in rational terms because of their marked degree of 'perceptual closure': they do not hear what they do not want to hear. They would not admit that, as the figures show, the social security benefits in EEC member countries are on balance much higher than in Britain and that unemployment benefits, in particular, out-distance the British benefits by up to twice the amount in every member country except Italy (see the tables in Kommission . . ., 1970b, pp. 81–4; and Department of Health and Social Security, 1970). If there is one country in the world which could legitimately have fears of attracting immigrants solely because of its high level of social security benefits, then it is Sweden —but not Britain.

May I say finally that I am not writing this book as a pro-Marketeer or as an anti-Marketeer. I am interested in the concept and actual development of free movement in the European Communities, because I see in it the greatest single contributory factor to the establishment 'of an ever closer union among the peoples of Europe', which the preamble of the Treaty of Rome postulates in its first sentence (I have tried to define this concept in Böhning, 1971b, p. 7). It is obvious that simple intermingling of ethnically different people does not make them accept each other: quite the

---

7 To which must also be assigned Mr. Wilson's infamous black-leg speech in Birmingham; see *The Times* (27 April 1971). See also a recent article in the *Police Review* (19 Nov. 1971, p. 1484), which saw 'lawbreakers and stolen property . . . [moving] freely in or out of the countries concerned', illegal immigrant traffic 'particularly in view of the large proportion of French and Dutch citizens who are non-Europeans', and 'vastly increased risk of Police conduct and reports being challenged in both civil and criminal proceedings'.

contrary, the working of the 'perceptual closure' often widens the social distance. I am convinced, however, that an enlightened policy and social climate accompanying the intra-European exchanges of people can lead to the kind of social interaction which first makes us accept our 'foreign neighbour' at the work-bench, then in our circle of friends, and finally in politics. I am equally convinced not only that the EEC has 'registered a distinct success' (Swann, 1970, p. 66) in economic and political terms in this much overlooked area, but also that the first signs of this intra-European acceptance are already visible.

PART ONE

THE DEVELOPMENT OF THE EEC FREE MOVEMENT OF LABOUR SYSTEM AND THE IMMIGRATION OF WORKERS INTO CONTINENTAL COUNTRIES AND THE UNITED KINGDOM

2

The EEC's System of Freedom of Movement

The specific programme of Articles 48 and 49 was inserted in the Treaty of Rome on the insistence of Italy, and that country has naturally been pushing ahead its implementation. It found a willing ally in the Commission and in the desperate manpower shortages north of the Alps. The two articles themselves are little more than a liberal-capitalist prescription for bringing manpower shortages and surpluses into balance within a given free trade area. The responsible member of the Commission, Mr. L. Levi-Sandri, originally interpreted the Treaty provisions in this sense: '...freedom of movement for workers as envisaged by the Treaty implies a regime the nature of which is to limit maximally the possibility of uncontrolled and useless movements' (*BEC*, June 1961).

The Council promulgated its first regulation in this field, No. 15/61, on 16 August 1961. (See *Journal Officiel des Communautés Européennes*, No. 57, 1961; and for a non-authentic English text, the Foreign Office translation of this Regulation [H.M.S.O., 1962] relating to first steps for the achievement of free movement of workers within the Community. See also Dahlberg, 1968, and Feldstein, 1967.) Its provisions were in force between September 1961 and May 1964 and applied principally to non-seasonal and non-frontier workers. They authorized nationals of member states to accept offers of employment 'if no suitable worker from the regular labour force of the other Member State is available ... within a maximum of three weeks from the time the vacancy was registered at the Employment Exchange' (Article 1). Furthermore, EEC nationals were entitled to have their work permits renewed 'for the same type of work' after one year; after three years a worker should be permitted 'to take up another type of work if he is qualified for it'; and after four years he should receive an unrestricted work permit (Article 6). Discrimination on grounds of nationality was prohibited in respect of all conditions of work or employment. The worker's spouse and children under 21 were to be 'allowed to take up residence with him if he has normal dwellings for his family' (Article 11). (For the Dutch reservation here, see Dahlberg, 1968, pp. 314, 325.)

Regulation 15/61 also established the basic institutional framework: the European Office for Co-ordinating Vacancy Clearance, the Consultative Committee, and the Technical Committee. The European Office for Co-ordination, as it is commonly called, was a new institution within the Commission responsible for the technicalities of the Community-wide vacancy clearance.[1] It contained the seeds of a Community employment exchange but never came anywhere near fulfilling such a function. The Consultative Committee became a tripartite body with members from each country and was to function in an advisory capacity to the Commission in practically all matters relating to the migration of workers. The Technical Committee was to be composed only of representatives of each member government with the responsibility of 'assisting the Commission in the preparation, promotion and follow-up of all operations and technical measures required to give effect to this Regulation and any future amendments' (Article 36). In other words, it is a watch-dog where the governments are functioning on their own (and not in a tripartite committee together with employers and trade unionists).

Regulation 15/61 applied to the European territories of the member states. It did 'not affect any obligations incumbent upon Member States by reason of the special relations they maintain with certain non-European countries or territories in consequence of the institutional ties that exist, or have existed, between them' (Article 42[3]). The institutional ties with certain non-European countries or territories referred mainly to France's former possessions in Africa, and to the overseas provinces of the Netherlands, i.e. Surinam and the Dutch Antilles. France desired to maintain its practically uncontrolled migration system with 'Black Africa' and Algeria, and its

---

[1] As the Foreign Office translation noted correctly: vacancy clearance should be understood to refer not only to the matching of specific job seekers with unfilled vacancies, but also to the balancing of labour supply and demand on a macro-economic scale. The correct title of the institution is European Office for Co-ordinating the Balancing of Job-Offers and Job-Seekers.

completely uncontrolled internal migration between the metropolitan and the Overseas Departments. It does not seem to have asked for the inclusion of Algerians and/or its own citizens from the Overseas Departments in the EEC free movement system for which Article 227 (2) (2) of the Treaty requires a unanimous decision of the Council. The Netherlands pursued a similar policy. It is worthwhile to elaborate this particular point here before considering in detail the future EEC plans and the problem of UK nationality. Surinam and the Dutch Antilles are constituent parts of the Kingdom of the Netherlands. Surinamese and Dutch Antillians are Dutch citizens according to Dutch law. They have the same passports as other Dutch and only from the place of birth noted in the passport can it be deduced that these Dutch citizens were born overseas— and a look at the bearer will indicate his ancestry. The Netherlands ratified the Treaty of Rome on behalf of the Kingdom in Europe and Netherlands New Guinea. A Declaration annexed to the Treaty expressed the intention of having both Surinam and the Dutch Antilles associated with the Community under Part IV of the Treaty.[2] The Netherlands seemed to anticipate the future independence of these two overseas provinces. As independence would have entailed separate citizenships and as this would hardly have animated the five partners of the Netherlands to extend the privileges of free movement to these West Indian peoples, the Dutch Government suggested in September 1961, when the association agreement with Surinam was thrashed out,[3] not to have the Surinamese included in the free movement system because of their likely exclusion at the time of independence. The Council naturally agreed to this request. The Dutch Antilles were associated separately with the Community in 1964 (*JOCE*, No. 150, 1964) and added to the list of countries and territories in Annex IV of the Treaty. This agreement implicitly excludes the Dutch Antillians from the EEC free movement system, because no agreement to the contrary has been published according to Article 135. Speaking to leading Dutch citizens from Surinam, one finds no awareness of their exclusion from the EEC's freedom of movement, and Dutch officials

[2] In Part IV, Article 135 states: 'Subject to the provisions relating to public health, public security or public policy, freedom of movement within Member States for workers from the countries and territories (associated with the Community), and within the countries and territories for workers from Member States, shall be governed by agreements to be concluded subsequently with the unanimous approval of Member States.'

[3] Surinam became an associate member on 1 September 1962.

roundly deny it and refer to the near impossibility of differentiating by passports. However, other officials are prepared to admit that the Dutch Government is currently considering introducing immigration controls between Surinam and the Low Countries, which would contrast oddly with free movement within the Community.

The 1961 Regulation achieved little in terms of free movement. It was a true reflection of the Treaty provisions, did not go much further than various national migration systems had gone anyway for a larger number of foreign workers, and was exclusively intra-European in its applicability. During the subsequent years, similar regimes were established for seasonal and frontier workers and other special categories of worker, but already on 25 March 1964 a new regulation was approved by the Council which constituted a certain breakthrough: it brought permanent, seasonal, and frontier workers under one regime and was in force between May 1964 and November 1968. (See *JOCE*, No. 62, 1964; and see also the Foreign Office translation of EEC Regulation No. 38/64 [London, H.M.S.O., 1964] on the freedom of movement of workers within the Community, for a non-authentic English version.)

Article 1 of Regulation 38/64 not only authorized Community workers to take up notified vacancies, but it gave them the *right* to do so—and without local labour having a priority of three weeks. This meant that for all practical purposes a rudimentary freedom of movement was established: work permits were not restricted to employers (except perhaps for the first year) or regions and were automatically renewable (Article 22). National authorities could no longer refuse permission to work or to change work except temporarily in regions or occupations where a serious danger to the balance of employment existed. The exemption clause (Article 2) was in fact invoked by various countries a number of times (KEG, 1966a, 1967a, 1968a) but, though still superseding Article 1, it was in itself not absolute (see Articles 2 [3], 3, 4, 5, and 6). Equality of treatment was reinforced and broadened as was the authorization for family reunion. Apart from the spouse and children under 21, 'dependent ascendants and descendants of the worker and his spouse' (Article 17 [1] [b]) were to be allowed to join the bread-winner if 'normal housing' was available. The European Office for Co-ordination and the two Committees kept their place and function.

A new aspect was the establishment of a *de facto* Community priority over recruitment by member states from non-EEC countries. Italy, with the support of the Commission, managed to have an article (30 [2]) inserted which gave labour surplus areas fifteen days to indicate whether they could fill listed Community vacancies— if they could not do this, member states were free to recruit in third countries. Although this was a very uncertain procedure with no practical means of enforcement, it presented in effect an entirely new aspect not foreseen in the Treaty of Rome.

Article 53 (3) of Regulation 38/64 repeated the wording of Article 42 (3) of the 1961 Regulation (see above p. 11), but it added a second paragraph:

Workers from such [non-European] countries or territories who, in accordance with this provision, carry on a wage-earning employment on the territory of one of these Member States cannot invoke the benefit of the provisions of this Regulation in the territory of other Member States.

In other words, this Regulation, too, applied only to the European territories of the Six. Dahlberg (1968, p. 322) writes: 'Germany and Italy were successful in having an article inserted (Article 53) which prevented salaried workers from French and Dutch territories and former colonies from claiming the benefits of the new regulation.' (He was presumably referring to Article 53 [3] [2].) In fact, France again does not seem to have pressed the inclusion of its citizens from overseas, for the decision on this problem was specifically reserved in Article 58.

The negotiations in the Community leading up to the present Regulation No. 1612/68 were protracted. Encouraged by its successes in 1961 and 1964, the Commission put forward a bold proposal. In 1961 it had managed to anchor the principle of family reunion in the regulation, of which the Treaty said nothing. In 1964 it laid the basis for a Community priority and common labour market, again without explicit support from the Treaty. In 1968 it threw overboard the somewhat mercantilistic principle of confining free movement to vacancies registered at employment exchanges and it dropped the requirement of 'normal housing' for family reunion. In other words, it took a greater leap forward than was required on purely economic grounds.

Article 1 of Regulation 1612/68 states:

(1) Any national of a Member State, irrespective of his place of residence, shall have the right to take up an activity as an employed person, and to pursue such activity within the territory of another Member State in accordance with the provisions laid down by law, regulation or administrative action governing the employment of that State. (2) He shall, in particular, be eligible for employment vacancies in the territory of another Member State with the same priority as nationals of that State. (See European Communities, Secondary Legislation, English Text, Part 10, Social Affairs [H.M.S.O., 1972].)

Since November 1968, workers from member countries have the right[4] to move to any other member country and seek work there without being restricted to notified vacancies. There is, however, an understanding by the Council that in order to forestall abuse of this provision, a residence permit, which is still required, should not be issued if the worker has not found employment within three months, that is, the unsuccessful job-seeker could be treated after three months as a tourist who had overstayed his permission to stay. A worker who has found a job, either before entry or within three months of entry, will automatically be issued a residence permit of five years' validity unless his exclusion can be justified on grounds of public policy, public security, or public health. These limitations are explained in more detail in the discussion of Directive 64/221 below (pp. 20–1). The entire work permit procedure is abolished for Community workers for ever.

The meaning of 'worker' in this context needs some clarification. Worker is defined not in terms of international law or in terms of the municipal law of the various member states, but has acquired a distinct meaning according to *Community law*. It refers to all blue-collar and white-collar workers—that is, wage-earners and salary-earners, respectively—other than those employed in 'the public service' (Article 48 [4] of the Treaty). The public service is taken to mean not the industrial labour force in nationalized industries, but civil servants in local or national government whose activities can be defined in analogy to Article 55 of the Treaty (which relates primarily to the right of establishment), i.e. 'occupations which involve . . . even occasionally, the exercise of official authority'. The self-employed do not fall under the provisions for freedom

---

[4] French: ' . . . a le *droit* d'accéder à une activité salariée et de l'exercer'. German: ' . . . *berechtigt*, eine Tätigkeit im Lohn-oder Gehaltsverhältnis . . . aufzunehmen und auszuüben'.

of movement for workers; rather they come under separate Treaty provisions (Articles 52–58), and the same applies to persons rendering services (Articles 59–66 of the Treaty). Neither category necessarily tallies with national or international usage—but this only serves to show that the EEC is in effect creating a distinct kind of Community law, a law which becomes operative in member countries not on sufferance (as international law) but through an autonomous legislative process.

The requirement not to discriminate against Community workers on grounds of nationality, already embodied in Regulations 15/61 and 38/64, is broadened to cover practically all aspects of work and life except the sphere of civil rights and voting.[5] Specifically, equality of treatment is required for remuneration, dismissal, vocational training and rehabilitation, tax and social security benefits, trade union membership and rights, and access to public and private housing.

The provision of Regulation 1612/68 relating to family reunion is largely self-explanatory and worth quoting in full.

(1) The following shall, irrespective of their nationality, have the right to take up residence with a worker who is a national of one Member State employed in the territory of another Member State: (a) his spouse and their children under the age of 21 years or dependent children; (b) dependent relatives in the ascending line of the worker and his spouse. (2) Member States shall encourage the admission of any members of the family not coming within the provisions of paragraph 1 if dependent on the worker referred to above or living under his roof in the country whence he comes. (3) For the purposes of paragraphs 1 and 2, the worker must have available for his family housing considered as normal for national workers in the region where he is employed; this provision, however, must not give rise to discrimination between national workers and workers from the other Member States.

The circle of immediate relatives covered by this Article 10 is not different from that of Regulation 38/64, despite the altered wording (see above). It includes the spouse, minor children as well as dependent older children, and the couple's parents and grandparents who are dependent on the bread-winner. Paragraph 2 tries to take care of the extended family system. Paragraph 3 incorporates one of the compromises of Community politics which leaves everyone formally satisfied and the reality of Community life strengthened

---

[5] Articles 7–9 of Regulation 1612/68. These must also be seen in relation to the recently modified regime for social security of migrant workers; see Regulation 1408/71, below pp. 23–4.

with some progress towards greater 'harmonization'. The draft of the Commission, which contained no proviso for normal housing (Rochcau, 1968, p. 14), was objected to by the Netherlands and Germany on account of their housing shortages. Italy would not accept the reinsertion of the normal housing requirement unless it was also stated that this must not lead to discrimination on grounds of nationality. The legal stalemate represents in fact a victory for Italy and the Commission as the Dutch and German administrations are not controlling the reunion of families from Common Market countries.

In the legalistic atmosphere of Brussels, the sort of compromise embodied in Article 10(3) often opens up the way for a later, more definite step towards the non-static aims of the Community as perceived by the Commission. Article 16(2) is a case in point. Whereas Regulation 38/64 established no more than a *de facto* priority for Community workers, Regulation 1612/68 contains a *de jure* requirement not to offer jobs processed through the Community vacancy clearance system to workers from non-member countries within eighteen days from receipt of the offer by the services of a member with labour surpluses. There are still many exceptions to this rule (seasonal immigrants in France, frontier workers from non-member states, family ties between established and prospective workers, and so on), and Italy is manifestly unhappy with its implementation. It seems that any further progress would require a strengthening of the role of the Commission in this field.

The European Office for Co-ordination, the Consultative Committee, and the Technical Committee still have essentially the same functions as at their time of inception in 1961. But with the establishment of a common labour market for migrant workers in 1968, the hitherto unilateral right of member countries to exempt regions or occupations from the application of the regulations, passed over to the Community as a whole. It is again worthwhile to quote the text of Article 20, Regulation 1612/68, in full.

(1) When a Member State undergoes or foresees disturbances on its labour market which could seriously threaten the standard of living and level of employment in a given region or occupation, that State shall inform the Commission and the other Member States thereof and shall supply them with all appropriate particulars. (2) The Member States and the Commission shall take all suitable informative measures so that Community workers shall not apply for employment in the said region

B

or occupation. (3) Without prejudice to the application of the provisions of the Treaty and of the Protocols annexed thereto, the Member State referred to in paragraph 1 may request the Commission to state that, in order to restore to normal the situation in the said region or occupation, the operation of the balancing machinery provided for in Articles 15, 16 and 17 should be partially or totally suspended. The Commission shall decide on the suspension as such and on the duration thereof not later than two weeks after receiving such request. Any Member State may, within a strict time-limit of two weeks, request the Council to annul or amend any such decision. The Council shall take a decision on any such request within two weeks. (4) Where such suspension does take place, the employment services of the other Member States which have indicated that they have workers available shall not take any action to fill vacancies communicated directly to them by employers in the Member State referred to in paragraph 1.

If informing potential migrants is insufficient to prevent them from moving into endangered areas or occupations, the country concerned may request the Commission to suspend the *vacancy clearance system* with a provision for appeal to the Council. However, the individual's *right to freedom of movement* remains enforceable in the courts.[6]

The provisions relating to 'institutional ties' and territorial applicability were carried over from the earlier regulations essentially unchanged. (See Article 42[3] of Regulation 1612/68 and above pp. 11–13 and 14.) But on 15 October 1968 the Council finally decided to have the *départements français d'outre-mer* included in the free movement system (*JOCE*, No. L257, 1968). Thus, French citizens from Guiana, Martinique, Guadeloupe, and Réunion enjoy the right to move freely throughout the European area of the EEC (and European Community workers are entitled to move without hindrance to the French Overseas Departments). But people from the *territoires d'outre-mer*, i.e. islands in the Pacific under French colonial rule were not given the same right.

This system of freedom of movement for workers represents a truly remarkable advance into one of the most sensitive areas of every modern nation-state. Whereas hitherto migration of workers was handled by the authorities of the receiving country, freedom of movement has become a Community affair. The notion of

6 The reference to the Treaty, etc., in Article 20(3) does not impair this right either; the Treaty provision in question authorized unilateral protective measures (Article 226) only for the *transitional* period—and logically so, as Regulation 1612/68 came into force eighteen months before the deadline. The reference to 'protocols' seems to apply mainly to Luxembourg's special population problems, which does not curtail the right to free movement as such.

'immigrant' or 'temporary migrant' has been replaced by that of the *Community worker*. The same commissioner who in 1961 saw free movement in terms of a factor of production, proclaimed in 1968 that it constituted 'an incipient form—still embryonic and imperfect —of European citizenship' (L. Levi-Sandri, in *BEC*, No. 11, 1968, p. 6; above p. 10 and Wedel,[7] 1970, p. 464).

Of course, the success of the Commission would scarcely have been possible without the explicit provisions of the Treaty. Article 49 empowered it to issue directives *or* regulations. The Commission was shrewd enough to commence with a regulation and subsequently to accommodate the main features of the system in these instruments. Directives are binding on national authorities only with respect to the aims of the legislation; they leave the choice of form and methods to the national legislator. Regulations, however, are more than guidelines (see Article 189 of Treaty). They are to apply generally, i.e. they have normative character; they are binding in their entirety, i.e. all parts are valid and are the final wording of the law; and they take direct effect in each member state, i.e. the legislation becomes effective and applicable without the requirement of transformation into municipal law. The national legislatures cannot change the wording of a regulation and they have to heed its content in all subsequent national legislation. All that is left to the national authorities is the form of publication—but publication there must be because regulations directly create rights and obligations for the citizens of member countries. Moreover, direct applicability and normative character also mean that regulations supersede any norm of municipal law to the contrary. The Court of Justice in Luxembourg has also extended the notion of direct applicability to those provisions of directives which are directly effective in the sense that national legislators have no enabling power over expressly given rights. (See L. J. Brinkhorst's report in *Common Market Law Review* [Vol. 8, No. 3, July 1971], pp. 380–92, on Case 9/70 [*Grad v. Finanzamt Traunstein*, Decision of 6 October 1970] and Case 33/70 [*S.A.C.E.* v. *Ministry of Finance of the Italian Republic*, Decision of 17 December 1970].)

An examination of the EEC's system of freedom of movement would not be complete without consideration of the accompanying and other relevant legislation. This comprises the Council's Directive

---

[7] '. . . a triumph of social ideas over purely economic and utilitarian conceptions.'

64/221 of February 1964 to co-ordinate special measures in respect of movement and residence of foreigners, justified on grounds of public policy, public security, or public health; the Directive 68/360 of October 1968 on the abolition of restrictions on the movement and residence of workers of member states and their families within the Community; the Regulation 1251/70 of June 1970 concerning the right of workers to remain in the territory of a member state after having been employed there (Böhning and Stephen, 1971a); and the Regulation 1408/71 of June 1971 on the application of social security systems for workers and their families who migrate within the Community (*JOCE*, No. L149, 1971).

Directive 64/221 established the guidelines for the three basic limitations on free movement (and the right of establishment and to supply services) contained in Articles 48(3) and 56(1) of the Treaty. As a general norm it stated that grounds of public policy, public security, or public health 'shall not be invoked to serve economic ends' (Article 2[2]).[8] This means that the refusal of entry or renewal of a residence permit, or the removal from a member country, on grounds of economic policy in general or because the person concerned is a charge on the public purse, is illegal for EEC nationals. The diseases and disabilities likely to endanger public health are enumerated in this Directive and refer mainly to severe infectious diseases. However, these diseases can only justify refusal of entry or issue of initial residence permit. 'Diseases or disabilities occurring after the initial residence permit has been issued shall not justify refusal to renew the residence permit or deportation from the territory' (Article 4[2]).

Whereas public health is dealt with exhaustively by Directive 64/221, public policy and public security are circumscribed only in a negative way. Firstly, they cannot, as indicated, be invoked for economic reasons; secondly, any grounds 'shall be based exclusively on the personal conduct of the individual concerned' (Article 3[1]); and thirdly, the fact that there have been convictions shall not by itself justify the taking of such measures (Article 3[2]). Nevertheless, this means that member countries are not free to denote as public policy or public security what they think fit within their own national

---

8 This would seem to be an example of a provision in a directive with direct applicability, which would also seem to hold true for Articles 3 to 7 of Directive 64/221.

concepts.[9] Rather, it means that public policy and public security have become a concept of *Community law* with respect to EEC nationals (Campbell, 1971, p. 228; and Lyon-Caen, 1967) and that an 'alignment of procedures' (Preamble to Directive 64/221) is required. This is also visible in the last of the important aspects of the Directive which imposes upon member countries the obligation to establish an appeals procedure for cases falling under it.

Regulations 15/61 and 38/64 had both been accompanied by a Directive of the Council indicating the required abolition of restrictions on movements and residence (*JOCE*, No. 80, 1961, and No. 62, 1964). When Regulation 1612/68 came into being, the Council thought it

appropriate to adopt, in regard to the abolition of restrictions still existing as regards movement and residence within the Community, measures which conform to the rights and privileges accorded by the said Regulation to nationals of any Member State who move with a view to working as an employed person and to members of their family (Preamble to Directive 68/360).

Apart from reiterating the right to emigration and the abolition of visa requirements, Directive 68/360 confirmed the *right of residence* in the country of employment for persons covered by the free movement system (Article 4[1]). This entails the complete abrogation of restrictions relating to the geographical area or duration of validity of the residence permit: permits must be valid for the whole of the territory for at least five years and be automatically renewable. Temporary and seasonal workers may be issued with a temporary residence permit, but this does not impair the right of residence as such. Further,

a residence permit which is still valid may not be withdrawn from a worker solely on the grounds that he is no longer in employment, either because he is temporarily incapable of work as a result of illness or accident, or because he is involuntarily unemployed, this being duly confirmed by the competent labour office. When the residence permit is renewed for the first time the period of residence may be restricted,

---

[9] The French notion, for example, of *ordre public* encompasses everything that can be subsumed under the 'public good', while the Germanic law sees as *öffentliche Ordnung* only such norms whose enforcement is undeniable and necessary in the interests of the state.

but not less than twelve months if the worker has been involuntarily unemployed in the host Member State for more than twelve consecutive months (Article 7).

The latter provision shows that the Community is still some way from accepting all repercussions of a common labour market for migrant workers, which is understandable in view of the fact that tax and social security benefits differ significantly between various member countries and that, therefore, one wants to forestall movements motivated solely by differential benefit levels. The entire Directive is, of course, subject to the limitations of the right to freedom of movement: public policy, public security, and public health (see preceding paragraphs).

Somewhat belatedly the Council adopted in mid-1970 the regulation on the *right of stay*, which was based on the explicit provisions of Article 48(3)(d) of the Treaty. Naturally its provisions did not apply to workers alone but to their families as well because of the precedent of the regulations relating to free movement. Community workers are given the right to remain permanently in their country of employment without prior naturalization upon reaching the age limit for entitlement to old-age pension,[10] provided they have resided continuously for at least three years in that country and have been employed there during the last twelve months. 'Continuous' residence is not affected by a total of three months' absence per year or periods of involuntary unemployment or military service. Secondly, a Community worker is entitled to permanent residence after two years' continuous residence if he has to retire because of permanent incapacity to work; and 'if such incapacity is the result of an industrial accident or an occupational disease entitling him to a pension for which an institution of that State is entirely or partially liable, no condition shall be imposed as to length of residence' (Article 2[1] [b] of Regulation 1251/70). Lastly, frontier workers who have commuted for at least three years are also entitled to permanent residence. For female dependants the conditions as to length of residence and employment do not apply if the worker's spouse is a national of the receiving country or has lost the nationality of that country by her marriage to that worker. Spouses and children themselves have the right to stay indefinitely in the receiving country if and when

10 Which is 65 years for the Six, except in Italy where it is 60 years, and five years less for women than for men in Italy and Belgium.

the bread-winner acquires this right and to do so even after his decease. If the bread-winner dies before acquiring the right of stay, other less stringent conditions apply (see Article 3 [2]). Workers and families are allowed a two-year period of grace, after entitlement has commenced, in which to decide where to settle.

In this Regulation the Community has shown its progressive stance compared with the legislation previously applicable in most Western and Middle European countries. The rights and privileges accorded to EEC nationals have naturally led to misgivings on the side of migrant workers from third countries—and to a sort of EEC consciousness on the side of some Community workers: an Italian working with German Railways recently wrote on the back of a questionnaire: 'Here I am cleaning these carriages and all those Greeks are sitting in the offices. I shouldn't have to do this work as a citizen of the EEC!' National governments have found that 'owing to the prestige of [the EEC's] legislation' (Doublet, 1965, p. 290),[11] they are forced to liberalize their system towards workers from non-member countries, too. As will be shown in Chapter 6, the Commission itself is beginning to adopt initiatives in this field.

Finally, in mid-1971, the Community extensively modified its regime for the social security of migrant workers, which, as the third regulation ever to be adopted by the Council in 1959, had previously given EEC workers some assurance that their entitlements would not be forfeited by moving throughout the Common Market. Regulation 1408/71, which is also applicable to the French Overseas Departments, goes further, covering family allowances, unemployment, health and maternity, disablement, accidents at work and occupational diseases, old age, orphanage and widowhood, and death grants; it does not cover national assistance schemes, war pensions, and civil service schemes. As a rule, workers and their dependants are entitled to benefits on a *pro rata temporis* basis regardless of place of residence. While this generally means that a migrant worker is paid, or accumulates, benefits according to the system in force at his place of employment, and regardless of whether or not his dependants have joined him, an exemption is made in the case of French family allowances. A non-French EEC citizen working or unemployed in France will be paid the full French family allowance only for those dependants who reside with him; otherwise he receives the amount paid in the dependants' country of residence. The main

[11] Doublet is former Chairman of the *Office national d'immigration*.

features of the unemployment system are that time spent working in another Community country is to be taken into account for purposes of determining qualifying periods and that payment levels are according to the country of last employment unless the worker migrates during a spell of unemployment. In the latter case the former country of employment will continue to pay workers who have been involuntarily unemployed for at least four weeks for a further period of three months at most (see Articles 69 et seq.). A pensioner can draw his pension anywhere in the Community; and if his benefits accumulated in various member countries do not reach the minimum level of pension of his usual place of residence, he is entitled to a payment which bridges the gap.

The EEC's system of freedom of movement thus described is certainly not final in the sense that no improvements are contemplated. But the basic legal features are solidly established and will scarcely undergo any major changes during the next decade. The enlargement of the Community has provided no reason for rethinking the system on the side of the Community; and the Conservative Government was prepared to accept it (see HC Deb., 20 May 1971, col. 342, for Mr. Rippon's statement). The next chapters will examine whether or not these Regulations have had a marked effect on the migration streams into and among the Six. Yet, even if it were found that labour movements are 'dominated by economic and social factors, rather than by regulations', as paragraph 143 of the White Paper of July 1971 (Cmnd. 4715), *The United Kingdom and the European Community,* somewhat surprisingly put it, then one should realize that not having had this system would have meant a lot more personal hardship and psychological unease for the people falling under it—the migrants as well as the administrators—and would have robbed Europe of a pace-setter. There are actually a number of cases where EEC citizens have claimed their rights as Community workers (Campbell, 1971) and there are even a few cases where, after exhausting the national legal systems, they have used the ultimate means of complaint and appealed to the Commission. This, in my opinion, testifies to the fact that freedom of movement for workers within the Community is more than a piece of paper: it is becoming a social reality.

3

Immigration of Workers in European Countries

The international migration of workers is characterized by essentially the same determinants the world over. The situation in traditional immigration countries like Australia or Canada differs from that of Europe only by degree. Non-communist Europe itself presents a much more homogeneous picture than is generally recognized, regardless of the policies pursued and the immigrant populations involved—and with the immigration of some 50,000 Poles, Czechs, and Hungarians into East Germany and a lesser number into Yugoslavia, one can already detect the same features there. In this chapter the situation in the Six will be surveyed in alphabetical order, especially for the period since 1958, i.e. since the Treaty of Rome came into force. The situation in two non-EEC countries—Britain, of course, and Switzerland—will be examined for the same period in order to see whether there are any marked differences in the size, composition, direction, and permanence of migration streams inside and outside the Common Market. (For a general survey, see Bouscaren, 1969, who lacks, however, a systematic framework; and Rose, 1969, whose book includes some suspect data. The best, shortest, and most up-to-date survey is provided in the Community Relations Commission's quarterly *New Community*, Vol. 1, No. 1, October 1971.) Particular attention will be paid to immigration from non-European countries.

As this book is primarily concerned with Britain's entry into the EEC, the effects on the other applicants and the repercussions of their entry on the development within the enlarged Common Market will not be analysed in detail. It can be assumed that the effect of the entry of Denmark, Norway, and Ireland on the migratory patterns within the Community will be negligible (leaving aside the unresolved problem of Northern Ireland). All three countries are relatively small: Denmark has 5 million inhabitants, of which 2.3 millions are in civilian employment; Norway has a population of 4 millions with 1.5 millions in civilian employment; and Ireland's population of 3 millions has only just over 1 million in civilian employment. Ireland, it is true, is a traditional emigration country, but its intra-European migration streams are exclusively tied up with Britain. Germany, the biggest labour importer on the Continent, employed no more than 700 Irish in 1971 (0.0003% of the immigrant labour force). Norway is a marginal importer of foreign workers. In 1970 it employed about 30,000 foreigners, 50% of them in its merchant marine. Half of Norway's immigrant workers come from the Nordic countries, which form a common labour market similar to that of the EEC; but 50% of the foreign sailors are Chinese and Spaniards (Danielson, 1970, p. 13). Recently the number of Pakistanis has increased markedly in Norway to about 1,000 (Karadia, 1971, p. 344). In 1971, Germany employed 1,400 Norwegians and in the UK about 3,500 were registered as aliens. Less than 1,000 are annually admitted into the UK as workers, the majority as seasonal workers. Denmark is also a marginal importer of foreign labour, but the trend in the number of foreign workers has been rising steadily—and despite recent measures to bring their employment more into line with the labour market situation. Whereas in 1963 no more than 11,500 foreigners were employed in Denmark, the number had risen to 35,500 at the beginning of 1971, and together with dependants amounted to 50,000 (none of these figures includes people from other Nordic countries who are not subject to registration). Surprisingly, some 3,000 British workers were amongst them, plus over 1,500 dependants. Germany employed 3,700 Danes in mid-1971, and less than 3,000 were registered as aliens in the UK. Under 1,000 Danish workers are admitted into this country per year, slightly less than half of them as seasonal workers. So, the numerical impact of Danish, Norwegian, and Irish migrants on the continental streams is quite insignificant and there are no reasons to assume that there will be developments after their entry into the EEC that are radically different from the present. It may be noted in parenthesis that both Sweden and Austria, the two major labour-receiving countries not considered in this book, are also unlikely to be affected by the enlargement of the EEC. Neither of them is seeking accession to the system of freedom of movement for workers in its arrangement with the Common Market.

(a) BELGIUM

Since the middle of the nineteenth century, foreigners have been immigrating into Belgium in line with the industrialization of the country. In 1900, over 200,000 foreigners were resident in Belgium (3.1% of the population), 93% of them coming from neighbouring countries. After World War I the number first dropped and then increased again, with Italians playing an increasingly important role (37,000 out of 340,000 in 1938). After World War II the number increased further and Italians played a still more important part, especially in the coal-mines of the Charbonnage where they often provided most of the underground labour force. During the post-war period Belgium, particularly its French-speaking part, began to see immigration more in terms of its demographic situation and population requirements. It adopted a fairly liberal migration policy and favoured permanent immigration and integration despite its relatively high level of population density. This can be seen by comparing the number of employed foreigners between the counts of 1961 and 1967 (see Table 3–1) with the number of resident foreigners over the age of twelve counted by the census on 1 January 1964 (with figures for 1 January 1969 in brackets). The census enumerated 362,900 (455,600) foreigners, of which 136,200 (176,300) were Italians, 44,100 French, 35,900 Dutch, 27,000 (47,700) Spaniards, 12,600 (13,800) Greeks, 10,800 (11,300) Turks, 9,500 Germans, 7,300 British subjects, 5,000 (21,000) Moroccans, and 2,800 (3,200) Congolese (Bouscaren, 1969, pp. 81, 84; *Migration Today*, No. 14, Spring 1970). Since 1969, however, it seems that Belgium has been having second thoughts on its immigration policy and is attempting to reassert the primacy of the labour market for non-EEC workers.

In fact the annual intake of foreign workers has been very much in line with economic requirements, as Table 3–1 indicates. During the boom years of the mid-sixties as many as 40,000 first work permits were issued to foreigners, whereas the figure was down to 8,000 during the trough at the end of the fifties. Net immigration was negative during the latter period. The influx from the traditional labour suppliers of the EEC, especially from Germany and France, has been less variable than that from the more recent countries of

Table 3-1: Number of newly entering foreign workers 1958–1970, and number of employed foreign workers in 1961, 1967, 1968, and 1969 in *Belgium*, by nationality, in thousands.

	1958	1959	1960	1961	61: empl.[b]	1962	1963	1964	1965	1966	1967	67: empl.[c]	1968[d]	68: empl.[e]	1969[d]	69: empl.	1970
France	1.7	1.3	1.3	1.6	22.9	1.9	2.2	2.7	3.2	3.5	3.7	14.8	2.5	15.0	–	–	–
Germany	1.2	0.5	0.6	0.5	–	0.5	0.8	0.9	0.9	1.3	1.3	–	0.8	4.5	–	–	–
Italy	5.9	2.8	3.9	6.0	69.1	8.3	7.4	8.4	11.0	9.9	7.9	68.2	3.1	70.0	–	–	–
EEC[a]	8.8	4.6	5.8	8.1	–	10.7	10.4	12.0	15.0	14.7	12.9	--	6.5	104.4[f]	(7.5)[g]	117.0[f]	(6.5)[g]
Greece	2.2	0.07	0.1	0.4	3.6	3.9	4.0	1.9	1.3	0.8	0.7	6.4	0.06	6.5	0.09	–	0.1
Turkey	0.01	0.01	0	0.01	0.1	0.06	5.1	7.0	4.1	1.5	0.7	7.3	0.05	8.0	0.1	–	0.6
Utd. Kingd.	0.3	0.2	0.2	0.2	–	0.4	0.6	0.5	0.5	0.5	0.6	–	–	–	0.3	–	0.3
Spain	2.1	0.7	1.1	1.7	7.2	5.1	7.9	8.0	8.9	4.4	3.0	25.7	0.7	27.0	0.7	–	0.8
Portugal	0.08	0.05	0.07	0.08	–	0.1	0.3	0.7	0.7	0.6	0.6	–	0.2	–	0.1	–	0.3
Extra-Eur.	0.4	0.2	0.2	0.4	–	0.7	3.6	9.0	6.6	3.5	2.8	–	–	–	–	–	–
Other	3.0	1.2	1.4	1.5	–	1.5	1.4	1.6	1.6	1.5	1.3	–	1.3	–	1.2	–	2.3
OVERALL	16.9	7.0	8.9	12.4	164.4[f]	22.5	33.3	40.7	38.7	27.5	22.6	181.6[f]	8.8	182.0[f]	10.0	208.0[f]	10.9
% empl'ees	–	–	–	5.7%	5.7%	5.8%	6.0%	6.5%	6.9%	7.0%	6.9%	6.9%	6.7%	6.7%	6.7%	6.7%	6.9%

a = Excluding Luxembourg and the Netherlands (Common Labour Market).
b = End of year.
c = Mid-year.
d = Permanent workers.
e = Average of 1968.
f = Including Luxembourg and the Netherlands (20,400 Dutch in 1961; 13,500 in 1967 and 1968).
g = EEC estimate.
Source: Statistisches Amt . . . (1969); Kommission . . . (1970a, 1971a).

origin, like Spain and Turkey, or from the extra-European countries, which shot up to 22% of the total in 1964 but seems to have settled at the 10% mark now. Decolonization left Belgium with no 'colour and citizenship' problem. The fairly stationary level of the Italian work-force in conjunction with an annual intake of between 5% and 15% of this work-force, points to a mean length of stay of around ten years (disregarding naturalizations, deaths, and retirements). Belgium realizes that it faces a long-term immigration problem in economic terms, for immigrant workers are not solely employed in the old and declining mining industry but also in the modern factories in the North and West of the country; and with the foreign work-force standing at 7% of the total, the number of new immigrants called upon to fill the gaps of returning migrants is considerable.

(b) FRANCE

France's recent immigration history also begins in the nineteenth century. Since 1820 it has had a positive migration balance. Right from the start it was seen as a remedy to the decrease in population growth consequent upon the fall in birth rates. France was for a long time the only European country which considered itself a country of immigration. It encouraged the immigration of families and the reunion of separated families, and had a very liberal naturalization regime. A policy of *deliberate* integration was rather conspicuous by its absence. France relied on the method of 'natural attrition', i.e. it left immigrants to find their way around on their own. Besides permanent immigrants, France has always employed a large number of seasonal workers, mainly in agriculture and construction. Its 'open door' has not diminished the close correlation between its manpower requirements and the volume of immigration—in fact consequent upon the economic recession of the early thirties it repatriated a large number of Eastern Europeans whom it had called upon during the twenties.

The close link between the economy and immigration is also visible for the time since 1945 (G. and S. Castles, 1971; McDonald, 1969; and de la Presle, 1971). Nowadays there are about 3.5 million immigrants in France and up to 300,000 workers have entered annually in recent years. The number of seasonal new entrants seems to have become stabilized below the 50% mark.[1] After the War the

---

[1] On the other hand, France is also in receipt of a considerable 'brain drain'; see Blandy (1968).

bulk of the immigrants came from Italy, and since the end of the fifties they have come primarily from Spain; however, in recent years the Portuguese have become increasingly important (see Table 3–2). The fluctuations in the proportions of new migrants of different nationalities are more likely to reflect changing conditions in the sending countries and in competing labour-receiving countries rather than conditions in France itself. The drop in the share of recruits amongst permanent immigrants is largely attributable to increased clandestine migration from Portugal (and the willingness of the French to 'regularize' the position of these migrants after entry).

Table 3–2: Number of newly entering foreign workers, permanent plus seasonal workers (first row), the proportion of permanent new entrants who were recruited (second row), and number of employed foreign workers in 1968, in *France*, by nationality, in thousands.

	1958	1959	1960	1961	1962	1963	1964	1965	1966	1967	1968	68: empl.	1969	1970
Belgium	8.4	7.0	7.0	6.5	5.2	4.3	3.9	3.3	2.6	2.2	1.9	–	1.7	1.7
Germany	1.1	1.0	1.0	1.3	1.6	2.0	2.1	2.1	1.7	1.7	1.5	–	1.5	1.6
Italy	88.1	56.4	52.5	47.1	36.2	21.0	17.1	22.9	16.5	13.3	8.3	219.2	7.8	6.7
perm. recr.	62%	58%	57%	58%	49%	30%	19%	24%	20%	18%	9%	–	6%	2%
Luxbg.	0.01	0.02	0.01	–	–	–	0.03	0.03	0.04	0.02	0.04	–	0.04	0.05
Netherld.	0.2	0.2	0.2	0.2	0.3	0.3	0.4	0.4	0.4	0.4	0.3	–	0.3	0.4
EEC	97.9	64.5	60.7	55.2	43.2	27.6	23.5	28.6	21.2	17.7	12.0	262.4	11.4	10.4
Greece	–	–	–	–	–	–	0.8	0.6	0.6	0.4	0.4	–	0.3	0.3
Turkey	–	–	–	–	–	–	0.2	0.4	0.6	1.2	1.7	3.5	2.6	14.1
Utd. Kingd.	–	–	–	–	–	–	0.7	0.7	0.8	1.0	–	–	–	–
Yugosla.	0.5	0.3	0.2	0.2	0.5	2.0	3.9	6.7	10.1	10.0	9.3	31.1	12.1	10.9
perm. recr.	–	–	–	–	–	–	–	6%d	17%	22%	34%	–	75%	77%
Spain	41.1[a]	36.6[a]	90.6	106.0	137.9	144.9	173.3	168.9	148.4	127.3	138.6	252.9	146.3	140.0
perm. recr.	39%	29%	34%	43%	46%	34%	24%	18%	25%	23%	27%	–	57%	61%
Portugal	5.1	3.5	5.0	8.0	14.4	27.1	47.5	51.5	48.0	37.9	34.0	170.1	83.9	91.6
perm. recr.	74%	59%	48%	62%	47%	41%	33%	23%	25%	22%	6%	–	9%	10%
Other	1.7	3.1	2.2	6.4	6.2	15.2	24.8	26.2	26.1	16.3	27.0	438.1	44.1	42.0
OVERALL[e]	146.3	108.0	158.7	175.8	202.2	216.8	274.7	283.6	255.8	211.8	223.0	1,158.1	300.7	309.3
perm. recr.	55%	46%	41%	47%	47%	35%	29%	21%	23%	21%	17%	–	27%	37%
% seasonal[b]	43%	59%	69%	55%	46%	47%	44%	46%	49%	54%	58%	–	44%	44%
Women[c]	9%	17%	18%	17%	–	16%	14%	15%	15%	17%	18%	–	–	–

– = Not available.
a = Seasonal grape harvesters not counted prior to 1960.
b = Seasonal as percentage of total new entrants.
c = Non-seasonal female new entrants as percentage of total non-seasonal new entrants.
d = Recruits of last quarter as percentage of permanent entrants of whole year.
e = New entrants data exclude Algerians, Black Africans, and Laotians.
Source: *Annuaire Statistique de la France*; *Statistiques du Travail et de la Sécurité Sociale*; Statistisches Amt . . . (1969); Kommission . . . (1970a, 1971a).

This drop is also visible for Italy and for Spain and in the Italian case derives more from the mature character of the migration stream than from the freeing of movements within the EEC. The remarkable drop in the absolute number of Italian new entrants finds its explanation in the Italian boom at the beginning of the sixties and the pull of German wage levels during that decade. A great many of the present-day Italian new entrants are people from areas of traditional emigration to France joining up with friends and relatives who migrated during the fifties and early sixties. Greeks and Turks have never played a very significant role in France's immigration, but France has recently tapped the Yugoslav migration potential. Female labour has never yet played an important part either. This may be due largely to the origin of most migrants: female labour in traditional areas of Italy and the Iberian peninsula is the exception rather than the rule and this holds true even more for Moslem countries. The 'tendency toward a more widespread distribution of imported labour throughout the economy' (McDonald, 1969, p. 122) is likely to entail a relatively larger number of female immigrant workers, especially in the sectors of light industry and services. On the other hand, the French administration has recently become worried that the large-scale import and easy availability of foreign labour may slow down the rationalization of French industry and it is considering measures to prevent such a development. This may well result in a cut-back in the number of new immigrants and/or their confinement to the hard and dirty jobs of heavy industry and construction.

France's coloured immigrants divide neatly into three groups. First of all there are the North Africans: Algerians, Moroccans, and Tunisians being the most important group numerically. Then there are the people of Francophone Black Africa, i.e. people from former French colonies and dependencies. Lastly, there are the Black French from the four Overseas Departments: Martinique, Guadeloupe, Réunion, and Guiana (Delerm, 1964; *Rapport Annuel 1970* ... ; G. and S. Castles, 1971).

Since Algeria gained its independence in 1962, the number of Algerians in France has paradoxically doubled to around 670,000. Originally Algerians were completely free to come and go to France (and were even included in the original EEC Regulation on social security of migrant workers). At the end of 1968 a Franco-Algerian agreement limited the annual intake to 35,000 workers and subjected their stay to limitations on grounds of *ordre public,* public security, and public health modelled on the lines of the EEC provisions. At the time of independence some 40,000 Algerian Moslems, who had fought on the French side, fled to France (McDonald, 1965, p. 148). As French citizens their number is difficult to establish today but may be assumed to be considerably higher than it was shortly after independence. In addition to Algerians, about 150,000 Moroccans and 100,000 Tunisians are resident in France, more than half of whom are economically active. Altogether close to a million non-naturalized North Africans are living in France and half a million are working there.

People from fifteen countries of Black Africa[2] enjoy free access to France where they can obtain ('recover' as the French law calls it) French nationality through an act of declaration. This left-over from France's colonial time has not led to great social problems because the number of people taking advantage of this situation is relatively small. Prospective workers from Mali, Mauritania, and Senegal are subject to a medical examination before departure and are issued with a labour contract. In 1968 and 1969, 3,445 and 5,093 workers, respectively, entered metropolitan France from these three countries, while at the same time 5,335 and 5,423, respectively, left the country so that the migration balance was negative. For migrants from the remaining twelve countries a medical examination or work contract is not required. In 1968 and 1969, 11,481 and 13,358 workers, respectively, entered France from these countries and only 8,671 and 8,303, respectively, left, so that the migratory balance was positive and more than outweighed the losses to Mali, Mauritania, and Senegal. Delerm estimated in 1964 that the workers and dependants from Black Africa numbered about 45,000, to which he added 3,500 trainees, 11,000 students, and at least the same number of former students and their offspring who stayed in France (Delerm, 1964, p. 524). Today the number of 50,000 Black African workers and dependants is not considered an overestimate. As was indicated in the previous chapter, migrants from these countries do not enjoy the right to move freely throughout the EEC unless, of course, they acquire French citizenship, which only 1,200 persons seem to have done so far (*Rapport Annuel 1970 . . .*, p. 298).

Migrations from the French Overseas Departments to the metro-

---

[2] Cameroons, Central African Republic, Congo (Brazzaville), Dahomey, Gabon, Guinea, Ivory Coast, Madagascar, Mali, Mauritania, Niger, Chad, Senegal, Togo, and Upper Volta.

polis are completely free of any controls or restrictions. During the sixties, between 11,000 and 13,000 workers arrived each year, many of them under the auspices of a development programme. Their number in France is almost impossible to determine, but it may be estimated to have totalled less than 100,000 in 1964, if the natural increase in France is taken into account (Delerm, 1964, pp. 517, 522, 524). However, not all of these immigrants are coloured, as a sizeable but unknown proportion of white French is included in the number of migrants from the Overseas Departments. Today the number of coloured French from the Overseas Departments resident in metropolitan France may have reached 100,000.

(c) GERMANY

At the end of the nineteenth century the industrialization of unified Germany set in motion a large intra-*Reich* movement from the East to the Ruhr which included many Poles, first from within the German borders and later from the Polish provinces of Russia. At the turn of the century, large contingents of seasonal workers were hired in Eastern Europe for temporary employment in agriculture. Italians, too, were prominent amongst foreign workers in Germany, amounting to 128,300 out of 873,000 in mid-1907 (Merx, 1967). During the inter-war period the employment of foreigners declined slightly and slumped to 366,000 during the great depression. After World War II the division of Germany brought with it the influx of over 10 million refugees from the former German territories in Eastern Europe and 3 million refugees from the German Democratic Republic. By mid-1955 not more than 80,000 foreign workers were counted in the Federal Republic of Germany ('Germany' in this book). Germany was not in receipt of a structurally determined immigration. Since around 1958 (Böhning, 1970c, 1971c, 1971d), a tremendous increase has taken place in terms of both gross and net migration and today over 2.25 million foreign workers are employed in Germany. They are accompanied by 1 million inactive dependants, the majority of whom are children. Both Yugoslavs and Turks now outnumber Italians, who formed over 40% of the foreign work-force some ten years ago.

A widespread recruitment system in the Mediterranean area generally provides around two-fifths of the total annual intake of foreigners and between 50% and 90% of the intake from the Mediterranean

Table 3-3: Number of newly entering foreign workers (first row), the proportion of recruited new entrants (in brackets), and number of employed foreign workers at mid-year (second row), in the *Federal Republic of Germany*, by nationality, in thousands.

	1958[a]	1959	1960	1961	1962	1963	1964	1965	1966	1967	1968[b]	1969[b]	1970[b]
Belgium	0.5	0.7	2.1	3.6	3.6	2.7	2.9	3.6	2.9	2.0	0.8	0.9	2.0[c]
	2.0	2.3	2.7	4.9	6.4	6.7	6.7	6.6	7.3	6.2	6.2	7.1	8.7
France	1.2	2.6	6.5	10.8	10.2	9.8	10.9	15.6	13.2	7.8	5.1	6.2	8.0[c]
	3.9	6.8	9.3	14.5	19.4	20.1	21.1	25.8	29.3	23.5	24.2	28.7	36.2
Italy	19.5	42.5	141.3	165.8	165.3	134.9	142.1	204.3	165.5	58.5	130.2	136.2	168.3[c]
(% recr.)	(50)	(59)	(66)	(65)	(46)	(24)	(19)	(13)	(8)	(7)	(8)	(8)	(4)[c]
	25.6	48.8	121.7	207.7	266.0	299.2	289.3	359.8	399.2	274.3	287.4	340.2	375.8
Luxbg.	0.06	0.06	0.2	0.1	0.2	0.2	0.2	0.2	0.2	0.1	0.2	0.2	0.3[c]
	0.5	0.6	0.6	0.7	0.8	0.9	0.9	1.0	1.0	0.9	0.9	1.1	1.2
Netherld.	8.3	7.9	16.5	28.5	29.3	27.4	25.2	22.9	15.7	6.9	3.4	3.9	8.4[c]
	28.1	29.7	33.6	44.7	52.9	58.1	60.4	59.6	58.5	44.9	44.7	49.9	56.5
EEC	29.5	53.7	166.6	208.8	208.6	175.0	181.2	246.5	197.4	75.4	139.7	147.4	187.0[c]
	60.0	88.2	167.9	272.5	345.0	385.0	378.4	452.7	495.3	349.7	363.5	426.9	477.5
Greece	1.5	2.5	23.4	36.6	47.6	58.0	65.1	61.8	39.7	7.6	37.3	65.1	64.0
(% recr.)	-	-	(41)	(58)	(67)	(70)	(62)	(54)	(68)	(26)	(65)	(79)	(78)
	2.8	4.1	13.0	40.8	69.1	106.2	143.9	181.7	196.2	146.8	136.2	174.3	229.4
Turkey	-	-	-	7.1	15.3	27.9	62.9	59.8	43.5	14.8	62.4	121.5	123.6
(% recr.)	-	-	-	(31)	(72)	(84)	(87)	(76)	(75)	(49)	(67)	(81)	(77)
	-	-	2.5	5.2	15.3	27.1	69.2	121.1	158.0	137.1	139.3	213.0	328.0
Untd. Kingd.	1.1	1.5	2.1	2.6	3.0	3.7	3.6	4.5	4.7	3.7	4.1	4.8	5.9
	2.0	2.6	3.2	4.1	5.1	6.1	6.7	7.6	8.8	8.6	9.1	10.9	13.3
Yugosl.	3.4	4.2	4.4	10.0	25.1	19.4	17.5	31.0	50.9	15.4	76.8	192.2	202.4
(% recr.)	-	-	-	-	-	-	-	-	-	-	-	(35)	(53)
	4.8	7.3	8.8	12.9	23.6	44.4	53.1	64.1	96.7	97.7	99.7	226.3	389.0
Spain	1.2	1.9	26.7	51.2	55.0	51.7	65.9	65.1	38.6	7.8	32.0	50.1	48.8
(% recr.)	-	-	(41)	(53)	(66)	(68)	(68)	(62)	(69)	(42)	(73)	(84)	(83)
	1.5	2.2	9.5	48.4	87.3	117.5	144.3	180.6	185.3	129.1	112.0	135.5	165.9
Portugal	-	-	-	0.9	1.0	1.5	3.9	11.1	9.2	1.8	6.7	13.2	20.1
(% recr.)	-	-	-	-	-	-	(58)	(74)	(80)	(46)	(70)	(86)	(90)
	-	-	0.3	0.7	1.4	2.2	3.5	10.5	19.8	18.5	18.7	26.4	40.2
Extra-Eur.	3.4	5.0	8.9	15.7	17.0	15.0	14.2	15.0	13.6	8.6	10.7	15.1	24.7
	4.1	6.5	9.9	16.5	26.7	35.5	41.6	47.8	50.2	43.9	44.3	49.0	61.1
Other	14.5	16.5	27.4	27.6	24.0	25.3	28.0	30.1	27.2	16.8	21.2	36.7	37.4
	51.9	55.9	64.3	106.3	81.6	87.2	92.2	98.3	103.7	92.3	92.0	109.8	134.5
OVERALL	54.6	85.3	259.5	360.5	396.6	377.5	442.3	524.9	424.8	151.9	390.9	646.1	713.9
(% recr.)	(18)	(30)	(43)	(43)	(39)	(38)	(38)	(29)	(25)	(11)	(27)	(43)	(45)
	127.1	166.8	279.4	507.4	655.5	811.2	932.9	1,164.4	1,314.0	1,023.7	1,014.8	1,372.1	1,838.9
% women	16%	15%	15%	15%	19%	22%	21%	25%	29%	35%	28%	26%	25%
	-	19%	15%	14%	18%	21%	22%	23%	25%	29%	30%	29%	29%
% emp'ees	0.6%	0.8%	1.3%	2.3%	3.0%	3.6%	4.1%	5.5%	6.1%	4.9%	4.9%	6.4%	8.5%

- = Not available or not applicable. a = Excluding Saar.
b = New entrants excluding frontier workers (21,400 in 1968; 29,200 in 1969; 8,600 in 1970). c = Estimated.
Source: *Amtliche Nachrichten*.

countries themselves (see Table 3–3). As in the case of France, the share of new entrants from Italy has fallen steadily in recent years. In Germany, too, this decline had set in before 1964, i.e. before the EEC significantly freed the movements of workers. But the maturing of the migration stream must have played a smaller part during the first half of the sixties in Germany than it had done in France, where the maturing had reached its last stage while in Germany it was still in its early stages (see next chapter). In Germany it was the desperate labour shortage which made officials close their eyes when Italians coming in as tourists found work and applied for work and residence permits *ex post facto*. (In the case of Spaniards in France it was the willingness of the French authorities to regularize the position of spontaneous immigrants.) But Spaniards and other people from countries not neighbouring on Germany found it rather more difficult to spill over into Germany than did the Italians, and they may also have met with a less lenient attitude on the side of the German authorities (quite apart from the fact that countries like Turkey, and sometimes Greece, kept a very tight control over emigration which they wanted to channel through the official procedures). An Italian lured to Germany by higher wages may often have found the official recruitment system too slow and perhaps too selective—about 9% of the applicants have been refused over the last fifteen years—and since the message had passed down the 'grapevine' that there was little risk of being turned back at the border or after having found a job, he was more likely to jump on a train which brought him to Munich in hours than to take his place in the official queue. Conversely, a Spaniard, Portuguese, or Greek faced a long and uncertain journey without assurance of obtaining employment and was therefore more likely to choose the official procedure where at least he had a 90% chance of getting a job in the next few months or weeks. It is fairly certain that the freeing of movements within the EEC has had no or very little significant autonomous influence upon the degree of organized versus spontaneous immigration on the side of the Italians. If there was an EEC effect in this respect in the second half of the sixties, then it was additional to the maturing and became effective only in conjunction with the acute demand for labour in Germany.

Germany is in many ways Europe's most typical labour-receiving country. In the beginning there was an unspoken assumption that Germany was not a country of immigration. It considered the import of foreign labour as a temporary expedient with which to overcome unusual demand pressure and believed that the migrants would return home when the economy returned to its normal pace. When the influx gathered momentum and workers continued to stay longer and longer, no German official missed the chance of prefacing his remarks on the subject with the adjuration that Germany was not a country of immigration. The economic recession of 1967 seemed at the outset to confirm the original notion of *Konjunkturpuffer*, i.e. the import of foreign labour when it is needed during a boom and its re-export during a recession. In fact, it showed that, although official recruitment was down to 17,200, altogether 151,900 new workers were engaged during 1967 (see Table 3–3); and the return flow was only very slightly larger than it would have been during boom conditions, due to the fact that some foreigners went home earlier than anticipated because they were unable to do overtime or even full time (while some 30,000 stayed on as unemployed). The net decrease of about 200,000 in the total of employed foreigners was not due to the dismissal of foreigners by employers but was almost wholly the result of a fall in the number of new immigrants. After the recession the number of newly entering immigrant workers climbed even higher than before and the essentially structural requirement for foreign workers became evident as well as the largely circulatory character of the migration.[3] However, the official attitude remained unchanged and the more the social reality showed Germany as a country of immigration, the louder were the official denials that this was or ever should be the case. Meanwhile the human and social problems had become so pressing that they could not be left in the hands of social workers or the labour market authorities alone, and the need for a concept and policy of integration became imperative. An expendable labour force takes its problems away with it when it is re-exported, and it does not require special governmental attention during its temporary sojourn so long as employers and trade unions are satisfied with their respective stakes; the housing and living conditions of temporary immigrants can be rationalized by reference to their desire to save, and discrimination can be excused on grounds of short stay and only partial participation in the life of the society; but when the facts belie the notion of

---

[3] Forty per cent of the Italians, Greeks, Spaniards, and Turks who entered Germany during the first three quarters of 1968 had worked in Germany before; see Table 32 in Böhning (1971d).

temporary immigration, the rationalizations and excuses carry no conviction and the lack of policies compounds social problems. The German civil servants probably realized this long before the politicians—and the labour market administrators, in particular, had quite early on started to deal with the foreign work-force in a much more liberal way than the wording of the law and the reasoning behind it would seem to permit. Finally, in early 1970, the outline of an integration policy was developed, representing the lowest common denominator between the various interests involved. The politicians gave their blessing (but little money), and the publication of this policy was surrounded by frequent official statements that Germany was not a country of immigration (*Bundesarbeitsblatt*, No. 4, 1970). However, the log-jam had been broken, and one year later the same official publication carried another series of articles (*Bundesarbeitsblatt*, Nos. 7–8, 1971; and also Deutscher Städtetag, 1971) in which there was grudging acknowledgement of the fact that Germany had become a country of immigration and that one needed to integrate the foreign workers socially and politically—either pluralistically or by way of assimilation. The realization that migrant workers had already settled in German towns, that Germany had acquired a permanent foreign work-force with a decreasing element of rotation, and that in the foreseeable future this work-force was more likely to grow than to stagnate or decrease, made the change in the official stance inevitable. The change itself is not dramatic; it gives immigrants no more than is their due. Acts of positive discrimination (outside the employer's responsibility) are still considered to be politically unfeasible. But at least the atmosphere has changed and a beginning has been made.

The movement of immigrant workers into Germany because of economic factors is not in question. Ninety-six per cent of the variance in the number of new entrants over the period 1957–68 was explained by German labour demand (Böhning, 1970d, note 2, p. 199).[4] As in the case of France, the variations in the share of new immigrants of different nationalities are less likely to be related, at given levels of demand, to conditions in the receiving country than to conditions in the sending countries and other immigration countries. For example, the increase in the proportion of Italians in 1965

[4] On the other hand, it is also clear that the size of the foreign work-force itself is only weakly related to German labour demand and the same holds true for the return flow; see Böhning (1970d), p. 193.

and 1966 reflected both the economic setback in Italy and the Swiss measures to stabilize their foreign work-force; and the present-day preponderance of new entrants from Yugoslavia and Turkey reflects the drying up of the Italian source compared with the abundant supplies in those two countries. At varying levels of demand for labour, the receiving country's selectivity becomes more important and effects fluctuations in the shares of different nationalities which are related to the stage in the development of the sending countries. As the skill level of a labour force rises in line with the level of development, and as migration streams generally reflect the skill composition of the population at source,[5] the receiving country is likely to admit proportionately more immigrants from developed countries during periods of economic recessions because low-skill jobs are not in demand. For example, during 1967 the proportion of new entrants from Germany's neighbours rose steeply, whereas the proportion of Greeks and Spaniards fell considerably while that of the Italians fell only slightly, possibly reflecting Italy's 'two nations' (Böhning, 1970d, p. 197; and Table 5–3 below).

Germany was spared a colour and citizenship problem due to its loss of colonies after World War I. During the post-World War II period, non-Europeans were as a rule not considered for employment in Germany. There are, however, a few telling exceptions to this rule. Firstly, people from the white Commonwealth, the United States, and Israel are not treated differently from Europeans; secondly, doctors and nurses, and skilled workers whose employment constitutes a demonstrable need are given preferential treatment; thirdly, trainees are generally welcome; and fourthly, specific contingents of people are admitted from time to time for reasons of foreign policy (e.g. Moroccans and Tunisians) or because the Ministry for Overseas Development is unable to procure financial aid and offers to employ a certain number of workers for a fixed period instead. Thus, there have been contingents of Chilean miners from time to time. The employment of these people has a habit of becoming semi-permanent and irreversible. Moroccans and Tunisians now come to Germany on a fairly regular basis within the framework of the recruitment

---

[5] If anything, the skill level of the migrant population is usually higher than that of the non-migrant population; see Böhning (1971d). The brain drain is an extreme example of this. Blandy (1968, p. 186) comes to essentially the same conclusion. Distortions arise mainly from the different phases of maturity of a migration stream; see below Chapter 4.

agreements of 1963 and 1965, respectively, although it is in these two countries that the recruitment is first stopped when economic activity begins to fall. In mid-1971, 11,000 Moroccans and 10,000 Tunisians were employed in Germany, one in fifty of the former and one in ten of the latter being women. At the beginning of 1971, 14,000 workers in nursing and auxiliary occupations were foreigners, of whom 3,200 were Koreans, 1,300 Filipinos, and 900 Indians. Altogether there may be some 60,000 coloured workers in Germany today, 10% of whom are trainees: 8,000 come from the New Commonwealth, including 4,500 Indians, 1,000 Nigerians, 800 Pakistanis, 700 Ghanaians, over 100 West Indians, and some smaller groups.

(d) ITALY

Italy is on the way to becoming an immigration country, too. Economically determined emigration of nationals and immigration of foreigners do not exclude each other. Thousands of British, German, and Dutch workers are leaving their countries every year while at the same time thousands of foreign workers are entering their countries, and the same holds true for countries like Yugoslavia, Spain, and Italy and, of course, for the brain drain generally. In the case of Italy it is not yet clear whether a replacement migration is taking place, i.e. whether immigrants are filling gaps left by emigrants who according to economic indicators were not subject to any economic 'push'; or whether the immigrants comprise largely white-collar workers, i.e. personnel sent by foreign firms establishing themselves in the booming North; or whether the immigration is already following the pattern of countries north of the Alps. The comparatively large number and (decreasing) proportion of Germans and Britons would seem to point to the second explanation (white-collar business migration). However, these could equally be fairly skilled workers filling the gaps left by Italians who could not resist the myth of migration. In any case there is little doubt that the variations in the over-all number of immigrants closely reflect the state of the economy (see Table 3–4). With 30,000 foreign workers out of a labour force of some 19 millions, one can hardly speak of a structurally determined immigration as opposed to an immigration of random size and for idiosyncratic reasons. But one must expect Italy to enter the rank of labour-receiving countries long before its internal surplus of labour has been absorbed abroad or at home: in the same way that other countries imported labour

Table 3-4: Number of newly entering foreign workers 1958-1970, and number of employed foreign workers 1965-1968, in *Italy*, by nationality.

	1958	1959	1960	1961	1962	1963	1964	1965	65: empl.	1966	66: empl.	1967	67: empl.	1968	68: empl.	1969	1970
Belgium	8	16	6	25	55	69	42	61	-	66	-	54	-	86	391	73	73
France	122	89	93	193	382	530	410	564	2,323	556	2,457	479	2,533	826	2,754	672	464
Germany	300	484	533	588	902	1,170	948	938	5,255	899	5,329	854	5,591	1,109	5,951	1,037	797
Luxbg.	1	2	1	0	2	11	5	5	-	6	-	9	-	3	25	4	9
Netherld.	23	77	66	35	80	249	331	232	-	299	-	273	-	322	907	292	262
EEC	454	668	699	841	1,421	2,029	1,736	1,800	-	1,826	-	1,669	-	2,346	10,028	2,078	1,605
Greece	-	-	-	-	-	132	177	119	-	104	-	121	-	133	637	112	135
Turkey	-	-	-	-	-	-	28	17	-	20	-	11	-	18	129	29	35
Utd. Kingd.	173	103	114	135	341	406	297	-	2,630	637	2,771	-	3,007	-	3,301	-	-
Yugosl.	-	-	-	-	-	212	578	-	1,039	-	1,133	-	1,440	-	1,781	1,948	2,007
Spain	-	-	-	-	-	317	670	412	1,137	328	1,225	262	1,277	291	1,402	424	463
Portugal	-	-	-	-	-	30	53	52	-	72	-	148	-	169	203	246	518
Extra-Eur.	117	124	175	166	441	587	620	-	-	-	-	-	-	-	-	-	-
Other	246	207	145	221	681	583	912	2,530	15,612	2,193	15,903	3,042	16,779	4,448	15,617	3,534	4,190
OVERALL	990	1,102	1,133	1,363	2,884	4,296	5,071	4,930	27,996	5,180	28,818	5,253	30,627	7,405	33,098	8,371	8,954

Source: Statistisches Amt . . . (1969); Kommission . . . (1970a, 1971a).

at times of excess supply because of the scarcity of some occupations and the non-transferability of skills from surplus occupations.

(e) LUXEMBOURG

During the second half of the sixties, Luxembourg employed about the same number of foreigners as Italy, but of course in tiny Luxembourg these workers constituted almost 30% of all wage and salary earners (see Table 3–5) and in Italy less than 0.3%. Luxembourg's

Table 3–5: Number of newly entering foreign workers, and total number of employed foreign workers and employed Italians, in *Luxembourg*, by nationality.

	1958	1959	1960	1961	1962	1963	1964	1965	1966	1967	1968	1969	1970
Italy	8,736	8,194	8,111	9,823	5,427	4,911	3,939	4,275	3,347	1,375	1,113	855	551
empl.	-	-	-	10,517	11,364	10,660	11,310	12,340	12,454	11,716	11,300	11,100	11,000
EEC[a]	12,384	11,793	11,809	12,823	7,197	6,971	7,172	7,495	6,134	3,261	2,900	2,173	1,745
Untd. Kingd.	21	18	21	33	22	97	78	46	34	-	-	-	-
Other Eur.	344	268	431	523	779	1,526	3,055	1,912	1,508	586	-	(2,077)[c]	(3,554)[c]
Extra-Eur.[b]	67	52	48 *	73	71	171	306	215	138	134	-	-	-
OVERALL empl.	12,816	12,131	12,309	13,452	8,069	8,765	10,611	9,668	7,814	3,981	3,898	4,479	5,592
empl.	-	-	-	20,900	22,402	22,789	25,258	28,106	29,427	27,891	28,600	30,100	33,100
% employees	-	~	-	22%	23%	23%	25%	27%	28%	27%	27%	28%	29%

a = Excluding Belgium and the Netherlands (Common Labour Market).
b = Including stateless and those of unknown nationality.
c — Greece, Yugoslavia, Portugal, and Spain.
Source: Statistisches Amt . . . (1969); Kommission . . . (1970a, 1971a).

history of immigration closely resembles that of Belgium except that Luxembourg has never encouraged immigration for demographic reasons and has made it rather difficult for foreigners to settle permanently. Because of its population problems (340,000 inhabitants), Luxembourg secured special consideration as regards the right of Community workers to settle there permanently under the EEC free movement system. (See Protocol concerning the Grand Duchy of Luxembourg, annexed to Treaty of Rome, and Article 9 of Regulation 1251/70 which exempts Luxembourg from that Regulation.) The reunion of migrant families is, however, often easier in Luxembourg than in surrounding countries because the housing shortage is less acute.

In 1930 Luxembourg was host to 15,000 foreigners, mainly from neighbouring countries. In the fifties the immigration of workers gathered momentum again, coming mainly from Italy. Today, barely 10% of the number of Italians who annually entered ten years ago, go into Luxembourg and the number in employment is falling. Portuguese and Spaniards are taking their place. Manufacturing, construction, and services each employ about one-third of the foreigners, though there are also a few workers in agriculture.

(f) THE NETHERLANDS

The peak of Dutch emigration had hardly passed in 1956 when the Netherlands started to experience an unknown degree of labour scarcity and became a labour-receiving country. At the beginning of the last decade, the immigration gathered momentum with Italy providing between 20% and 40% of the new entrants. However, it was quickly overtaken by Spain and, since 1964, by Turkey (see Table 3–6). The Italian work-force has become stationary at the 11,000 level. There are at least twice as many workers from neighbouring Belgium and Luxembourg in the Netherlands as from Italy (Bouscaren, 1969, p. 72; ter Heide, 1971; Bagley, 1971a, 1971b; Hogebrink, 1970).

Recruitment agreements have been concluded with most Mediterranean countries. They have not been very successful because of the intense German competition and because the Dutch agents were searching predominantly for young single workers. All Dutch governments have favoured temporary immigration of workers without their families, and rapid turnover rather than permanent settlement. A memorandum presented to the Dutch Parliament by the Ministers of Social Affairs and National Health, Justice, Economic Affairs, and Culture, Recreation, and Social Work, states: 'It should be kept in mind that the demographic situation in the Netherlands does not make the stimulation of immigration desirable. . . . The Netherlands is definitely not an immigration country' (*Nota buitenlandse werknemers*, Document 10504, 14 Jan. 1970, p. 9). Thus, the reunion of separated families from non-EEC countries is particularly difficult, requiring at least two years' employment in the Low Countries plus assurance of at least another year's employment plus the willingness of the local authority to offer housing. Because of its recency and the harsh attitude of the Dutch authorities, the migration stream into the Netherlands is maturing only slowly. Thirty per cent of the people from Mediterranean countries who left the Netherlands during 1966–7, i.e. during the economic stagnation, had stayed less than twelve months; 84% had stayed less than three years; and 97%, less than six years (ter Heide, 1971, p. 4).

Table 3–6: Number of newly entering foreign workers (first row) and number of employed foreign workers at end of year (second row), in the *Netherlands*, by nationality, in thousands.

	1958	1959	1960	1961	1962	1963	1964	1965	1966	1967	1968	1969[f]	1970[f]
France	0.1	0.2	0.2	0.3	0.3	0.2	0.7	0.6	0.6	1.5	0.6	0.4	0.4[g]
	0.3	0.3	0.4	0.6	0.5	0.5	0.6	0.9	0.9	1.8	1.7	-	--
Germany	2.0	1.9	2.1	2.0	1.8	2.0	2.8	2.2	2.1	2.7	2.6	2.2	2.5[g]
	8.1	7.5	8.3	8.0	7.4	7.7	7.9	8.3	9.1	10.6	11.7	-	-
Italy	0.9	0.3	1.4	4.5	3.2	2.6	3.2	2.7	2.1	1.4	1.4	1.6	1.2[g]
	2.7	1.9	2.7	5.6	6.7	6.8	7.2	8.1	8.5	8.7	9.5	-	-
EEC[a]	3.0	2.4	3.7	6.8	5.3	4.8	6.7	5.5	4.9	5.6	4.7	4.2	4.1[g]
	11.1	9.7	11.4	14.2	14.6	15.0	15.7	17.3	18.5	21.1	22.9	-	-
Greece	-	-	-	-	-	1.5	1.9	0.9	0.6	0.2	0.3	0.5	0.5
	-	-	-	-	0.4	1.5	2.4	2.0	2.1	1.6	1.6	1.4	1.3
Turkey	-	-	-	-	-	0.7	4.9	4.3	6.9	1.3	3.7	5.7	6.9
	0.01	0.01	0.02	0.07	0.2	0.7	4.6	7.3	12.2	10.2	13.6	16.5	18.5
Untd. Kingd.[h]	0.5	0.4	0.7	0.7	1.0	1.1	1.4	1.0	1.5	1.3	-	-	-
	1.1	1.1	1.3	1.3	1.7	1.9	2.3	2.2	2.5	2.5	2.7	3.1	3.1
Yugosl.	-	-	-	-	-	0.4	0.2	0.7	0.9	0.5	-	-	-
	-	-	-	-	-	0.6	0.8	1.0	1.1	0.9	1.4	3.4	6.2
Spain	-	-	-	-	-	5.5	9.4	9.9	8.0	2.4	2.3	4.6	7.1
	0.07	0.07	0.2	1.3	4.0	7.2	12.8	16.5	17.1	12.9	12.1	11.8	13.4
Portugal	-	-	-	-	-	0.2	0.4	0.8	1.1	0.7	0.4	0.6	1.0
	-	-	-	-	-	0.3	0.5	1.1	1.8	2.2	2.3	2.1	2.6
Extra-Europ.[b]	-	-	-	-	-	1.7	4.6	6.5	11.0	4.1	-	-	-
Other	1.6	1.9	2.5	4.0	7.1	1.2	1.4	1.6	1.3	1.2	8.5	12.9	17.6
	11.5	10.4	11.2	11.1	11.1	10.8	12.5	15.8	21.0	20.7	23.7	12.1	26.2
OVERALL	5.1	4.7	6.9	11.5	13.4	17.1	30.9	31.2	36.2	17.3	19.9	27.7	37.2
	23.8	21.3	24.1	28.0	32.0	38.0	51.6	63.2	76.3	72.1	80.3	60.1[i]	71.3[i]
% women[c]	24%	24%	33%	19%	17%	15%	12%	10%	10%	12%	13%	12%	15%
% emp'ees	0.7%	0.6%	0.7%	0.8%	0.9%	1.1%	1.4%	1.7%	2.0%	1.9%	2.1%	1.5%	1.8%
Surinamese Dutch Ant.[d]	-	-	13.7	14.7	16.3	18.4	20.8	24.7	28.3	31.6	35.2	40.7	47.6
Amboinese[e]	-	-	19.2	19.9	20.0	20.3	21.2	21.6	22.1	22.5	25.5	25.9	26.3

a = Excluding Belgium and Luxembourg (Common Labour Market) and frontier workers.
b = New entrants.
c = Employed females as percentage of total employed.
d = Resident in the Netherlands.
e = Resident in the Netherlands.
f = Employment data: less than five years in the Netherlands.
g = EEC estimate.
h = Excluding Chinese of British citizenship: 363 British Chinese were employed in 1968, 641 in 1969, and 684 in 1970.
i = Excluding all EEC citizens.
Source: Statistisches Amt ... (1969); Kommission ... (1970a, 1971a); *Sociale Maandstatistiek*; and *Stafbureau statistiek*.

In relative terms, coloured immigrants play a much more important role in the Netherlands than in France. With the end of World
War II and the independence of Indonesia, some 200,000 Indonesian
Dutch fled to the Low Countries. They were followed by about
12,500 Ambonese (Molukkers), whose number grew to 19,000 in
1960 and to just under 30,000 in 1971 (see Table 3–6). The Indonesian Dutch were assimilated quickly by a deliberate and
enlightened policy. The Ambonese sought to retain their own
cultural identity and group cohesion in the hope of returning to
their islands. A second group of coloured immigrants comes from
Latin America, i.e. Surinam and the Dutch Antilles (see pp. 11–13
above). People from these overseas parts of the Netherlands can
freely enter the European parts and have done so increasingly in
recent years (see Table 3–6). The immigration from Surinam dates
back to the early nineteenth century, when it was a middle-class
migration and quite small (van Amersfoort, 1968). During the early
post-war years the middle-class character still predominated, but
since 1955 Dutch companies have recruited workers from Surinam
and the composition of the migration stream is now more akin to
that of Mediterranean workers in the Netherlands. Surinam has
about 370,000 inhabitants, but a further 45,000 are estimated to
live in the Low Countries, 36,000 of whom are workers and 9,000
dependants. Out of those 45,000, an increasing proportion is repre-
sented by Hindustanis, perhaps 7,000 today. Hindustanis and Creoles
comprise 35% of the population in Surinam. Dutch Antillians have
migrated to the Netherlands only recently. During the mid-fifties the
rationalization of the oil refineries set free a large number of workers
and the migration stream has consequently been largely working
class. Today an estimated 8,000 workers and 2,000 dependants are
living in the Low Countries. Thus, there are altogether 285,000
coloured Dutchmen in the Netherlands at the time of writing
(200,000 Indonesian Dutch, 30,000 Ambonese, and 55,000 West
Indians) or 2.2% of the total population of 13 millions. In addition,
there were in mid-1970 about 18,000 Moroccans and over 80,000
Europeans in Europe's most densely populated country, and the
illiberal stand of the Dutch Government towards immigrants other
than its own citizens or EEC nationals becomes easily explicable by
these figures, especially if one takes into account that the natural
increase of the Dutch population is estimated to bring it up to 17

millions by the year 2,000, with 500 people per square kilometre or more than twice the present British density!

(g) NON-EEC COUNTRIES: SWITZERLAND AND BRITAIN

The survey of the Six has revealed no obvious indications that migration streams into and among Community countries are subject to a special EEC effect. This theme will be elaborated upon in a later chapter. Here the experience of the two most important non-EEC countries with large labour immigrations will be examined briefly to see whether the development outside the Six was markedly different from that of the Six. Other countries, Sweden and Austria for example, could be adduced, too, but the information available is not yet sufficient to give a clear picture of the Swedish and Austrian scenes. Austria began importing labour in 1962 and its foreign work-force has grown steadily to a level of about 130,000 (Mayer, 1971, pp. 7–9, 13–14), about half of whom are Yugoslavs and 10% Turks. The number of Italians has always been small and fell below the 1,000 mark in 1970. Sweden started to admit foreign workers soon after World War II and, with the exception of three periods of recession, has employed an increasing number of foreigners: 228,000 in 1970, half of whom were Finns and 10% Yugoslavs (Swedish Institute, 1970; Reinans, 1971).[6] Altogether 400,000 foreigners and 225,000 naturalized foreigners are living amongst 8 million Swedes today.

Switzerland has traditionally been a country of immigration for workers from neighbouring states (Bericht der Studienkommission ..., 1964; and Mayer, 1965; 1971). At the outbreak of World War I, 15% of the Swiss population was foreign. The deferment of investment programmes during World War II and the increased economic activity in the devastated neighbouring areas shortly after the War, led to an intense shortage of labour in Switzerland, which that country immediately started to fill with Italians from Northern Italy in the expectation that the boom would be temporary and that the Italians would return home after it had faded out. But the boom proved permanent and so did the Italians, except that their origin changed from North to South. During 1946, 48,800 Italians constituted 98% of Switzerland's foreign work-force; in 1957, five times that number of Italians, 247,800, constituted exactly two-thirds of the

---

6 There were 5,000 Italian workers and 3,000 dependants in Sweden at that time.

foreign workers; today about 350,000 Italians provide only a little over half the foreign workers. Since its peak in 1963–4, the number of Italians in Swiss employment has fallen by 100,000. This decrease is due, on the one side, to the deliberate Swiss policy, since 1963, of stabilizing the number of foreign workers, which first cut down on the number of new entrants and later imposed annual reductions on the number employed in most sectors of the economy. On the other side, there are also a considerable number of Italians each year who are taken off conditions, i.e. they are no longer subject to registration and are permitted to stay permanently, but are not naturalized Swiss citizens. The over-all number of permanently established foreigners has doubled to 158,000 in the last ten years; Italians can be assumed to make up half of these. Outside the staff of international organizations there are hardly any extra-European workers in Switzerland.

Like Germany and the Netherlands, Switzerland was originally interested primarily in single workers and discouraged family reunion and permanent settlement. The desired rotation of workers took on exploitative characteristics when, for example, a seasonal worker had to take his annual holiday over the Christmas period and this was regarded as the break in the seasonal employment requiring the worker to obtain a new seasonal permit upon his return. When the 1958 recession finally put paid to the notion of *Konjunkturpuffer* and the permanent character of the foreign work-force became indisputable, 'Switzerland found herself forced to liberalise the stringent rules against bringing in their families and to renew work permits indefinitely' (Mayer, 1971, p. 2). At the beginning of the sixties a Commission was convened to study the problem of foreign employees (Bericht der Studienkommission . . . , 1964). During the following years a general consensus emerged to stop the influx of new migrants and to give more help to those immigrants who show themselves able and willing to settle and assimilate. Within this framework the admittance of dependants has also been liberalized.[7] As Table 3–7 shows, the figure of new entrants has in fact decreased and the number of foreign workers subject to control has been stabilized. But if one takes into account the number of foreigners taken off conditions, then the foreign work-force is still growing

---

[7] One-third of all residence permits of twelve months' duration is nowadays in the hands of dependants, as against a quarter during the fifties (Mayer, 1971, p. 5).

Table 3–7: Number of newly entering foreign workers (permanent plus seasonal plus frontier workers), and number of employed foreign workers in August each year (permanent, seasonal, and frontier workers subject to control), in *Switzerland*, by nationality, in thousands.

	1958	1959	1960	1961	1962	1963	1964	1965	1966	1967	1968	1969	1970
France	-	-	-	-	-	-	-	20.6	22.0	27.7	32.1	34.4	40.0
	8.6	8.8	11.9	16.2	18.7	21.2	24.0	23.8	25.6	29.5	34.0	36.8	41.5
Germany	-	-	-	-	-	-	-	31.1	28.1	32.4	32.0	31.3	28.8
	76.2	71.4	72.4	73.5	77.7	78.4	78.6	67.7	58.4	59.1	60.4	57.2	53.0
Italy	-	-	-	-	-	-	-.	257.1	234.1	213.7	208.7	208.1	179.1
	235.8	242.8	303.1	392.1	454.4	472.1	474.3	448.5	432.8	425.2	409.3	398.9	371.8
Spain	-	-	-	-	-	-	-	38.8	34.8	31.3	38.5	54.5	68.3
	-	-	6.4	21.8	28.3	63.7	82.3	79.4	77.2	75.9	80.9	95.7	112.6
Other	-	-	-	-	-	-	-	27.6	27.5	34.8	34.6	42.9	40.8
	42.8	41.8	41.7	44.7	65.6	54.6	61.7	56.9	54.5	58.3	63.4	70.6	80.6
OVERALL	254.6	273.8	341.9	422.5	455.7	445.0	455.3	375.2	346.5	339.9	345.9	371.2	357.0
	363.4	364.8	435.5	548.3	644.7	690.0	720.9	676.3	648.5	648.1	648.1	659.2	659.5
% seasonal	48%	47%	46%	46%	49%	50%	52%	57%	55%	53%	50%	51%	56%
	29%	31%	32%	32%	30%	29%	29%	27%	25%	24%	22%	23%	23%
% women	32%	30%	27%	26%	25%	25%	24%	24%	24%	25%	26%	26%	25%
	38%	36%	34%	32%	31%	30%	30%	30%	31%	31%	31%	32%	32%
Established[a]	-	-	71.0	-	-	-	-	104.0	117.0	131.8	148.1	158.3	..

a = Taken off conditions, in December each year. 'Permanent' workers in the heading refers to holders of permits of twelve months' duration but not to permanently established aliens.

Source: *Statistisches Jahrbuch der Schweiz*; *La Vie Économique*.

slightly and the most recent measures of the Swiss administration aim at the stabilization of this total work-force, which amounts to 30% of all economically active Swiss. To some degree these measures were no doubt influenced by the Schwarzenbach movement on 'over-foreignization', but economists have been equally worried by the degree of 'over-dependence' on foreign workers in many factories and even whole sectors of the economy, where the non-managerial work-force is sometimes completely dependent upon the supply of foreigners.

The country on which Vera Lutz (1963) built her influential model of the economics of international migration has largely failed to fulfil her assumptions. As will be seen in the next chapter, this is mainly due to the economic and social dynamics of migration. The proportion of foreigners employed in low-productivity, low-paying jobs in Switzerland has been halved over the last fifteen years, while a larger and larger share of immigrant labour has found employment in the metal and machinery industry, for example. Moreover, whereas, in 1955, 75% of the workers with a twelve-month permit had stayed in Switzerland for less than three years and only 11% for five years or more, in 1969 the proportions had changed to 44% and 42%, respectively (Mayer, 1971, pp. 5, 11).

Statistics and other data on immigrant workers in Britain are still rather unsatisfactory as far as non-Commonwealth immigrants are concerned. Besides the Jews at the turn of the century and the coloured Commonwealth immigrants since the fifties, Europeans have played a minor but significant role as immigrants, though more in numerical than in social terms. The post-war wave of European 'Volunteer Workers' (Tannahill, 1958) is almost completely absorbed and forgotten,[8] and the employment of Italians shortly after the War has never developed into a large migration stream. (For Italians, see, for example, Barr, 1964; Chadwick-Jones, 1964; Brown, 1970; see also the forthcoming Runnymede publication by J. and L. Macdonald on Italian, Spanish, and Portuguese immigrants in Britain.)

The three sets of statistics available do not tally. The Department of Employment's *Gazette* gives figures on the number of work permits issued to foreigners still abroad, according to the prescribed procedure, and (formerly, in addition and without detailing its composition) the over-all number of work permits issued to foreigners already in the country. The first of these figures is usually a little higher than the number of permits actually taken up, which the Home Office establishes at the port of entry. But the Home Office misses out, it must be assumed, on those one in six whose permit is granted by the Department of Employment after entry, namely, hairdressers, workers in residential domestic service, agriculture, and horticulture, and low-skilled manual workers in textiles. On the other hand, the number of workers counted by the Home Office and the number of permits granted after entry (see Table 3–8) do not add up to the number of applications for National Insurance Cards by foreigners (Davison, 1963, pp. 49, 56). Needless to say, the number of aliens subject to the registration procedure includes both workers and dependants and gives, therefore, little indication of the size of the foreign work-force. The numbers of those who for one reason or another (marriage or four years' work in approved employment) are taken off conditions but are not yet naturalized, are not regularly published.

[8] Though Patterson (1968) found a few remnants.

Table 3–8: Number of newly entering foreign workers, permanent plus seasonal workers, 1958–1970 (first row), and number of foreigners registered at end of year 1961–1970 (second row), in the *United Kingdom*, by nationality, in thousands.

	1958	1959	1960	1961	1962	1963	1964	1965	1966	1967	1968	1969	1970
Belgium[a,b]	0.3	0.4	0.4	0.4	0.4	0.3	0.3	0.3	0.4	0.4	0.3	0.5	0.4
France	2.8	3.0	3.0	3.3	3.5	3.6	4.2	4.9	5.2	5.7	5.4	5.4	5.8
	-	-	-	7.9	9.1	9.4	10.8	12.2	13.2	13.5	13.5	13.6	13.9
Germany	10.3	9.5	9.0	8.0	7.5	6.0	5.8	5.7	5.5	5.1	4.6	4.2	3.9
	-	-	-	16.2	16.6	15.4	15.2	14.2	12.8	12.5	11.6	11.4	11.0
Italy	7.7	7.2	10.6	12.1	7.1	4.6	5.2	7.6	6.9	4.9	4.2	3.9	3.1
	-	-	-	29.8	30.9	28.6	25.8	24.6	24.5	23.5	21.2	18.0	14.8
Netherlands[b]	2.1	2.1	2.0	1.9	1.9	1.8	1.8	2.4	2.0	2.2	1.9	2.0	2.0
EEC	23.2	22.3	25.0	25.6	20.3	16.3	17.3	20.9	20.0	18.3	16.4	16.0	15.0
	-	-	-	58.1	61.1	58.2	56.9	56.7	56.2	55.5	52.3	48.7	45.6
Greece	0.2	0.2	0.3	0.5	0.4	0.5	0.5	0.5	0.6	0.5	0.4	0.4	0.5
	-	-	-	2.2	2.6	2.9	3.2	3.4	3.7	3.9	4.1	4.3	4.7
Turkey[b]	0.08	0.06	0.05	0.1	0.2	0.2	0.3	0.2	0.3	0.3	0.3	0.5	0.9
Yugosl.	0.6	0.4	0.3	0.3	0.3	0.4	0.4	0.6	0.8	1.0	1.4	1.4	1.7
	-	-	-	0.7	0.9	1.0	1.3	1.4	1.9	2.4	2.7	3.1	3.3
Spain	3.1	3.5	5.5	7.5	8.1	6.8	7.8	7.8	6.9	6.0	6.6	7.3	7.1
	-	-	-	16.6	22.0	24.4	26.3	26.6	24.8	22.8	21.4	21.2	22.0
Portugal[b]	0.3	0.4	0.5	0.6	0.5	0.6	0.8	1.1	1.1	1.0	0.7	1.1	1.7
Extra-Eur.	2.9	2.6	3.1	3.5	3.6	4.3	5.1	6.2	6.5	7.6	7.8	8.8	10.8
	-	-	-	25.3	30.3	36.0	41.3	46.1	51.0	54.8	57.3	62.9	73.3
Other[b]	11.1	10.9	11.3	11.3	10.9	10.6	10.4	11.6	12.4	11.2	11.5	12.4	9.8
OVERALL[c]	41.5	40.4	46.1	49.4	44.3	39.7	42.6	48.9	48.6	45.9	45.1	47.9	47.7
(DEP ab)[d]	-	-	-	(51.8)	(48.2)	(43.9)	(47.6)	(54.3)	(54.8)	(50.3)	(51.5)	(56.2)	(56.0)
(DEP in)[e]	-	-	-	(6.7)	(7.2)	(8.6)	(10.7)	(11.9)	(11.2)	(10.3)	(10.8)	(11.6)	(11.6)
	-	-	-	125.4	141.3	147.9	157.1	164.5	166.6	170.8	169.6	173.6	179.3
% seasonal[b,f]	35%	34%	32%	35%	38%	45%	44%	43%	45%	50%	50%	52%	48%
% women[b,f]	70%	76%	67%	62%	61%	61%	54%	47%	46%	47%	45%	44%	44%
Vouch. tot.[g]	(60.7)[i]	(66.0)[i]	(108.5)[i]	(144.5)[i]	5.1	30.1	14.7	12.9	5.5	5.0	4.7	4.0	4.0
I.P.W.W.[h]	(32.9)[k]	(34.4)[k]	(65.2)[k]	(92.0)[k]	3.3	25.4	10.6	8.6	3.8	3.6	3.0	2.2	1.6

a = Including Luxembourg.
b = New entrants data only.
c = Excluding Irish and permit-free categories.
d = Number of employment permissions granted to persons abroad by Ministry of Labour (etc.).
e = Number of employment permissions granted to foreigners already in the United Kingdom by Ministry of Labour (etc.).
f = Non-seasonal female new entrants as % of total non-seasonal new entrants.
g = Total number of voucher holders arriving in the UK.
h = Number of voucher holders arriving from India, Pakistan, the West Indies, and West Africa.
i = Persons arriving from Commonwealth countries who applied for National Insurance Cards.
k = Newly entering applicants for National Insurance Cards from India, Pakistan, the West Indies, and West Africa.

Source: *Statistics of Persons Entering and Leaving the United Kingdom*; *Commonwealth Immigrants Act 1962: Statistics*; *Annual Abstract of Statistics*; *Gazette*; and Davison (1963).

C

The available data suggest that a fairly steady and slightly growing stream, now standing at 60,000 foreigners, has entered the UK during the same time as the immigration from the New Commonwealth first reached its peak in 1961 and then much diminished. At the peak of the Italian immigration, also in 1961, Italians formed a quarter of the foreign migrant workers. Today their 3,000 annual entrants, 6.5% of the total, are too few to prevent the number of those Italians who are subject to control from declining. It is the Spaniards, in the main, who have taken their place, but here, too, one can notice a stabilization of the numbers (see Table 3–8).

The economic determination of the immigration of non-seasonal foreign workers into Britain is clearly visible (Peach, 1965)[9] even though it is not as strong as for Germany (Böhning, 1970d, p. 199). The lower degree of correlation with labour demand and the still large share of women (around 45% since 1965) point towards a different composition and motivation of the migration as compared with the Continent. Britain presumably experiences more of a middle-class and white-collar immigration over and above the random immigration for idiosyncratic reasons (for example, marriage, evasion of national service).

There is no doubt that the often canvassed dichotomy of coloured Commonwealth immigrants=permanent settlers, and foreign workers =temporary immigrants is false on both sides. Every economic migration stream has been accompanied by a return flow, and coloured Commonwealth immigrants are no exception to this rule. As far as foreign immigrants are concerned, there is (short of a survey) a fairly reliable way of establishing the approximate proportion of temporary versus permanent immigration from official statistics. A comparison of the number of non-seasonal new entrants and returnees for the period 1963–70 (see Table 3–9)[10] shows that for every two

[9] It also holds true for coloured Commonwealth immigrants.
[10] Non-seasonal new entrants were chosen so as to exclude the deliberately short-term migration of seasonal workers which is not at stake here. Non-seasonal new entrants *had* to be chosen to make this category congruent as far as possible with the category 'registered at end of year' (which presumably includes a few seasonal workers as well—a repetitive effect which should not result in significant distortions). The non-seasonal new entrants data comprise both workers and their dependants. Other persons also admitted for twelve months or more enumerated by the Home Office are not taken into account. They include such groups as *au pair* girls, students, ministers of religion, wives, minor children coming to join resident foreigners, and so on. Although most of these residual groups inflate the number of registered aliens, this should not result in a significant distortion of the results. There are doubt-

immigrating workers and their dependants (234,568) there was one returnee (111,569). However, the ratio of inflow to outflow within the same year, or even within the same medium-term period, does not give the exact proportion of permanent stayers as people intending to return may do so after a number of years. If one relates the number of persons taken off conditions to the population from which they originate, in this case the new entrants four years earlier,[11] one obtains a much more reliable estimate of the proportion of permanent settlers. For, if people are taken off controls, they are allowed to stay for permanent residence; and the fact that they intend to do so is borne out by the figures on the acquisition of UK citizenship, which follow closely the number of persons taken off controls. Taking into account the bias of the figures, it can be said that on average one-third of the foreign workers and their dependants who were permitted to enter the UK on a non-seasonal basis stay in this country for good. Over a quarter (27%) of the original immigrants (57,217 out of the 211,973 who immigrated in 1959–65), or over three-quarters (78%) of the definite stayers (57,217 out of the 73,736 who stayed from 1963–9), take out citizenship of the UK and Colonies and thereby signal their intention of becoming permanent settlers. The close correspondence between the figures for new entrants and the figures for people taken off controls after four years and acquisitions of UK citizenship after five years, is striking and inspires confidence in the results.

I would further estimate that if exactly comparable categories were available and if one were to relate the number of foreign workers annually entering and leaving this country to the number of foreign workers subject to registration, one would arrive at essentially

lessly some *au pairs* and students who stay on in this country and therefore become included in the figure of persons taken off conditions. On the other hand, most of the small number of dependent children of workers admitted are not included in the figure of registered aliens as they are under 16 years of age. My own 'guesstimate' is that the number of non-seasonal workers and dependants returning (c in Table 3–9) is a slight underestimate and the number of workers and dependants staying permanently a slight overestimate.

11 The two populations are not completely comparable. The number taken off controls is a cumulative figure where cases occurring after five or more years may be assumed to outweigh cases occurring during the first four years (e.g. marriages). However, the bias created thereby is estimated to be negligible over a longer period. New entrants data for the years 1959–62 are not included in Table 3–9. From 1959 onwards they are as follows: 27,596, 32,218, 34,246, and 31,382.

Table 3–9: Various indicators of length of stay of non-seasonal workers and their dependants in the *United Kingdom*, 1963–1970.

	New entrants	Current non-seasonal returnees	Definitive non-seasonal returnees within four years	Definitive non-seasonal stayers after four years	Proportion of definitive stayers in original new entrants	Acquisition of UK citizenship
	(a)	(b)	(c)	(d)	(e)	(f)
1963	25,197	11,446	20,450	7,146	26%	(n.a.)
1964	27,762	7,243	20,991	11,227	35%	8,855
1965	33,572	13,616	21,659	12,587	37%	8,565
1966	33,040	18,065	20,515	10,867	35%	7,448
1967	28,761	17,960	16,077	9,120	36%	9,914
1968	28,081	18,240	17,223	10,539	38%	8,058
1969	28,143	11,857	21,322	12,250	37%	7,498
1970	30,012	13,142	21,784	11,256	34%	6,879

a = Workers and dependants of workers admitted for twelve months.
b = Aliens registered at beginning of year (= end of preceding year) plus new entrants during year (a) minus those registered at end of year minus persons taken off controls during year (d).
c = New entrants (a) during year $x-4$ minus persons taken off controls (d) during year x. Four years are the minimum period for qualifying for indefinite leave to stay (d).
d = Persons taken off conditions: employment permit holders plus dependants plus children accompanying or joining parents.

$$e = \frac{\text{(d) in year } x}{\text{(a) in year } x-4} \times 100.$$

f = Naturalization and registration of aliens (excluding British Protected Persons) *in* the United Kingdom. Five years are the minimum period for qualifying for naturalization.
Source: *Statistics of Persons Entering and Leaving the United Kingdom*; *Annual Abstract of Statistics*; *Statistics of Persons Acquiring Citizenship of the United Kingdom and Colonies*; and Runnymede Trust (1971).

the same proportions as, for example, for Germany as a receiving country (Böhning, 1970c, Table 1). The differing assessments of these two countries—i.e. that Germany *is* a country of immigration and that Britain is supposedly a country where foreign workers stay only for a short time and do *not* settle—derive, in my opinion, from the different order of magnitude involved. During the sixties Germany admitted ten times as many foreign workers as Britain! The absolute number of settlers is proportionately higher and the public is accordingly more aware of them. But the two migration streams have basically the same characteristics, dynamics, and permanence.

A comparison of the British and Swiss scene with the situation in the Common Market countries reveals no marked differences as to the incidence, determination, and permanence of contemporary labour migration. The composition of the immigrant work-force naturally differs between countries for historical and geographical reasons, and for economic reasons the size of this work-force differs as well. All European countries have received Italians: Britain, Sweden, the Netherlands, and Austria less so than France, Belgium, Germany, and Switzerland. Sweden, the Netherlands, and Austria really started to import manpower when the peak of the Italian emigration was over at the beginning of the sixties, and their immigrant populations are consequently less dominated by the highly mobile Italian worker. France, Germany, and Switzerland have had Italian immigrants for almost one hundred years now; the migration to Belgium has been taking place since the end of World War I. These four countries have experienced a typical chain migration from Italy. Britain has experienced only a minute chain migration from Italy even though it imported labour on a large scale (from the New Commonwealth) when the Italian supply was still abundant. All European countries have seen at least a stabilization, if not decline, in the number of Italian immigrants in recent years.

4

Excursus: The Self-feeding Process of Economic Migration from Low-wage to Post-industrial Countries with a Liberal Capitalist Structure

It has already been indicated that the composition and permanence of a migration stream caused by economic differentials and motivations 'matures' over time and that migrations in different socio-political settings with different backgrounds and populations are denoted by characteristic dynamics. This chapter examines the structural causes of contemporary labour immigration into European countries and the ways in which supposedly temporary migrants turn, on a large scale, into permanent settlers. Migrants who from the outset had the intention of settling abroad permanently need not be considered here. However, they are few and far between on the European scene, with the possible exception of some sections of the coloured immigrant population in Britain. Apart from the trainees and seasonal migrants, almost all economic migrants in Europe are polyannual migrants in intention when they leave their countries of origin, but are not emigrants in the traditional sense (Böhning, 1971d). Yet, after a few years a third of the polyannual migrants to Britain settle permanently (see above p. 51); 42% of Switzerland's foreign workers with year-round permits are counted as having been continuously resident for over five years (see above pp. 47–8, 1969 figures); and 57% of Germany's male foreign workers and 39% of the females are shown as having been uninterruptedly resident for over four years (*Erfahrungsbericht 1969*, 1970, p. 49: 1968 figures). Somewhere there must be a mechanism in our post-industrial capitalist societies which makes polyannual migrants change their mind about returning home as quickly as possible.

A post-industrial society is denoted by a relatively small agricultural sector, a large semi-automated industrial sector which tends to decline in relative terms, and an equally large and expanding tertiary sector:

If one assumes that such a society:

firstly, has a liberal capitalist structure,

secondly, is committed to full employment and high real growth policies, and

thirdly, is not a traditional country of immigration and does not experience any significant immigration,

then it follows that:

fourthly, this society will run into endemic labour shortages in socially undesirable and low-wage jobs because it is unable to change its traditional job structure, and that,

fifthly, it will try to meet these labour shortages by engaging foreign workers from low-wage countries with labour surpluses, thereby,

sixthly, rigidifying the social job structure, forestalling an effective solution of the labour shortage problem, and setting in motion a process of migration which, under current trends of technological development, is unending and self-feeding.

This hypothesis can be exemplified by reference to Germany because the relevant data are available. The UK was approaching model conditions in the fifties but has since increasingly deviated from the essential assumption of *high* real growth (entailing a fast rising standard of living). Italy and Spain may provide a future test of the hypothesis, though in the case of Spain this will depend on its degree of liberalism.

Under an increasingly liberal regime of international trade, a society of the kind stipulated generally experiences a fast increase in the standard of living of its working-class population shortly after the transition of its economy from an industrial to a post-industrial one. The rising standard of living is achieved with the traditional social job structure, that is, the structure developed during the first stages of industrialization with socially undesirable and low-wage jobs at the bottom. In a fully employed economy, a noticeable increase in the standard of living has the following two effects. Firstly, it induces a growing gap between the rising expectations that go with an increase in the standard of living and better schooling, on the one side, and the undesirability of given jobs in terms of status, physical hardship, and pecuniary reward, on the other. Secondly, it gives workers the opportunity to leave undesirable jobs for those that are more socially acceptable and better paid, without much difficulty. Consequently workers drift into job openings which are more likely to fulfil their aspirations in respect of status and pay. The result is a partial labour shortage in socially undesirable jobs.

These symptoms of structural maladjustment are commonly overlooked in the beginning or accredited to partial demand situations. However, what *is* overlooked is the *systemic* character of these symptoms and the fact that they are indicative of an impending *general* labour shortage. The partial labour shortages may arise in different parts of the economy in different countries—in mining in Belgium, in tourism and private households in Switzerland, in agriculture in Germany—but they always make themselves felt first and foremost in sectors with a high concentration of undesirable and low-wage jobs. Sometimes these high concentrations are to be found in sectors of seasonal employment and low job security; and, at other times, in declining industries (which clouds the issue in the sense that the structural development of the economy and the structural maladjustment of the labour market go hand in hand). However, the signal of structural maladjustment may be given by any sector, including booming industries such as tourism or construction or the steel industry, because it is not the economic sector as such but the incidence of socially undesirable jobs that matters and there is practically no sector where there are no badly paid and undesirable jobs. Thus, the symptom of partial labour shortage is no less than a signal of impending general labour shortage. The speed and intensity of this development may be influenced by such external factors as demographic developments (e.g. losses of active population resulting from wars), but it is essentially independent of them.

A post-industrial capitalist society facing the first instances of endemic labour shortage has two options open to it. Firstly, it could pursue a revolutionary manpower policy by adapting its social job structure to post-industrial requirements, i.e. to pay a truly economic wage for undesirable jobs, taking into account the fact that market forces are largely inapplicable on the labour 'market' and that wage structures are determined socio-politically. Secondly, it could fill these jobs with foreign workers admitted not for settlement but for the specific purpose of filling the supposedly temporary shortages on the labour market (the *Konjunkturpuffer* approach). The alternative to the first option, namely, to permit large-scale unemployment and a considerable drop if not reversal in the real growth of the economy in order to stop the flight from undesirable jobs, is not feasible politically because it would catapult the party in power out of government[1] (this alternative would not fit in with the second assumption). The alternative to the *Konjunkturpuffer* option would be to have a settlement immigration related to economic needs. No government in a country which is not traditionally a country of immigration and which deliberately set out to invite aliens to settle inside its borders on purely economic grounds, would survive the onset of this immigration. Permanent settlement migration is usually not even considered because the labour shortage problem is seen as essentially short term.

The first option is one that does not commend itself to the political decision-makers on socio-political grounds. A drastic rearrangement of the social structure of jobs might require, for example, that a dustman be paid as much or more than an accountant or that an agricultural labourer be given the same status as a research assistant. Needless to say, capitalist societies are neither willing nor able to do this on the scale required in view of the social consequences anticipated.[2] Furthermore, under current technological conditions the problem cannot be solved by automation because many of the socially undesirable jobs are not open to automation, particularly in the service sector, and because automation often creates new low paid jobs. The present stage of semi-automation in manufacturing industries has given rise to many boring and frustrating activities which do not attract sufficient indigenous manpower. Hence, the second option seems the only way out. It also seems the easiest way out with the least political friction and the greatest degree of freedom of manoeuvre in relation to both its execution and the alternatives. Governments fall for this solution. They are under the illusion that the labour shortages which make themselves felt are basically temporary in character. Significantly, they usually permit the employ-

---

[1] Witness the fall of Chancellor Erhard at the end of 1966.
[2] It was instructive to hear the public outcry in April 1971 following British Leyland's decision to give lavatory attendants at the Longbridge works an annual salary of £1,500.

ment of foreigners in specific jobs long before full employment levels are reached in macro-economic quantitative terms.

Once the political decision has gone in favour of the foreign worker or *Konjunkturpuffer* approach, the self-feeding process of migration from the chosen labour surplus areas into the labour shortage jobs commences and it can only be reversed by a political decision which is incomparably more difficult to take—because of the increased internal and additional international constraints—than a decision to adopt a strongly reformist manpower policy when the first gaps in the labour market appeared.

There are two aspects to this self-feeding process. One, as already implied, relates to the structure of post-industrial societies and the other to the migratory process itself. These will now be examined in turn.

The foreign worker approach does not stop the secular drift of the indigenous labour force from socially undesirable jobs, for it does not deal with the cause of the problem. On the contrary, it actually reinforces the given social structure of jobs and may even accelerate the drift described. An indigenous worker will often feel less inhibited in changing jobs if he finds that he is working side by side with a foreigner and if he suspects that his employer has engaged him to keep wages down. Sentimental attachment is lowered, too, when it is obvious that vacant jobs are filled quickly. The social job structure remains fixed, the drift of the indigenous work-force continues, and the problem becomes less and less amenable to a reformist solution. The reshuffle that would have been necessary to meet the original labour shortage problem quickly reaches the proportions of upheaval. As the task becomes more formidable, the resolve to conquer it diminishes, which in turn reinforces the tendency to opt again and again for the import of foreign workers whenever there is a labour shortage.

After about six years of high real growth this process has usually worked its way through the whole of the economy. The initially isolated pockets of structural maladjustment, now filled with foreign workers, extend to all sectors of production. Table 4–1 shows how sectors that are underrepresented in the beginning attract an increasing share of the foreign work-force and how the concentrations in sectors of original labour import fade out. This development would be much clearer statistically if other factors could be held constant or if one compared the type of demand for foreign workers over time.

For example, in 1956, 95% of the foreigners recruited for employment in Germany were seasonal workers, mainly in agriculture. In 1970 over a third of the recruits were engaged in metal goods and the electricity industry, but less than 2% were in agriculture. In both years the absolute number of recruits for agriculture was about the same (5,800).

Table 4–1: Proportion of employed foreign workers by economic sector in the *Federal Republic of Germany*, in percentages.

		1958	1959	1960	1961	1962	1963	1964	1965	1966	1967	1968	1969	1970
Germany[a] (mid-year)	Agr. etc.	(5.7)	(4.7)	3.1	2.2	1.6	1.4	1.2	1.2	1.2	1.4	1.2	1.0	0.9
	Mining	(13.5)	(10.5)	7.8	7.3	6.5	6.1	6.2	5.5	4.9	4.4	3.8	3.3	3.2
	Metal goods	(12.1)	(11.8)	25.6	30.0	30.6	29.1	31.3	34.3	33.3	31.3	32.9	36.9	38.9
	Other manuf.	(24.3)	(22.4)	19.6	20.7	21.3	23.3	23.4	24.4	26.2	27.0	26.7	25.9	24.5
	Constr.	(14.3)[b]	(21.9)[b]	25.5	24.0	24.9	24.6	22.7	20.1	18.8	15.2	15.2	15.5	16.3
	Services	(30.1)[b]	(28.7)[b]	18.3	15.8	15.0	15.5	15.1	14.5	15.7	20.8	20.3	17.3	16.2

a = Figures for 1958 and 1959 relate to occupational groups.
b = Including not elsewhere classified.
Source: *Amtliche Nachrichten*.

This spreading of the employment of foreigners to all sectors of the economy is basically due to two factors. On the one hand, there is the well-known complementarity of jobs, which means that different grades of labour are dependent upon each other for the performance of one production process. Wherever this holds true and wherever this involves socially undesirable jobs, there is the likelihood that sooner or later foreign workers will have to be engaged if national workers leave the bottom grades.[3] Nurses emptying bedpans and building labourers fetching bricks and cement are cases in point. On the other hand, employers in mass-production processes who have hitherto not resorted to foreign labour realize that its easy availability in conjunction with an appropriate redesign of the production system would enable them to turn out far more goods than would otherwise be the case. They further subdivide many skilled jobs into simple components which can readily be taught to workers who have never before stood at a production line. Thus, the *pattern* of demand for labour *changes* towards the skills available or their lack. It is usually in the large firms in manufacturing industries, which can look further ahead and which can afford to take on a contingent of foreigners on a trial-and-error basis, where foreigners

[3] This was well seen by Lutz (1963, note 35, p. 30), but not as being sufficiently forceful to upset her two-sector model.

of all grades and levels of literacy are taught in a day or two how
to turn a screw or how to operate a lever. Often the production
process is already so much subdivided that no further redesigning
is required, the car industry being an example. In other cases
employers may completely redesign their whole production process
to adjust it to the kind of immigrant labour available (Cohen and
Jenner, 1968).[4] The general point here is that, apart from the fact
that there are undesirable and badly paid jobs in almost all sectors
of the economy, the semi-automated manufacturing industries of
today can easily adapt their mass-production processes to the kind
of skills offered; and if, say, semi-literate farmers from underdeveloped countries can offer no industrial skills at all, they can
still be put into a work place where no more than a repetitive manual
movement is required. In manufacturing industries the complementarity of jobs and the adjustability of production processes coincide
to a very high degree and the resulting concentration of foreign
workers in such jobs is no surprise: over 20% of Switzerland's
foreign workers are employed in metal goods and over 20% in other
manufacturing industries; over one-third of the foreign workers in
both the Netherlands and Germany are employed in metal goods,
and manufacturing industries as a whole absorb about two-thirds
of the foreign work-force in both countries. The complementarity of
jobs on its own, i.e. without the additional factor of adaptable mass-
production processes, comes to the fore in the construction industry:
one-third of Luxembourg's foreign workers are employed in construction; the proportion is as high as a quarter for Switzerland and stood
at that level in Germany during the first half of the sixties, but has
now fallen to one-sixth.

A breakdown of the total labour force by economic sectors reveals
that the import of foreigners has had a scaling effect. A breakdown
by socio-economic status, on the other hand, reveals an increasing

---

[4] This aspect of the debate on the economic effects of immigration has generally
been overlooked. Whether too many marginal firms are kept in business and
whether capital widening is preferred to capital deepening, depends more on
the nationally prevalent investment policy and on the degree to which firms
are sheltered from competition than on the import of labour in the lower
wage brackets. The construction industry, for example, has not been known
to be particularly exposed to international competition. The economics of
migration form the subject of a report which I am preparing for the OECD
Manpower and Social Affairs Directorate.

SELF-FEEDING PROCESS OF ECONOMIC MIGRATION   61

differential between the foreign and the indigenous work-force.[5] Taking the *total* distribution in terms of socio-economic status as the *structural* requirement of the economy, one finds a growing under-representation of the indigenous worker in the blue-collar sector in general and in unskilled and semi-skilled positions in particular, as Table 4–2 exemplifies. Between 1961, i.e. shortly after the large-scale engagement of foreigners had begun, and 1968, half a million

Table 4–2: The socio-economic composition of employees over the age of 15 residing in *West Germany* at 6 June 1961 and in autumn 1968, by sex, in percentages.

	MALES						FEMALES					
	TOTAL		GERMAN		FOREIGN		TOTAL		GERMAN		FOREIGN	
	1961	1968	1961	1968	1961	1968	1961	1968	1961	1968	1961	1968
Wage earners	63.4	60a)	62.8	58a)	86.8	90	49.2	43a)	49.0	41a)	69.6	86
Apprentices	6.5	6b)	6.6	6b)	2.7	2	7.7	7b)	7.8	7b)	5.4	–
Salary earners	22.0	26b)	22.3	27b)	10.5	8	40.9	48b)	41.1	49b)	24.9	12
Civil Servants	8.0	9	8.3	9	0.0	0	2.2	3	2.2	3	0.0	0
Overall	99.9	101b)	100.0	100b)	100.0	100	100.0	101b)	100.1	100a)	99.9	98

a = Decreasing absolute number.
b = Increasing absolute number (all foreign categories were increasing in absolute terms).
Source: Statistisches Bundesamt (1966); *Statistisches Jahrbuch für die Bundesrepublik Deutschland* (1966, 1970); *Erfahrungsbericht 1968* (1969); and the author's own computations.

German men and 600,000 German women left the broadly manual sector and were partly replaced by over 350,000 foreign men and over 200,000 foreign women. During the same period, 600,000 German men and half a million German women, as well as 20,000 foreign men and the same number of foreign women, entered into broadly white-collar positions. At the latter date, foreign men constituted a quarter of the group of unskilled male wage-earners, 10% of the semi-skilled, and 3% of the skilled wage-earners (overall 7.9%). Thus, over time, foreign workers become a more and

---

[5] Jones and Smith (1970) seemed to be somewhat surprised to find that Commonwealth immigration has had a scaling effect in terms of both industrial sectors and occupational groups as early as five or six years after it had commenced. Their analysis with respect to occupations is defective (mainly through lack of data) in so far as it takes account of only one dimension of this two-dimensional problem. One is very much reminded of the bird's-eye view of Paris which found that immigrants are distributed fairly evenly over the whole of the city when every Parisian knows that immigrants are living mainly in lofts and cellars, which you find everywhere in Paris.

more indispensable part of the labour force of post-industrial societies unless their employment is curtailed by a political act.

The second aspect of the self-feeding process relates to the migratory process itself. It is based upon the notion of chain migration but goes further than this in that it does not see the chain ending in one particular village or region; rather this chain extends to the whole of the labour-sending country. This might be called the 'maturity' of a migration. This aspect represents an autonomous contributory factor to the self-feeding process, i.e. it is not caused by the incidence of endemic labour shortage. Nevertheless, its momentum can keep the immigrant population growing long after the purposive recruitment of foreign workers has been curtailed politically or ended temporarily during a recession.

Migration is a social process: a migrant leaves one social context for another on the basis of a hierarchically ordered set of values. For economic migrants the socio-economic deprivations at home are often (though not necessarily) a sufficient condition of his out-migration. Lured by the prospects of an El Dorado magnified through hearsay, he sees himself as a *target worker*, that is, someone who goes abroad to earn as much money as possible, as quickly as possible, in order to return home. The target worker notion, of course, coincides perfectly with the *Konjunkturpuffer* approach of most European labour-receiving countries. What these two notions fail to take into account is the fact that migration leads to changes in the interactional system of the polyannual migrant. In the case of polyannual migrants coming from developing to post-industrial countries, this amounts potentially to a complete secondary socialization at the age of 20 or 30 (Böhning, 1971d). The secondary socialization is in many cases not very successful, but in almost all cases the migrant absorbs at least superficially some of the norms and values of the host society. In particular, he becomes part of the system of norms, values, and deprivations of a consumer society within a matter of a year or two. After about one year, most polyannual migrants realize that short-term participation in a high-wage economy does not once and for all eliminate their deprivation back home, however spartan their conduct in the country of employment. They decide to extend their stay abroad in the expectation of really amassing the big wage packets they have been hoping for and then returning home and starting a new life. By this time, however, a polyannual migrant has become subject to new deprivations, namely, those of the lower working class in the receiving country. Some of these deprivations are entirely new in the sense that he had never experienced them before entering a consumer society (e.g. he is made to want cameras, record players, tape recorders, electric shavers, and so on). Others are simply the extension or transference to the new milieu of the deprivations he experienced in his place of origin (e.g. those related to housing, schooling, and so on). So the migrant slowly becomes socialized in that unsocial game between the standard of living and the cost of living in a post-industrial society.

The polyannual migrant, then, is constantly torn between his desire to overcome his deprivations and his desire to return home to a social context where he must feel the deprivations even more deeply than when he left. The result is that again and again he extends his stay abroad, or he re-emigrates repeatedly after returning home for a short while. Finally this process will lead to a significant number of target workers tending to settle down in the receiving country, if not for ever at least until retirement age. The migrant becomes an immigrant.

This process is applicable to both single and married workers. The young single migrant tends to predominate in the early stages of migration. He is less constrained to take the decision to go abroad and he is also less inhibited when it comes to deciding whether to return 'now' or 'a little later'. Once the apparent success of migration to a particular receiving country makes the round back home, the married worker joins the stream, probably on his own and with the intention of returning home to wife and children as soon as possible. While abroad, he not only has the very human desire to be united again with his family, but he is also most likely to come to that typically lower working-class conclusion that if he wants to improve his lot, and if he is not to return home and admit failure, he will have to send for his wife and older children and will have to send them out to work where he is. He will convince his wife that this is the best solution, and thus over the years the majority of married migrant workers will be joined by their families. However hostile the immigration regulations are towards family reunion, a determined migrant will not be put off by them and will try to satisfy all the provisos: legally if possible, illegally if necessary. Also, in a liberal capitalist society, the inhuman regulations hindering family reunion are coming under increasing pressure from enlightened national and international opinion as well as employers themselves, who find that their foreign workers stay longer and are better workers —that is, more profitable—when they are reunited with their families.

The change from a strongly single to a strongly familial migration is illustrated by Table 4–3. In interpreting the figures here and in the subsequent Table 4–4, one should bear in mind that the migration from different countries to Germany started at different times (in Italy in the second half of the 1950s, in Greece and Spain in 1961, and in Turkey in 1962) and that different cultural systems restrain to a varying degree the travel and employment of women (e.g. in Anatolia more so than in the North of Italy). Therefore, the migration stream matures not so much for the receiving country as a whole but for each sending country separately, and the speed of maturing is influenced to some extent by the different constraints of the sending societies. In any case, it is clear that more and more of the married migrants in Germany were joined by their families during the sixties and that a constant proportion of the shrinking share of separated migrants wished their spouse to come and join them.

Looking at this process in more detail, one can see that a target worker migration stream matures in four stages, which are analytically distinct but historically intertwined in any actual situation and therefore difficult to disentangle empirically.[6] In the *first phase* young single workers, usually male (depending on the social system in the country of origin and the type of labour demand at destination), form the bulk of the migration. They come from the more industrialized and urbanized areas of the sending country, that is, the bigger towns with their more developed networks of internal and international communication, where employment opportunities abroad first become known and information from the emigrants is first relayed; these areas are thus the locus of the 'grapevine' which sets in motion a chain migration. As the first small batch of migrants originates from the more developed part of the sending country, it will comprise a considerably higher level of skills and more industrial

[6] In addition to the literature already quoted, there is a wealth of pertinent data in the reports prepared for the Working Group on Migration of the OECD Manpower and Social Affairs Directorate. For two sending countries not considered in Tables 4–3 and 4–4, see the reports by Baucic (1971) on the effects of emigration from Yugoslavia and by Allefresde (1971) on Finnish migration to Sweden. See also Reinans (1971), pp. 5 and 7.

skills than the non-migrant population as a whole. If these first migrants come into a country which has only just started to import labour, their duration of stay is likely to be very short, partly because the migration has not yet matured and partly because the first immigrants are likely to be employed in the most marginal positions. Turnover or the ratio of (temporary and permanent) returnees to the size of the foreign work-force is largely a function of

Table 4-3: Marital status of foreign workers in Germany and their desire to be reunited with their families, in percentages.

Sample Source	Date	Country of origin	Sex	Marital Status		Married with spouse in FRG[b]		Married without spouse in FRG		Proportion who want their spouses to join them in FRG		
				Single (I)	Married (II)	as % of I+II (III)	as % of II (IV)	as % of I+II (V)	as % of II (VI)	as % of I+II (VII)	as % of II (VIII)	as % of V (IX)
Delgado (1966),pp.17-18	Jan.-July 63	Spain	Male	57	40	22		21[a]				
	Jan.-July 63	Spain	Both	61	35	23		16[a]				
Deutscher Stadtetag(1964)	30 Sept. 63	All	Both			6-8				16-20		
Abadan(1966), pp.106-7	Nov. 63	Turkey	Both	41	56	17	10	42[a]	90[a]			
Hollenberg (1965),pp.210-222: social worker sample	Aug.-Sept. 64	Italy	Both	67	33		25		75[a]			50
	Aug.-Sept. 64	Spain	Both	50	50		5		95[a]			30
	Aug.-Sept. 64	Greece	Both	53	47		35		65[a]			55
	Aug.-Sept. 64	Turkey	Both	75	25		12		88[a]			10
	Aug.-Sept. 64	Average	Both	56	44	9	21		79[a]		18	41
employer sample	1964	Average	Both			0	20		80[a]		7	16
Erfahrungs-bericht 1967 (1968),p.19	30 Sept. 66	Italy	Male	40	60	24	39	36	60			
	30 Sept. 66	Spain	Male	34	66	30	45	36	55			
	30 Sept. 66	Greece	Male	25	75	51	68	24	32			
	30 Sept. 66	Turkey	Male	22	78	10	21	32	79			
	30 Sept. 66	Average	Male	33	67	28	41	39	60			
Aguirre (1968),pp.46-50	Oct.66-May 67	Spain	Male	36	62	30	47	33	53			
	Oct.66-May 67	Spain	Fem	66	31	16	52	15	48			
Hentschel et al. (1968), pp.47-8	Summer 1967	Italy	Male	56	44							65
	Summer 1967	Spain	Male	23	77		.					
	Summer 1967	Greece	Male	36	64		84		16[a]			86
	Summer 1967	Turkey	Male	35	65		20		80[a]			26
	Summer 1967	Average	Male	42	58		37		63[a]			55
Mehrländer (1969),pp.62-3, 127, 195	Aug.-Dec. 67	Spain	Both	36	64				38			
	Aug.-Dec. 67	Greece	Both	26	74				17			
	Aug.-Dec. 67	Italy	Male	37	63		55		45[a]			
	Aug.-Dec. 67	Spain	Male	29	71		62		38[a]			
	Aug.-Dec. 67	Greece	Male	22	78		83		17[a]			
	Aug.-Dec. 67	Turkey	Male	14	86		31		69[a]			
Erfahrungs-bericht 1969 (1970),pp.53, 64	30 Sept. 68	Italy	Male	36	64	35	54	29	45	21	46	
	30 Sept. 68	Spain	Male	26	74	44	60	30	41	20	50	
	30 Sept. 68	Greece	Male	22	78	61	78	17	22	15	67	
	30 Sept. 68	Turkey	Male	18	82	28	34	54	66	29	44	
	30 Sept. 68	Portugal	Male	22	78	34	44	44	57	36	54	
	30 Sept. 68	Average	Male	28	72	39	54	33	46	22	48	
Marplan (1970),p.4	Jan.-Feb. 70	Italy	Both	32	68		63		37[a]			
	Jan.-Feb. 70	Spain	Both	34	64		60		40[a]			
	Jan.-Feb. 70	Greece	Both	23	75		83		17[a]			
	Jan.-Feb. 70	Turkey	Both	29	71		53		47[a]			

a = Estimated: column V = $100-(I+III)$
column VI = $100-IV$.
b = FRG = Federal Republic of Germany.

the economy of the receiving country and is likely to be very high in marginal jobs. If the first migrants come into a country which is already employing other nationalities, their duration of stay is still likely to be short, but not so much on account of employment in marginal positions as these workers are likely to be employed in a wider variety of jobs.

In the *second phase* the migration stream ages slightly, its sex composition remains basically unchanged, but its composition in terms of marital status resembles more that of the non-migrant population (except that married workers are not necessarily accompanied by spouse and children). Duration of stay increases slightly but perceptibly as both single and married workers tend to extend their stay; turnover decreases accordingly. Looking at the second phase from the viewpoint of the sending country, one can discern the following development. Once the first emigrants return home, they talk in glowing terms to friends and neighbours about their experience, for to do otherwise would imply that their migration was a failure; then newspapers and radios carry reports, and more and more people in the area where the migration started and in neighbouring areas get to know about the luring opportunities. First of all, it is the hitherto hesitant married worker in the area of original emigration who decides to try his hand. The obvious solution is to leave wife and children behind, to go abroad for a definite period of up to one year, to save as much money as possible, and to return and start anew. As married workers are generally somewhat older than single workers, the migration stream shows a slightly higher average age. At the same time the word has gone round in other areas—probably those in close proximity to the area of original migration—that easy money is to be made in a certain labour importing country. Again it is predominantly the single (male) worker who is the first emigrant from the new catchment areas, the pioneer who returns—often only temporarily—to spread the word about high wages and living standards. The geographical extension of the areas of origin from the bigger towns to the surrounding smaller towns and countryside brings with it a greater variety, but lower level, of skill and socio-economic status. Yet it is still true that not only does each new chain of migration show a higher average skill level than its catchment area, but that the migration stream as a whole is more skilled than the general working population of the country from whence it comes.

Table 4–4: Indicators of the maturing migration stream into *Germany* for selected immigrant groups.

Indicator	Category	Country of origin	Sex	1962	1963	1964	1965	1966	1967	1968	1969
Mean age in years^a)	emp.^f)	Italy	Male	29.5	29.5	31.0	31.5		29.0	32.0	
	emp.	Spain	Male	29.5	30.5	31.5	32.0		34.0	35.0	
	emp.	Turkey	Male	29.0	29.5	30.5	31.0		29.0	34.5	
Sex composition (proportion of females)^b)	new^g)	Italy	Fem.				16.9	20.1	25.2	20.1	20.3
	new	Spain	Fem.				40.5	36.8	36.8	24.2	19.4
	new	Turkey	Fem.				21.7	20.4	18.5	24.6	21.2
	new	All	Fem.	23.2	28.1	25.9	32.6	41.1	53.2	39.3	35.9
	emp.	Italy	Fem.	9.0	11.3	13.8	15.0	17.3	21.6	22.1	22.9
	emp.	Spain	Fem.	24.4	28.4	29.0	28.7	30.7	35.2	36.2	32.6
	emp.	Turkey	Fem.	8.3	11.0	10.0	12.8	16.5	18.5	21.7	22.1
	emp.	All	Fem.	17.9	20.7	22.2	23.1	25.3	28.9	29.5	29.4
Mean duration of stay (in years/months)^c)	emp.	Italy	Male		(1/6)		1/5		2/11	4/8	
	emp.	Spain	Male		(1/6)		1/8		3/7	5/2	
	emp.	Turkey	Male		(0/9)		1/3		2/6	3/7	
	emp.	Italy	Fem.				1/2		2/0	2/11	
	emp.	Spain	Fem.				1/8		2/10	4/3	
	emp.	Turkey	Fem.				0/9		1/10	2/9	
Turnover (returnees divided by average size of work force)^d)	emp.	Italy	Both	0.42	0.50	0.44	0.39	0.44	0.60	0.29	0.29
	emp.	Spain	Both	0.28		0.28	0.24	0.25	0.31	0.22	0.15
	emp.	Turkey	Both		0.22	0.17	0.15	0.19	0.36	0.17	0.11
	emp.	All	Male		0.39	0.33	0.31	0.34	0.49	0.21	0.17
	emp.	All	Fem.		0.28	0.26	0.26	0.29	0.42	0.19	0.11
	emp.	All	Both	0.36	0.37	0.32	0.30	0.32	0.47	0.21	0.15
Turnover index (Turnover adjusted for labour demand)^dd) in '000	emp.	Italy	Both	231	267	268	253	237	181	142	217
	emp.	Spain	Both	154	149	146	162	167	151	107	112
	emp.	Turkey	Both		117	104	97	103	109	83	82
	emp.	All	Male		123	117	110	95	68	55	75
	emp.	All	Fem.		61	66	76	75	68	43	34
	emp.	All	Both	198	197	195	195	173	142	103	112
Ratio of active to inactive immigrants^e)	im.^h	Italy	Both					5.8:1		3.4:1	
	im.	Spain	Both					4.5:1		2.6:1	
	im.	Turkey	Both					6.4:1		3.8:1	
	im.	All	Both					4.5:1		3.5:1	

a = Source: *Erfahrungsbericht* (various); and Hentschel *et al.* (1968).

b = Source: *Erfahrungsbericht 1969* (1970); and *Amtliche Nachrichten* (various). At first sight the 'newly entering' data do not seem to conform to the hypothesized development. It should be borne in mind, however, that the figures shown are generally larger than the 'employed' figures and that differential turnover in terms of sex and marital status (see note d) accounts for much of the variation.

c = The bracketed 1963 male figures refer to both sexes! Source: *Erfahrungsbericht* (various).

d = Source: *Amtliche Nachrichten* (various); and Böhning (1971d), Table 32. It is interesting to note that the female figures are always smaller than the male figures. Given the fact that almost all married women were living with their husbands in Germany, while this holds true for only about half the married men, it can be assumed that married couples have a much lower return rate than single workers and, probably, married workers who are not accompanied by their spouses.

dd = The 'raw' figures for turnover cannot show the hypothesized development
clearly because they are influenced by the demand for labour. As labour
demand 'explained' the inflow of foreign workers into Germany almost
exclusively (see above pp. 36–7), the given turnover figures were scaled by
demand as measured by unfilled vacancies (annual average male and
female demand, respectively). Though the time periods do not coincide
exactly (September intervals are used for turnover), the results clearly
point to the hypothesized decreasing turnover.

e = Source: Böhning (1970c), Tables 2 and 5. The figures refer to employees
and their dependants (i.e. excluding employers and unpaid family workers).
The active population includes male plus female workers. The inactive
population includes inactive foreign wives of employed workers (I have
slightly adjusted my figures in the original Table 2 for this calculation:
a new survey showed that over-all 46% of the German wives of foreign
workers were active, while I had originally used the over-all figure of
34% for all female Germans; the absolute differences are slight) plus
inactive children of foreign parentage (here the available ratio for 1968
was applied to the given 1966 figures in my original Table 5 [1970c] to
obtain a rough estimate). Inactive husbands of employed wives and other
dependants were not considered.

f = Employed immigrants.

g = Newly entering workers.

h = Foreign workers and their dependants.

In the *third phase* the receiving country experiences a continuation
of the ageing of the migration stream and a change in the sex
composition in favour of the originally underrepresented sex, as
married workers send for their spouses. In this phase the hitherto
stable ratio of economically active to inactive immigrants begins to
fall: not so much because the wives or husbands of married
workers are inactive—they are predominantly taking up employment
themselves—but because younger children join their parents abroad.
Duration of stay increases further, especially for families, and turnover decreases considerably. Table 4–4 exemplifies this development for Germany. (For the change in marital composition, see
also Table 4–3 and Böhning, 1970c, pp. 18–21.) Its speed depends
on the intensity of the demand for labour in the receiving country
and business cycle fluctuations as well as the size of the sending
country and possible political interferences there.

In the third phase the married migrant who left the area of original
emigration during the second phase begins to realize that he has
exchanged one set of deprivations for another and that the desired
accumulation of money is taking place at a much slower speed
than he had imagined. In the receiving country he finds himself
at the bottom of the socio-economic ladder. To return home permanently after only a year abroad would mean that his emigration was

not successful in terms of the goals he set for himself when he left his home. Therefore, he decides to go back temporarily and tell his wife that more time is needed for him to achieve his goals. He might possibly suggest, or have indicated in an earlier letter, that two pairs of hands can earn more than one and that his wife should consider accompanying him abroad. This would put an end to their separation and together they could finish the job of earning a great amount of money much more quickly than he could do on his own; it would also eliminate the expense of maintaining two separate households. If the children cannot be cared for by grand-parents, they might just as well come along, too. They would surely receive a much better education in the receiving country than at home. Thus, after the first batch of predominantly single migrants and the subsequent wave of unaccompanied married workers one can then detect a wave of family reunion from the original area of emigration. At the same time the areas from which new migrants were first drawn when the receiving country had entered the second phase of maturing, now experience, during the third over-all phase, their second stage of maturing, i.e. married workers leave from here without their spouses, and so on. And also during the third over-all phase the remaining areas of the sending country that had hitherto not participated in this migration stream will be drawn into its ambit as the message spreads into the more backward and less accessible parts of the country. For them the development repeats itself by starting with young, single workers, and so on. This new and additional part of the migration stream depresses its skill level further and changes its composition more towards the kind of occupations prevalent in the backward areas. But it can still be seen that the skill level of the migrant population is on the balance higher than that of the non-migrant population (Böhning, 1971d, Tables 6 and 7). Whether or not the migration stream from the sending country as a whole finally comes to be dominated by the flows from the more backward areas depends on the size of those areas relative to the intermediate and most developed areas of the country concerned.

Up to the beginning of the third stage the migratory process is not self-feeding in the sense that more migrants are entering the receiving country than are wanted for work there. During the third stage the self-feeding process which is unrelated to the cause of labour demand commences, predominantly through the immigration of dependants. Moreover, by this time the immigration population has swollen so much that it induces significant infrastructural demands for housing, schooling, and consumer goods. This means that additional infrastructure and capacity will have to be provided and that additional demand for labour will be exerted, some of which can only be satisfied by importing additional workers.

Finally, longer stays and a significant extent of family reunion lead in the *fourth phase* of maturity to an enlargement of the immigrant population via the entry of employers, secular and religious leaders, and others. As the psychological comfort afforded by the company of their fellow countrymen leads the immigrant workers and families to settle in groups and colonies, there slowly arises a demand for ethnic shops, churches, schools, and other facilities. Each of these ethnic institutions will subsequently be staffed predominantly by ethnic workers, which means additional immigration both in terms of additional workers and additional non-workers. For this to materialize there must be present a significant number of ethnic immigrants, that is, a certain concentration over a given space. The threshold for the major European post-industrial societies seems to lie between 100,000 and 200,000 ethnic immigrants. When the fourth phase has begun for the labour-receiving country, the intermediate areas of the sending country only experience their third stage, i.e. family reunion, and the least developed areas only their second stage, i.e. the migration of married workers without families. The picture which I have painted in terms of an ideal type of development is of course less sharp as regards the distinction of developed/intermediate/backward areas if one has only aggregate data at one's disposal. And the fact that the four-stage development for the receiving country is composed of a staggered four-stage development for various areas of origin in the sending country makes the statistical picture slightly less impressive than if one could follow the maturing of the migration stream from a small controllable area.

It is worthwhile to consider briefly some of the implications for the return movement of target workers deriving from this four-stage model of maturity. There is unmistakable evidence that integration into the host society is largely a function of the level of skills and education: that is, the higher the level of skills and/or education of foreign workers entering the host society, the more quickly and easily they will become integrated into that society. These workers tend to extend their stay repeatedly until they finally settle (Hagmann, 1971; and Böhning, 1971d). Therefore, one can expect a disproportionate share of the original migrants from the most developed areas not to return permanently but to settle and possibly marry abroad. Furthermore, the married worker who overcomes the initial adjustment difficulties and who asks his wife and children to join him abroad, consciously or subconsciously opts for at least semi-permanent settlement. With his family he will be able to overcome further adjustment problems more easily and, once some of his children go to school in the receiving country, he begins to realize that they are slowly becoming alienated from their country of origin and that returning home would severely diminish their chances of living the life he wishes for them. Anyway, he himself becomes inextricably enmeshed in the demands and rewards of a consumer society, and after some years of employment abroad he is gradually but noticeably climbing the socio-economic ladder. Migrants from the backward areas of the country of origin have the least favourable educational and skill endowment, and their family structure may also retard the degree of family reunion more than is the case for married workers from the cities and intermediate areas. It is these people, ill equipped to be successful in a post-industrial society, who form a disproportionately large share of the returnees in terms of both permanent returnees and the large number of people who circulate on the European labour market without ever finding a comfortable niche.

A stream of economic migrants into our contemporary post-industrial societies is self-feeding and unrending because, on the one side, our job structures are becoming fossilized and the demand for labour can be restructured in low-skilled repetitive jobs to suit the potential supply, and, on the other side, because the repercussions on labour demand and the build-up of ethnic communities during maturation create, autonomously and additionally, demand for workers which was not foreseen when the labour import commenced and which can largely be satisfied only by the import of new workers.

5

The Effect of Freedom of Movement on Migratory Patterns in the Common Market

Having described the EEC's system of freedom of movement for workers and the experience of European countries in the field of labour immigration, one can now examine whether the Common Market has had any effect on the patterns of migration in the Six. The general question is whether the freeing of labour movements has entailed migratory movements which would not have occurred if that freeing had not taken place. The other question—whether the existence of the Common Market has had any effect on labour movements through the repercussions of increased economic activity on the demand for foreign labour—need not be considered separately. Any such effect can only have been of the same nature—that is, of increased migrations—as free movement effects and will therefore be subsumed in the following analysis. Trade effects deriving from the establishment of the customs union have certainly played a role in the high level of capacity utilization throughout the Community, though these effects are generally assumed to be small in aggregate terms, namely, of the order of 1 to 2% of the Gross National Product. The focus on migratory patterns means, of course, that this discussion will not consider the effects of the EEC freedom of movement legislation on trade union membership, non-discrimination, etc. (The experience of member countries up to the end of 1968 has been summarized in three reports by Altarelli, 1969, de Wenger, 1969, and de Haan, 1969. Generally, see the annual reports on free movement by the Commission [Kommission ..., 1966a, 1967a, 1968a, 1969a, 1970a, and 1971a].)

'Free movement effects' could have occurred, firstly, in respect of the volume, composition, and permanence of migrations among member countries by increasing migrations and changing their characteristics. Secondly, the volume, composition, and permanence of intra-Community movements (as a whole and for individual countries) could have been affected in relation to movements into the Six from outside the Community. And, lastly, freedom of movement could have influenced the degree to which intra-Community movements are organized or spontaneous. These analytically distinct questions can fruitfully be answered only if one recognizes their interrelatedness. The question of increased volume of intra-Community migration has two aspects. On the one hand, increased migration could result from the movement of persons hitherto deterred by immigration controls (*addition effect*). On the other hand, increased migration could result from the hypothesis that Community workers, who have priority over workers from third countries, are in a position to pick up jobs for which they might otherwise have had to queue, in which case a degree of replacement of third country workers by Community workers would obtain (*extra-substitution effect*).

In the case of extra-substitution it is obvious that free movement only brings forward the engagement of certain groups of workers but does not induce an increase in the migration stream as such (for then it would fall under the addition effect). In time the queue-jumping effect will have dissipated itself, unless there is always a sufficient number of eligible workers with the right sort of qualification applying for every new work-place and every vacated job—a most unlikely situation even in small labour markets and under conditions of less than full employment, let alone in a labour market of some 75 million people where the demand for labour far outstripped the supply in terms of both quantity and quality. It should also be borne in mind that employers in the Common Market are not obliged to notify national labour market authorities of job openings or to have them processed through the Community clearance machinery, and that they are under no obligation to engage Community citizens if they do not consider them suitable for the job. This is in effect what the Italian complaints regarding the eighteen days' Community priority are all about. They see large numbers of Community firms recruiting Turks and Yugoslavs and paying scant attention to the Community's job clearance system while there are thousands of Italians who, in their opinion, could and should be engaged in these jobs; whereas the employers maintain there are not enough Italians around to fill the openings and of those who are around, most lack suitable skills.[1] Community priority works in the same way as priority for national workers under a work permit system for foreigners. In previous chapters it was indicated repeatedly that foreigners were admitted everywhere long before the demand and supply situation was in numerical balance. This is due to the non-transferability of abundant skills, lack of training and re-training, and the still generally low degree of geographical mobility in European countries.[2] Neither Italy, with 25,000 non-EEC workers as opposed to 10,000 Community workers inside its borders, nor the Common Market as a whole, with slightly less than three million non-EEC workers as opposed to just under one million Community workers, is an exception to this rule.

The composition of intra-Community migrations could have been affected in many ways by the establishment of freedom of movement. The aforementioned addition and extra-substitution effects could have changed socio-economic or geographical characteristics. The focus here is usually on the incidence of family reunion and the degree to which economically inactive persons take advantage of the hitherto limited opportunities of following the bread-winner, which would represent an addition effect as defined above. The easier access to housing, etc., in conjunction with a *de facto* if not *de jure* discrimination towards migrants from extra-EEC countries, could also induce an additional number of people to move, or given numbers to move more quickly, than would otherwise be the case. However, the extent of family reunion and migration of inactive persons is in actual fact largely conditioned by the availability of

---

1 'It is characteristic that none of the more than 250 concrete job offers which the European Office for Co-ordination transmitted from Belgium to Italy have met with success. Belgium particularly wanted qualified workers in the metal industry, textiles and construction. There were no workers on the Italian labour market prepared to go to Belgium' (Kommission . . . , 1970a, p. 33). Or: 'The Italian employment exchanges put forward 11,764 applicants for 20,683 German job openings. Of these, 10,206 were accepted so that less than 50% of the vacancies could be filled' (Kommission . . . , 1970a, p. 29).
2 In fact, the import of foreign workers is one way of satisfying the occupational and geographical mobility requirements of an expanding economy, and governments have been happy to see that the frictions engendered by the rapid economic development in Europe's post-industrial societies are mediated for their own population by the inflow of foreign workers—this being one of the very mechanisms which causes the self-feeding process of migration. The sheltering of agriculture in France and Germany is only one of many examples in this field.

accommodation, and this seems to exert little differential impact on nationalities despite varying legal provisions. Accommodation is scarce in all Common Market countries with the possible exception of Luxembourg, and it is particularly scarce in the great conurbations where immigrant workers are concentrated. A newly entering Italian finds himself in basically the same position as a Portuguese or Moroccan, and his right to equality of treatment means little more than that he can take his place at the bottom of the waiting list. If he is found in inadequate housing, he is unlikely to be deported; but this also holds true for the Portuguese and Moroccans—otherwise there would be no *bidonvilles* all over Europe— for their labour is needed desperately and decreases in profitability through high rates of return.

The permanence of intra-Community migrations in terms of duration of stay could have been affected either directly, through the guaranteed extension of residence abroad, or indirectly, through increased migration of socio-economic groups that generally stay longer, i.e. skilled industrial workers and married workers with families as opposed to unskilled agricultural workers and single workers. (See above pp. 67 and 70–1 on differential rates of return.) On the other hand, it could also be hypothesized that freedom of movement has the effect of shortening the migrant's duration of stay. If workers have no need to fear refusal of permission to re-enter, they can leave their country of employment more readily for an indefinite period than if they feel they have to hang on to their jobs at all costs. More important, however, is the fact that the length of stay of polyannual migrants is determined by socio-economic factors in the way outlined in the previous chapter, and workers immigrating into EEC countries have not during the existence of the Common Market been subject to an arbitrary limitation of their stay. Residence permits have been renewed freely regardless of nationality and regardless of labour market conditions. The picture of Common Market employers firing foreigners at the first sign of a recession and of busy policemen deporting these people, derives more from imagination, historical reminiscences, and false analogies than from reality. No doubt there have been refusals of residence renewals as well as deportations, but these were predominantly related to reasons of public law and order rather than labour market conditions. As the discussion of the 1967 recession in Germany showed (see above p. 36), cutting down the inflow of foreign workers, together with the increased propensity to return, more than adequately achieves the desired reduction in the small part of the foreign work-force which is expendable. For the greater part, the foreign work-force remains indispensable even during a slump and any gaps made by returning foreigners must be filled quickly either by national workers (which they are reluctant to do in the expectation that the recession will soon be over), unemployed foreign workers, or foreigners desiring to enter.

Finally, it was said that free movement might affect the organized recruitment of Community workers, i.e. by increasing the proportion of spontaneous migrations. A brief evaluation of the French and German situation has already shown that the EEC system could have played but a small part and that the maturity of the migrations together with the geographical vicinity accounts for most of the decrease in the share of Italian recruits (see above pp. 31, 35). Once a migration stream is in its second stage for any particular sending area or village, the need to use the official recruitment procedure is greatly diminished. Pioneering single workers and unaccompanied married workers often find it safer and more convenient to use the official channel even if they are not required to do so. The reunion of families, on the other hand, and the migration of single and unaccompanied married workers in an established chain in many cases takes place outside and in spite of the prescribed procedure. By this stage the ethnic communities and communications are so well established that the official channel is looked upon either as unnecessary or as positively obstructive. The official procedure has a much reduced attraction if the migrant can make the way to and across the border of the receiving country on his own. This is not to say that free movement has no influence whatsoever on the degree of spontaneous migration in terms of inducing people who had previously intended to use the official channel to go on their own (*intra-substitution effect*) and in terms of animating people, who had so far been deterred by the prospect of an official procedure, to migrate (*addition effect*). Rather, it is to say that any such effect is likely to be small compared with other factors determining the degree of organized *v*. spontaneous migration.

The preceding paragraphs have made clear that the popular picture—that freedom of movement necessarily leads to increased migratory exchanges under given conditions of demand for labour, and possibly leads also to the immigration of groups of people which the work permit procedure might have eliminated—is rather oversimplified. The contrary hypothesis that free movement may enable workers to shorten their stay abroad and to return, at least temporarily, is usually not even considered. Now, it is impossible to develop here a sophisticated analysis of the main addition and intra- or extra-substitution effects of freedom of movement in the EEC. One would need to control a number of economic and political variables and to take into account the differential maturing of various migration streams. One would also need to know much more about the composition and permanence of immigration streams from different labour-sending countries. The data for this are simply not available and the exercise would easily fill a book of its own. Therefore, the less ambitious question shall be posed, that is, whether there has been an increase in intra-Community migrations over the years which is likely to be attributable to the establishment of free movement, whatever the origin (addition or substitution) of this increase. The limited data available fortunately refer to the number of people entering the Six, so that the supposed increase can be measured at source and is not distorted by differential length of stay. The obvious method is to relate, for each country, intra-Community migrations to migrations from outside the Community into the Six, and to compare intra-Community migrations amongst themselves where the push to emigrate differed sharply. If freedom of movement has had any addition or substitution effects, the proportion of new entrants from inside the Community should, *ceteris paribus*, have increased relative to immigrants from extra-Community countries. And as Italy was the only substantial labour surplus area in the EEC, where a large number of people was considering emigration, it should, *ceteris paribus*, have increased its share of new entrants relative to other member countries (an addition effect). In both respects the increase ought to be visible around 1964–5 and 1969–70, that is, shortly after the Common Market decontrolled labour movements in two big steps.

In *Belgium* the origin of new entrants has fluctuated strongly since the inception of the Common Market. Table 5–1 shows how the share of entrants from EEC countries (other than Benelux countries) rapidly fell from two-thirds of the whole at the turn of the last decade to below one-third in 1963 and 1964, but then surpassed its former level within three or four years. This development seems to confirm the existence of free movement effects for

Belgium and to point towards a significant extra-substitution effect over and above any addition effect. Belgium is perhaps the only country of the Six which has deliberately worked towards this extra-substitution effect:

...the number of newly entering workers from third countries has increased only marginally in 1969 compared with the preceding year despite accelerated economic growth and an increase in the demand for labour. The Belgian authorities attribute this development primarily to the freedom of movement for workers in the Community which went hand in hand with a more severe application of the law relating to the employment of workers from third countries (Kommission..., 1970a, p. 13).

Table 5-1: Origin of newly entering foreign workers in *Belgium*, by nationality, in percentages.

		1958	1959	1960	1961	1962	1963	1964	1965	1966	1967	1968[b]
France		10.1	18.6	14.6	12.9	8.4	6.6	6.6	8.3	12.7	16.4	28.4
Germany		7.1	7.1	6.7	4.0	2.2	2.4	2.2	2.3	4.7	5.8	9.1
Italy		34.9	40.0	43.8	48.4	36.9	22.2	20.6	28.4	36.0	35.0	35.2
EEC		52.1	65.7	65.2	65.3	47.6	31.2	29.5	38.8	53.5	57.1	73.9
EEC = 100%	France	19.3	28.3	22.4	19.8	17.8	21.2	22.5	21.3	23.8	28.7	38.5
	Germany	13.6	10.9	10.3	6.2	4.7	7.7	7.5	6.0	8.8	10.1	12.3
	Italy	67.0	60.9	67.2	74.1	77.6	71.2	70.0	73.3	67.3	61.2	47.7
Utd. Kingd.		1.8	2.9	2.2	1.6	1.8	1.8	1.2	1.3	1.8	2.7	–
Other Eur.[a]		43.8	28.6	30.3	29.8	47.6	56.2	47.1	42.9	32.0	27.9	26.1
Extra-Eur.		2.4	2.9	2.2	3.2	3.1	10.8	22.1	17.1	12.7	12.4	–
OVERALL		100.1	100.1	99.9	99.9	100.1	100.0	99.9	100.1	100.0	100.1	100.0

a = Including stateless and those of unknown nationality.
b = Permanent workers only.
Source: Table 3-1.

However, the picture is not as clear as it seems at first sight. Firstly, there are very strong variations in the absolute number of workers admitted annually from all foreign countries taken together (cf. Table 3-1), but here the number of Community citizens is much more stable in comparison with non-EEC immigrants. Moreover, EEC numbers have been falling since 1965. It seems, therefore, that the intensity of Belgium's demand for foreign labour played a very important role in determining the origin of the migrants. Whenever the long-established streams from Italy did not yield enough new manpower, e.g. during the period 1962 to 1966, Belgium resorted to the import of labour from other European and extra-European countries. At times of low demand for labour the share of new entrants from developed countries increased sharply because these workers have on average a higher level of skill and are also suitable for employment in white-collar positions. Secondly, Italy's share of intra-Community immigrants has shown a tendency to decline since 1962, but from that date the proportion of French new entrants has steadily increased to a point where almost as many non-seasonal immigrants enter Belgium from France as from Italy. Here the opposite of the hypothesized addition effect has taken place in terms of both absolute numbers (decreasing since 1965) and proportions relative to other Common Market migrants (Italians decreasing since 1962). In conclusion, it can be said that Belgium has probably experienced a comparatively small but nevertheless significant free movement effect, i.e. an increase in the volume of intra-Community migrations which would not have occurred otherwise; but this effect is obscured by the changing economic circumstances in Belgium and in the major sending countries.

Table 5–2: Origin of newly entering foreign workers in *France*, by nationality, in percentages.

		1958	1959	1960	1961	1962	1963	1964	1965	1966	1967	1968	1969	1970
Belgium		5.7	6.5	4.4	3.7	2.6	2.0	1.4	1.2	1.0	1.0	0.9	0.6	0.5
Germany		0.8	0.9	0.6	0.7	0.8	0.9	0.8	0.7	0.7	0.8	0.7	0.5	0.5
Italy		60.2	52.2	33.1	26.8	17.9	9.7	6.2	8.1	6.5	6.3	3.7	2.8	2.2
Netherld.		0.1	0.2	0.1	0.1	0.1	0.1	0.1	0.1	0.2	0.2	0.1	0.1	0.1
EEC		66.9	59.7	38.2	31.4	21.4	12.7	8.6	10.1	8.3	8.4	5.4	3.4	3.4
EEC = 100%	Belgium	8.6	10.9	11.5	11.8	12.0	15.6	16.6	11.5	12.2	12.4	15.8	14.9	16.3
	Germany	1.1	1.6	1.6	2.4	3.7	7.2	8.9	7.3	8.0	9.6	12.5	13.2	15.4
	Italy	90.0	87.4	86.5	85.3	83.8	76.0	72.8	80.1	77.8	75.1	69.2	68.4	64.4
	Netherld.	0.2	0.3	0.3	0.4	0.7	1.1	1.7	1.4	1.9	2.3	2.5	2.6	3.8
Other Eur.[b]		31.9	37.4	60.4	65.0	75.6	80.3	82.4	80.7	81.5	83.9	82.5	81.5	83.1
OVERALL[c]		(98.8)	(97.1)	(98.6)	(96.4)	(97.0)	(93.0)	(91.0)	(90.8)	(89.8)	(92.3)	(87.9)	(84.9)	(86.5)

b = European countries given in Table 3–2.
c = Difference to 100% comprises 'Other' in Table 3–2.
Source: Table 3–2.

The picture for *France* is less equivocal (see Table 5–2). There the share of new immigrants from EEC countries has declined relative to third countries from two-thirds of the total in 1958 to a mere 3% in 1970. During this period the absolute number of workers entering France from all countries taken together has steadily increased to twice its 1958 level, while the absolute number of Common Market immigrants has fallen by 90%. The fall in the absolute and relative number of Community workers is itself nine-tenths attributable to the decrease in Italian immigration. Comparing the intra-Community migrations, one can see that all countries *except* Italy have increased their proportions of new entrants, even Belgium whose citizens tended to decrease in absolute numbers. The increase was of course most noticeable for Germans and the Dutch whose absolute numbers tended to increase marginally. Relative to other Community countries, the Italian domination has decreased from nine-tenths in 1958 to two-thirds twelve years later. The temporary reversal of the decline in 1965 resulted mainly from the slump of the Italian economy in 1964. Thus, the presumption for France must be that free movement effects have not occurred on any noticeable scale.

The picture for *Germany* (see Table 5–3) is again a little more

Table 5–3: Origin of newly entering foreign workers (first row) and of employed foreign workers (second row) in the *Federal Republic of Germany*, by nationality, in percentages.

	1958	1959	1960	1961	1962	1963	1964	1965	1966	1967	1968[b]	1969[b]	1970[b]
Belgium	0.9	0.8	0.8	1.0	0.9	0.7	0.7	0.7	0.7	1.3	0.2	0.1	0.3
	1.6	1.4	1.0	1.0	1.0	0.8	0.7	0.6	0.6	0.6	0.6	0.5	0.5
France	2.2	3.0	2.5	3.0	2.6	2.6	2.5	3.0	3.1	5.1	1.3	1.0	1.1
	3.1	4.1	3.3	2.9	3.0	2.5	2.3	2.2	2.2	2.3	2.4	2.1	2.0
Italy	35.7	49.8	54.5	46.0	41.7	35.7	32.1	38.9	39.0	38.5	33.3	21.1	23.6
	20.1	29.3	43.6	40.9	40.6	36.9	31.0	30.9	30.4	26.8	28.3	24.8	20.4
Netherld.	15.2	9.3	6.4	7.9	7.4	7.3	5.7	4.4	3.7	4.5	0.9	0.6	1.2
	22.1	17.8	12.0	8.8	8.1	7.2	6.5	5.1	4.5	4.4	4.4	3.6	3.1
EEC	54.0	63.0	64.2	57.9	52.6	46.4	41.0	47.0	46.5	49.6	35.7	22.8	26.2
	47.2	52.9	60.1	53.7	52.7	47.5	40.6	38.9	37.7	34.2	35.8	31.1	26.0
EEC = 100% Belgium	1.7	1.3	1.3	1.7	1.7	1.5	1.6	1.5	1.5	2.7	0.6	0.6	1.1
(New entr- France	4.1	4.8	3.9	5.2	4.9	5.6	6.0	6.3	6.7	10.3	3.7	4.2	4.3
ants data Italy	66.1	79.1	84.8	79.4	79.2	77.1	78.4	82.9	83.8	77.6	93.2	92.4	90.0
only) Netherld.	28.1	14.7	9.9	13.6	14.0	15.7	13.9	9.3	8.0	9.2	2.4	2.6	4.5
Utd. Kingd.	2.0	1.8	0.8	0.7	0.8	1.0	0.8	0.9	1.1	2.4	1.0	0.7	0.8
	1.6	1.6	1.1	0.8	0.8	0.8	0.7	0.7	0.7	0.8	0.9	0.8	0.7
Other Eur.[a]	37.7	29.4	31.6	37.0	42.4	48.7	55.0	49.3	49.2	42.3	60.5	74.1	69.5
	48.0	41.7	35.2	42.2	42.5	47.4	54.3	56.4	57.8	60.7	58.9	64.5	70.0
Extra-Eur.	6.2	5.9	3.4	4.4	4.3	4.0	3.2	2.9	3.2	5.7	2.7	2.3	3.5
	3.2	3.9	3.5	3.3	4.1	4.4	4.5	4.1	3.8	4.3	4.4	3.6	3.3
OVERALL	99.9	100.1	100.0	100.0	100.1	100.1	100.0	100.1	100.0	100.0	99.9	99.9	100.0
	100.0	100.1	99.9	100.0	100.1	100.1	100.1	100.1	100.0	100.0	100.0	100.0	100.0

a = Including stateless and those of unknown nationality.
b = Excluding frontier workers in new entrants data.
Source: Table 3–3.

complicated. The Community provided over half the new entrants from 1958 to 1962, but only a quarter at the end of the sixties.[3] The absolute number of Belgian, Dutch, and French new entrants tends to decrease from the mid-sixties onwards and that of the Italian new entrants from the beginning of the decade. The trend in the Italian decline was temporarily reversed in 1965 and 1970 when on both occasions an overheated German economy and an uncertain economic situation in Italy—inflation in 1964 and strikes in the autumn of 1969—coincided and induced a large outflow of Italians to Germany. It is clear that the increases in intra-Community migrations are not primarily the consequence of freedom of movement and that they are smaller than the increase in movements from outside the EEC into Germany. Comparing intra-Community migrations, one detects a fairly consistent increase in the proportion of Italians from 66% to around 90% (taking account of the exclusion of frontier workers in the data). This would seem to point to an addition effect here. Short of an econometric analysis, it is difficult to say whether Germany has experienced significant free movement effect or whether the intense demand for labour would have caused the same development if Italians had had to negotiate the work permit hurdle. Germany has probably been subject to a small but insignificant free movement effect.

Italy's case provides an interesting parallel if one disregards the minute size of its immigration compared with that of Germany or France. From its peak of over 60% at the beginning of the sixties, the share of EEC citizens has declined consistently to 18% at the end of the decade. In absolute terms the size of intra-Community immigration has tended to increase slightly since 1964. Amongst intra-Community migrations the Dutch have secured a larger and larger share (see Table 5–6) and the French proportion has also

3 If one compares the relative figures for new entrants and employed foreigners, assuming that variations in the rates of return do not distort the employment figures, one notices that the new entrants figures are twice as often higher than the employment figures in the case of EEC countries than in the case of other European countries and that only in two cases out of thirteen are the Italian employment figures higher than the new entrants figures (in 1963 and 1969). This would seem to suggest that the duration of stay of EEC workers in general and of Italians in particular has not lengthened disproportionately relative to that of comparable immigration populations and that free movement has had no significant impact in this respect. See also Table 4–4 above, where the turnover figures do not reflect a free movement effect either when compared between Italians and other nationalities.

tended to increase, while the German share has decreased in relative terms. It is difficult to establish the cause of these variations without knowing more about the motives and composition of this immigration. The developments for the Netherlands and Germany, for example, are not explicable by differential labour market conditions as demand conditions in the two countries generally vary in unison because of the high degree of interdependence of the two economies. The question of free movement effects in Italy must be left unanswered for the time being.

Table 5–4: Origin of newly entering foreign workers in *Italy*, by nationality, in percentages.

	1958	1959	1960	1961	1962	1963	1964	1965	1966	1967	1968	1969	1970
Belgium	0.8	1.5	0.5	1.8	1.9	1.6	0.8	1.2	1.3	1.0	1.2	0.9	0.8
France	12.3	8.1	8.2	14.2	13.2	12.3	8.1	11.4	10.7	9.1	11.2	8.0	5.2
Germany	30.3	43.9	47.0	43.1	31.3	27.2	18.7	19.0	17.4	16.3	15.0	12.4	8.9
Netherld.	2.3	7.0	5.8	2.6	2.8	5.8	6.5	4.7	5.8	5.2	4.3	3.5	2.9
EEC	45.9	60.6	61.7	61.7	49.3	47.2	34.2	36.5	35.3	31.8	31.7	24.8	17.9
EEC = 100% Belgium	1.8	2.4	0.9	3.0	3.9	3.4	2.4	3.4	3.6	3.2	3.7	3.5	4.5
France	26.9	13.3	13.3	22.9	26.9	26.1	23.6	31.3	30.4	28.7	35.2	32.3	28.9
Germany	66.1	72.5	76.3	69.9	63.5	57.7	54.6	52.1	49.2	51.2	47.3	49.9	49.7
Netherld.	5.1	11.5	9.4	4.2	5.6	12.3	19.1	12.9	16.3	16.4	13.7	14.1	16.3
Other	54.1	39.4	38.3	38.3	50.7	52.8	65.8	63.5	64.7	68.2	68.3	75.2	82.1
OVERALL	100.0	100.0	100.0	100.0	100.0	100.0	100.0	100.0	100.0	100.0	100.0	100.0	100.0

Source: Table 3–4.

The neighbouring EEC countries and Italy provided almost all new entrants to the foreign labour force in *Luxembourg* at the time of inception of the Common Market and for much of the sixties, but recently their share has fallen to below one-third. The relative decline visible for France and Germany also holds true for this small country with proportionally the largest foreign work-force. The absolute number of new entrants from Common Market countries is falling, too. The figures do not suggest that an addition effect has obtained in the case of Italians relative to other Common Market migrations. Their share of intra-Community migrations has declined from over three-quarters to less than 10%, though more gradually and less steeply than the share of the EEC as a whole (see Table 5–5). Neither in 1964–5 nor in 1969 are there any unequivocal free movement effects and the question must therefore be left open for Luxembourg, too.

Table 5–5: Origin of newly entering foreign workers, and share of Italian workers in foreign labour force, in *Luxembourg*, by nationality, in percentages.

	1958	1959	1960	1961	1962	1963	1964	1965	1966	1967	1968	1969	1970
Italy: new	68.2	67.5	65.9	73.0	67.3	56.0	37.1	44.2	42.8	34.5	28.6	19.1	9.9
: emp.	-	-	-	50.3	50.7	46.8	44.8	43.0	42.3	42.0	39.5	36.9	33.2
EEC	96.6	97.2	95.9	95.3	89.2	79.5	67.6	77.5	78.5	81.9	74.4	48.5	31.2
Italy: new	70.5	69.5	68.7	76.6	75.4	70.4	54.9	57.0	54.6	42.2	38.4	39.3	31.6
Utd. Kingd.	0.2	0.1	0.2	0.2	0.3	1.1	0.7	0.5	0.4	-	-	-	-
Other Eur.	2.7	2.2	3.5	3.9	9.7	17.4	28.8	19.8	19.3	14.7	-	(46.4)[a]	(63.6)[a]
Extra-Eur.	0.5	0.4	0.4	0.5	0.9	2.0	2.9	2.2	1.8	3.4	-	-	
OVERALL	100.0	99.9	100.0	99.9	100.1	100.0	100.0	100.0	100.0	100.0	(100.0)	(100.0)	(100.0)

a = Greece, Spain, Portugal, Yugoslavia.
Source: Table 3–5.

The development of the *Netherlands* shows some peculiar characteristics. On the one hand, one can see the familiar decline of the proportion of new entrants from EEC countries relative to third countries, except when the recession of 1967 temporarily favoured the immigration of workers from developed countries, i.e. mainly from Germany and France. On the other hand, there is a reversal of the absolute and relative decrease in newly entering Italians in 1968 and 1969 *vis-à-vis* the Community as a whole (see Table 5–6); but it is not sustained in 1970. The Netherlands have never exerted any particular attraction for the Italian population and the wage pull has been smaller than for neighbouring Germany or Switzerland. It seems, therefore, that an incipient addition effect has existed with respect to Italian immigration but that it has never developed further because Italians were deflected from the Netherlands to Germany and Switzerland by high wages and established ethnic communities—Southern and Western Germany and Switzerland acting as intervening opportunities. The low ratio of new entrants to a still slightly increasing number of employed Italians in recent years (see Table 3–6) seems to point to a free movement effect in terms of increased duration of stay. Today the Italian workforce has probably a lower rate of external turnover in the Low Countries than in Germany, although the migration stream appeared to mature more slowly in the former country.

Table 5–6: Origin of newly entering foreign workers (first row) and of employed foreign workers (second row), in the *Netherlands*, by nationality, in percentages.

	1958	1959	1960	1961	1962	1963	1964	1965	1966	1967	1968	1969	1970
France	2.0	4.3	2.9	2.6	2.2	1.2	2.3	1.9	1.7	8.7	3.0	1.4	1.1
	1.3	1.4	1.7	2.1	1.6	1.3	1.2	1.4	1.2	2.5	2.1	-	-
Germany	39.2	40.4	30.4	17.4	13.4	11.7	9.1	7.1	5.8	15.6	13.1	7.9	6.7
	34.0	35.2	34.4	28.6	23.1	20.3	15.3	13.1	11.9	14.7	14.6	-	-
Italy	17.6	6.4	20.3	39.1	23.9	20.9	15.2	10.4	8.7	5.8	8.1	5.8	3.2
	11.3	8.9	11.2	20.0	20.9	17.9	14.0	12.8	11.1	12.1	11.8	-	-
EEC	58.8	51.1	53.6	59.1	39.6	28.1	21.7	17.6	13.5	32.4	23.6	15.2	11.0
	46.6	45.5	47.3	50.7	45.6	39.5	30.4	27.4	24.2	29.3	28.5	-	-
EEC = 100% France	3.3	8.3	5.4	4.4	5.7	4.2	10.4	10.9	12.2	26.8	12.8	9.5	9.8
(new entrants Germany	66.7	79.2	56.8	29.4	34.0	41.7	41.8	40.0	42.9	48.2	55.3	52.4	61.0
data only) Italy	30.0	12.5	37.8	66.2	60.4	54.2	47.8	49.1	42.9	25.0	29.8	38.1	29.3
Utd. Kingd.	9.8	8.5	10.1	6.1	7.5	6.4	4.5	3.2	4.1	7.5	-	-	-
	4.6	5.2	5.4	4.6	5.3	5.0	4.5	3.5	3.3	3.5	3.4	(5.2)	(4.3)
Other	31.4	40.4	36.2	34.8	53.0	65.5	73.8	79.2	82.3	60.1	76.4	84.8	89.0
	48.7	49.3	47.3	44.6	49.1	55.5	65.1	69.1	72.5	67.3	68.1	-	-
OVERALL	100.0	100.0	99.9	100.0	100.1	100.0	100.0	100.0	99.9	100.0	100.0	100.0	100.0
	99.9	100.0	100.0	99.9	100.0	100.0	100.0	100.0	100.0	100.1	100.0	-	

Source: Table 3–6.

The evaluation of free movement effects can be broadened by taking into account the development in non-EEC countries. For once, Swiss data are insufficient and the UK must therefore carry the comparison alone. Table 5–7 shows that the proportion of Community immigrants has declined less rapidly in *Great Britain* than in any EEC country (excepting Belgium and disregarding Commonwealth immigration): the share of the EEC countries fell by a mere 20 points from its level of 55% at the end of the fifties. At that time Italians were temporarily the most prominent group, comprising a quarter of all new entrants. Today there are more Germans and almost twice as many Frenchmen entering the country as compared with Italians. The proportionate decline in new entrants from the EEC in general and Italy in particular was less steep because Britain's demand for foreign labour was less intense than that of the continental countries and there was no need to search for large numbers of non-EEC workers when the Italian supply began to dry up.

So, one finds that inside and outside the Community the volume of migrations involving Common Market workers has many similar characteristics. First of all, the number of Italians has at least be-

Table 5–7: Origin of newly entering foreign workers in the *United Kingdom*, by nationality, in percentages.

	1958	1959	1960	1961	1962	1963	1964	1965	1966	1967	1968	1969	1970
France	6.7	7.4	6.5	6.7	7.9	9.1	9.9	10.0	10.7	12.4	12.0	11.3	12.2
Germany	24.8	23.5	19.5	16.2	16.9	15.1	13.6	11.7	11.3	11.1	10.2	8.8	8.2
Italy	18.6	17.8	23.0	24.5	16.0	11.6	12.2	15.5	14.2	10.7	9.3	8.1	6.5
Netherld.	5.1	5.2	4.3	3.8	4.3	4.5	4.2	4.9	4.1	4.8	4.2	4.2	4.2
EEC[b]	55.9	55.2	54.2	51.8	45.8	41.1	40.6	42.7	41.2	39.9	36.4	33.4	31.9
Other Eur.[a]	37.1	38.4	39.0	41.1	46.0	48.1	47.4	44.6	45.5	43.6	46.3	48.2	45.5
Extra-Eur.	7.0	6.4	6.7	7.1	8.1	10.8	12.0	12.7	13.4	16.6	17.3	18.4	22.6
OVERALL	100.0	100.0	99.9	100.0	99.9	100.0	100.0	100.0	100.1	100.1	100.0	100.0	100.0

a = Including the stateless and those of unknown nationality.
b = Including Belgium and Luxembourg.
Source: Table 3–8.

come stable if it is not already in decline: in Belgium both the newly entering and employed figures for Italians show a tendency to stabilize; in Germany and the Netherlands the new entrants figures tend to fall and the employment figures to become stable; in France and Luxembourg inside the Community, and Britain and Switzerland outside the Community, both sets of figures are falling for Italians. It is perhaps somewhat surprising to find that it is the French who are now participating more widely in intra-European migration than they did ten or twelve years ago. In Belgium, Italy, the Netherlands, Switzerland, and Britain, the number of newly entering French workers has tended to rise, sometimes quite dramatically; and the plateau of 7,000 to 8,000 in Germany is also much higher than it was at the time of inception of the Common Market. This development would appear to be attributable primarily to increased mobility on the side of French society rather than any free movement effects, as it applies to both EEC and non-EEC countries. The decrease in the number of Italian migrants, on the other hand, derives clearly from Italy's rapid economic development, especially in the North. The setbacks of 1964 and 1969–70 were due, respectively, to the inflationary situation following the boom of 1962–3 and the strikes of autumn 1969. On both occasions the number of emigrants rose sharply and the number of returnees declined, and on both occasions the economy was slow to recover. But the 1962–3 boom gave advance warning of the end of large-scale Italian emigration. From that moment on, the importance of the 'push' factor was diminished drastically relative to the 'pull' factors in other European countries.

The existence of free movement effects is clearly visible on a significant scale only for Belgium and in this case it is probably due as much to a deliberate Belgian policy as to the simple removal of the work permit procedure. Free movement effects are also noticeable for Germany and the Netherlands, although to a smaller extent and in the case of the Low Countries more in relation to the increased length of stay than the volume of migration. Luxembourg and Italy present no clear picture, but in France's case it can be safely assumed that free movement has had no significant effects. The temporary rise in the figures of new Italian immigrants after 1964 in all countries except the Netherlands, and in 1969–70 in most Community countries, though coinciding with the freeing of movements inside the EEC, must be attributed primarily to the economic crises in Italy and not to the Common Market measures. This is testified by the fact that Italians increased in both absolute and relative numbers in Britain in 1965 and that Italian emigration to overseas countries also showed an increase in 1965 and 1970. Furthermore, other intra-Community movements did not as a rule increase absolutely and relatively in 1965 or 1969, though the French are an exception to this rule in 1965 in Belgium, Germany, and Italy, as are the Belgians in Italy in that year and the Dutch in Germany in 1969.

The most certain conclusion of the preceding chapters is that migrations in the European Community under free movement conditions are determined predominantly by the demand for labour as regards the size of the migrations, by the availability of housing as regards the extent of separation of families, and by the maturity of the migration as regards the permanence of stay. The key factor is labour demand: when demand is low, no degree of freedom of movement can help significant numbers of redundant workers to find suitable employment; when demand is high, citizens of Community countries have in post-war Europe needed no freedom of movement to find work, to be able to send for their wives and children, and to stay as long as they wished. Under conditions of high demand, freedom of movement has an enabling function which assumes significant proportions only if receiving countries have previously strictly controlled the in-movement and residence of foreign workers and/or if sending countries have a really large surplus of workers willing and able to fill the positions in question.

PART TWO

THE FUTURE DEVELOPMENT OF THE EEC
FREE MOVEMENT OF LABOUR SYSTEM AND
THE SUPPLY AND DEMAND SITUATION
IN THE MAIN COUNTRIES

6

The Future of Freedom of Movement
in the EEC

Freedom of movement for workers had been achieved in legal terms in 1968. Equal treatment and equal opportunities did not remain mere paperwork—Community workers took up opportunities to a slightly larger extent in at least Belgium, Germany, and the Netherlands. Of course, in many cases this was a choice constrained by the socio-economic conditions in the sending areas (but the European Community set out to make it a truly free choice through its general economic and social policy which sought to restructure backward economic areas and to raise the living standards of people residing in those areas more quickly). In other respects the choice was constrained by the imperfect workings of the Community's common labour market and by the socio-economic conditions in the receiving areas, particularly as regards the reception and integration of migrant workers. The envisaged future development in the areas of the common labour market and the integration of migrant workers, is of immediate interest to our subject and will therefore be reported on as far as the Commission has formulated and published its plans. But prior to this an often overlooked *definitum* needs to be mentioned: namely, that the EEC has agreed to extend the free movement system to workers of two countries with which it concluded association agreements, Greece and Turkey. Other association agreements do not as yet include any stipulations relating to free movement. The Yaoundé Convention only recognizes the right of establishment for the self-employed and only on a reciprocal basis.

At the time of writing, the negotiations between the EEC and the six countries of the EFTA—Austria, Finland, Iceland, Portugal, Sweden, and Switzerland—which do not desire to become members of the EEC but are looking for some special free trade relationship, had not produced any final decisions as to the extension of this special relationship into the field of migrant workers. The EEC generally, and Italy in particular, want to see the principle of equality of treatment applied to Community workers in those six countries and are prepared to give equal rights to their nationals in the Common Market. This would uphold the work permit barrier for movements between the enlarged Community and the remaining EFTA members[1] whilst removing most controls after entry. It is interesting to note that Switzerland—which over ten or twelve years ago rejected an economic union with the Community on account of, *inter alia,* the free movement provisions of the Treaty of Rome—has reportedly begun to align its internal control system with that of the Common Market, i.e. giving greater rights and finally the same rights to foreigners as to Swiss nationals, while clamping down on the in-movements of workers from outside Switzerland, *because* it anticipates some sort of relationship with the enlarged European Community in this field.

The association agreement between Greece and the EEC of 9 July 1961 stipulates in Article 44:

> Freedom of movement for workers according to articles 48 and 49 of the Treaty setting up the Community shall be secured between Member States and Greece at such time and according to such procedure as laid down by the Council of Association but not earlier than at the end of the transitional period ... (Kommission, Europäische ... n.d., p. 43).

The transitional period foreseen was twelve years and, as the agreement came into force on 1 November 1962, the establishment of some degree of free movement would have commenced at the end of 1974 had not the coup of the Colonels in Athens intervened and obliged the European Community to suspend the association agreement with Greece. Today it is widely assumed that if and when Greece has a more democratic regime the association will require renegotiation. In that case it is likely that the free movement

---

[1] Except for Denmark and Norway, on the one side, and Sweden, Iceland, and Finland, on the other, which established and intend to maintain the Common Nordic Labour Market between them.

provisions will be more definite and detailed. The speed of introducing freedom of movement may well depend on the willingness of the Greek Government itself. During the sixties Greece was the Mediterranean country most concerned about the depletion of its army reserves and agricultural labour force through the emigration of the young and able-bodied.

The agreement between Turkey and the EEC of 12 September 1963 states in Article 12: 'The Contracting Parties agree that in order to secure by stages freedom of movement for workers between them they shall be guided by articles 48, 49 and 50 of the Treaty setting up the Community' (Kommission, *Abkommen zur Gründung* ...). The additional protocol signed on 23 November 1970 in Brussels specifies in Article 36:

> Freedom of movement for workers between the Member States of the Community and Turkey shall be secured by stages according to the principles laid down in article 12 of the Association Agreement between the end of the twelfth and the end of the twenty-second year after the coming into force of the said agreement. The Council of Association decides upon its implementation (Der Assoziationsrat, p. D29).

The transitional period in the Turkish case is also twelve years so that freedom of movement is to be established between 1 January 1976 and the end of 1985. This means that three years after Britain's envisaged entry into the Common Market there is certain to be a progressive abolition of the work permit procedure for Turks in member countries of the enlarged EEC and for Community workers in Turkey. As the association agreements form a constituent part of the Community's life, Britain as a prospective member had to agree to accede to their principles and contents. How far it has sought 'transitional provisions and any other adaptations that may need to be made' is not known (*The United Kingdom and the European Community*, para. 146). After entry, Britain will of course have voting rights in the Council of Association and therefore be able to pursue its interests there. However, Lord Windlesham was certainly mistaken in saying during the last stages of the Immigration Bill that 'if the United Kingdom were to join the EEC we should then have a say in deciding *whether* the free movement of labour provisions should be extended to Turkey and Greece' (HL Deb., 11 Oct. 1971, col. 225; my italics). The question is not one of *whether* but of *when*! Britain on its own would not be able to raise this to a question of overriding national importance permitting the use of the veto. A retrograde step is conceivable only if a number of member countries become seriously worried about the potential influx of Turks—there are already almost half a million Turkish workers in Germany, with a waiting list of well over one million—or if the Turkish Government found that large-scale migrations were disadvantageous. Turkey has so far been fairly satisfied with the results of large-scale emigration, which it sees primarily as balancing out its trade deficit. The tight control exercised by the Turkish authorities over the emigration and return of their workers has this very reason as its basis. There is little prospect of a change of heart on the side of the Six, which after all concluded the additional protocol only one year ago, and Lord Windlesham's further words should therefore be taken with a pinch of salt:

> It is not likely that there will be an early move to allow Turks and Greeks to move into EEC countries under the free movement of labour provisions. Implementation of this part of the Agreements is likely to be held back until economic conditions in Turkey and Greece approach more nearly to those in EEC countries (HL Deb., 11 Oct. 1971, col. 225).

Some measures complementing the bare freedom of movement have already been taken by the European Community in the field of residence and social security (see above pp. 21–4). These measures were based on Treaty provisions. On 17 March 1971 the new member of the Commission responsible for Social Affairs, Albert Coppé, gave an account to the European Parliament of the Commission's future plans concerning the migration and free movement of workers and in this case specific Treaty provisions were barely adduced as legitimation while the underlying *ultima ratio* of the Treaty of Rome came to the fore. To some extent this development in the social sphere is the natural growth from the earlier achievements of the EEC and to some extent it was spurred by the planned achievement of economic and monetary union.[2] Migration and free movement of workers play only a secondary role in bringing about the social integration that must go hand in hand with economic

---

[2] 'The economic and social aspects of the process of integration will, of necessity, become increasingly inseparable. The success of the whole process will be jeopardised if economic and monetary integration and social integration do not take place simultaneously' (Commission of the European Communities, 1971, p. 7). See also *BEC* (No. 5, 1971), pp. 5–10, 13–19, and 28–33.

integration, whereas the plans for bringing about more social integration directly bear on the freedom of movement. More important, some of the measures contemplated for migrant workers are already a step ahead of the envisaged social integration of the Community in that they seek, on the one hand, to give the embryonic form of European citizenship embodied in freedom of movement a political birth-help and, on the other hand, to draw workers from third countries into the ambit of the free movement system.

The first main priority of the programme of Community social policy is the speedier achievement of the common labour market (*CEC*, 1971, p. 58). The Standing Committee on Employment, set up after the First European Conference on Employment in Luxembourg in April 1970, is also to be seen in this context. In the absence of controls on workers' movements, the efficiency of a common labour market hinges on its transparency, i.e. whether and to what degree labour market indicators can be transmitted throughout the region so that they reach participants and can be acted upon by them. Accordingly, the increase of labour market transparency is one of the first objectives of the Commission and this should be of enormous benefit to potential migrants.

Secondly and more directly, recognizing that urgent and co-ordinated measures are needed to deal with the problems of foreign immigration, the Commission states its aim to prevent or stop any discrimination and to ensure a better integration of migrant workers and their families into their new living and working environment. 'This will call for a series of measures to provide the people concerned with more information and to improve their welcome, accommodation and social and cultural integration, and the provision of crash vocational training courses' (*CEC*, 1971, pp. 59; 23, 47).[3]

Thirdly,

as part of measures to strengthen the Community, the governments of Member States and the Community institutions should give thought to the possibility of gradually extending the rights and obligations associated with the possession of nationality to the nationals of other Member States resident on their territory. Representation at local level, for instance, would fulfil a profound aspiration of the migrant population (*CEC*, 1971, p. 47).

---

[3] 'Specific programmes will have to be worked out for such matters as vocational training, education for adaptation to children's cultural problems, the cultural advancement of adults, decent housing and integration into the host society.'

This indeed goes far beyond anything foreseen in the Treaty of Rome and it may even be thought to go beyond the notion of free movement. Yet, freedom of movement is the right of workers and their dependants to choose their place of work and residence as they think fit for the improvement of their living and working conditions and for the furtherance of their social advancement; and to divorce the political from the social and economic spheres would mean artificially separating parts of a social totality which stand and fall together. The truly revolutionary step forward in this proposal is the abandonment of prior naturalization, that is, the often tenuous and formal test of allegiance.

And lastly, I have already indicated that the underprivileged position of migrant workers from third countries compared with that of Community workers has given officials and migrants alike an uneasy feeling when confronted with situations involving discrimination on the grounds of nationality. A Greek, for example, is naturally annoyed when after a year or two he still has to ask for permission to change jobs while he sees his Italian colleague free to do so as he pleases. And an official is often placed in an impossible position by having to refuse, for example, a wife's entry in the case of a non-EEC worker when on the merits of the case he would have much preferred to grant permission to him than to the recent Italian immigrant who he knows cannot find decent accommodation either and whom he suspects will probably house his family in a place scheduled for demolition. Governments of member countries have already been under pressure to liberalize their post-entry control system for non-EEC workers, and even the Swiss have felt the force of the advancing Community system. The Commission presumably sensed that it could play a valuable and successful co-ordinating role here and therefore proposed that 'the benefits enjoyed by Community workers will have to be extended by stages to the whole Community's immigrant labour force, starting with workers from associated countries and entirely without prejudice to Community preference as regards recruitment' (CEC, 1971, p. 47).[4]   In other words, control on entry will be

---

[4] Incidentally, immigration policy towards third countries remains for the time being the prerogative of individual member countries. The Commission suggested in 1970 that because Italy could not satisfy the excess demand for labour in the Community and more workers would have to be imported from outside, the Community should address itself immediately to the problem of co-ordinating the immigration and recruitment policy of

maintained but control after entry is to be progressively dismantled, to the level currently applicable to Community workers, for workers from present[5] and future[6] associated countries, and finally for all non-EEC workers.[7] Here the Commission is on sound economic and pragmatic political grounds and it could even argue that 'the scope of paragraph 1 of Article 48 is clearly and intentionally wider than that of paragraph 2 and ... that the general objectives of the Treaty could be advanced by permitting free movement of labour regardless of nationality' (Campbell, 1971, p. 226; and above note 3, p. 4).

Of course, these four points are so far only part of the Commission's plan, and whether the Council of Ministers will come to a positive decision is an open question. It will probably look benevolently upon the first two suggestions, pass some innocuous directives, and nothing substantially new will happen. Taking the field of integration and vocational training of migrant workers as an example, national and international organizations in Europe have been enunciating similar principles for ten years or more—everybody is theoretically against discrimination and for increased vocational training, but nobody actually does much about it. Britain as a member of the Community will surely not raise its voice against such general aims.

Neither is Britain likely to object to the proposed enfranchisement of non-naturalized migrants from other Common Market countries. Re-

member states in third countries. It saw this as part and parcel of the employment policy and particularly in terms of distortion of competition as some members went out to recruit non-Community workers on a large scale while others with fewer means were left behind to pick up the crumbs from the table of the rich. See Kommission . . . (1970a), p. 48; and Stephen (1970), p. 12. So far this proposal has not progressed beyond preparatory studies by the Commission.

5 Greece and Turkey, of course; Surinam and the Dutch Antilles; the eighteen countries encompassed by the Yaoundé Convention, i.e. the fifteen countries of Black Africa enjoying privileged entry in France (see page 32, note 2) except Guinea, plus Burundi, Congo (Kinshasa), Rwanda, and Somalia; the three countries under the Arusha Convention, i.e. Kenya, Tanzania, and Uganda; and Morocco, Tunisia, and Malta.

6 Probably Algeria and the independent Commonwealth countries in Africa, the Caribbean, the Indian Ocean (but not India and Pakistan, for example), and the Pacific as well as all British dependent territories except Gibraltar and Hong Kong; cf. *The United Kingdom and the European Community*, para. 117–8.

7 The proposal to give equal rights to citizens of the remaining EFTA countries also belongs to this category; cf. above pp. 88–9.

sistance is far more probable from the side of those continental members who have made it very difficult to acquire their nationality. There will probably be long disputes about the residence qualifications for voting rights for polyannual migrants and about the admissibility of foreign candidates and parties, and so on. In Germany, for example, it is illegal for foreigners to form political associations. Although Britain permits only 'British subjects' to vote and stand in local authority or general elections, well over a million of what it considers 'immigrants' already have these rights—namely, citizens of independent Commonwealth countries resident in the UK—due to the fact that the status of 'British subject' and 'Commonwealth citizen' is interchangeable in British law. Even the Immigration Act 1971 did not terminate the right to vote and stand in elections for Commonwealth citizens admitted only temporarily and under restrictions. Furthermore, resident citizens of the Republic of Ireland enjoy the same rights. It appears, therefore, that future British governments would be easily reconciled to extending voting rights to the small number of EEC nationals in these islands.

The fourth proposal, however, may meet with stiff British opposition. The present Conservative Government has just given a great deal of parliamentary time to passing the Immigration Act 1971, the main practical effect of which is to subject the small remaining trickle of (non-patrial) Commonwealth immigrant workers to a job control from which they had hitherto been free, while also sharpening the deportation procedure for both Commonwealth and foreign immigrants. It is unlikely that any British government will be well disposed towards reversing this development in the near future and putting both non-patrial Commonwealth immigrants and the bulk of the current intake of foreign workers on the same footing as that smaller part of the intake which comprises EEC citizens. Lord Windlesham rejected an amendment to the Immigration Bill which proposed that Commonwealth immigrants be given, subject to control, the same rights after entry as EEC nationals (HL Deb., 11 Oct. 1971, col. 219–34). It will not be as easy to reject such a proposal if and when it comes before the Council of the European Community. Clearly this does not constitute a case of overriding national importance where the veto may be invoked. And unanimity according to Article 135 of the Treaty (see page 12, note 2 above) is not required because the control of movement from a third country into the Community remains unaffected. The extent of the British opposition probably depends on the degree of equalization foreseen for the first stages. Giving equality of treatment with respect to, for example, trade union membership will not irk any British government. Cancelling the restrictions on job changes and residences could well embarrass a Conservative Government which has just told the electorate, with the tacit agreement of trade unions, how terribly important these restrictions are. Allowing all immigrant workers to move about freely in the Community's territory is surely unacceptable to current British thinking.

7

The Socio-demographic Background

To tackle the question of the likely size and directions of future migrations across the Channel, one has to explore the possible imbalances between labour supply and labour demand here and on the Continent, and the motivations of potential migrants. This is not primarily a question of regulations and restrictions: free movement provisions in contemporary Europe have an enabling character in a situation where previous regulations have not substantially held back migrations between members of the European Community. Rather —leaving the consideration of motivations to the last section of the book—it is foremost a question of economic development and policy. But it is also to a large extent a question of the demographic and social development in the countries under review. The relationships between economic development and population changes are obvious in the case of underdeveloped countries, but they exist, no less, though perhaps more subtly, in the case of present-day European societies. The link between rising living standards and the import of foreign workers for menial jobs has already been referred to. Other examples are the advent of a baby boom, which may throw thousands of people on the labour market, or the adding of a further year of compulsory education, which may deplete the labour market of thousands. This chapter will therefore examine the socio-demographic development in the most relevant member countries of the enlarged Community in order to pinpoint likely imbalances in supply and demand of labour up to the year 1980. Fairly reliable demographic, social, and economic forecasts are available for a medium-term time span of ten years. Most components of the

demographic development affecting the labour market are already
with us, such as new entrants and age-specific death rates. Social
changes affecting the labour market and people's outlook on work
are more difficult to predict, and depend in turn on the demographic
and economic development. Short-term economic forecasts have become a subject for jokes rather than serious discussions, but this
should not blind one to the fact that medium or longer term
developments average out some of the short-term fluctuations and
are therefore more accurate although, perhaps, less specific. The
following projections are generally based on the social and economic
trends visible in the second half of the sixties.

It so happens that the two continental countries with the greatest
degree of imbalance between demand and supply of labour are also
the countries with the largest populations, the greatest number of
immigrants and emigrants, respectively, and the fastest rising living
standards in hitherto buoyant economies—that is, Germany and
Italy. Britain apart, they will form the focus of the following analysis. France also requires some special attention as it falls in almost
the same category as Germany. Luxembourg need not be considered
specifically because of its small size. The same holds true for Ireland, Denmark, and Norway (see above, p. 26). Greece and Turkey,
the two potential labour suppliers for the EEC under free movement, also need not be considered in detail because their demographic and economic development up to 1980 is unlikely to undergo any major changes and because by that time complete freedom
of movement may not have been established between them and the
enlarged Community. Greece's economically active population is
about the size of Belgium's (see Table 7–1), and the population
growth in both countries is of the same proportions. Greece, of
course, has exported one-tenth of its active population into other
European countries, while also providing immigrants for, among
others, Australia and Canada. Industrialization and urbanization,
which increase women's participation in the non-agricultural labour
force and thereby diminish their level of fertility (Safilios-Rothschild,
1971), are not foreseen to affect significantly Greece's emigration potential in the coming decade. The same picture obtains for
the much larger population of Turkey, where at present over one
million people are on the waiting list for employment in Germany.
With a crude birth rate as high as forty per thousand and a crude
death rate of fifteen per thousand, the majority of the population

living in small rural communities (56% in villages of less than 2,000 inhabitants), and the vast majority of the active population engaged in agriculture (over 70%, with 58% of all males), Turkey's emigration potential is unlikely to be affected in the foreseeable future even if the economic development were much faster than it is already. Turkey has in fact begun to repeat the experience of Western European countries with respect to fertility differentials.

In the three metropolitan centres [Ankara, Istanbul, and Izmir] that have gone farthest in fertility decline, there were extremely wide fertility differentials by social class. The differentials were less pronounced in other urban areas where fertility levels were also higher. In rural areas where fertility was the highest, there were no differentials between socio-economic groups (Timur, 1971, p. 24).

But in aggregate terms, 'reductions in fertility are unlikely unless profound and rapid changes in the economic and social structure have been attained' (Timur, 1971, p. 25). Danieli (1971) estimated that if Greece and Turkey were to follow the development path of Europe's industrialized countries, they would have a labour surplus of 270,000 to 670,000 and 4.3 to 5.3 millions, respectively, by the year 1980.

(a) BELGIUM

The natural increase in the Belgian population up to 1980 is comparatively small, that is, less than 500,000 (see Table 7-1). The growth in the indigenous labour force is likely to be very small in the first half of the seventies, but will be more pronounced towards the end of the decade (Werner, 1971).[1] The projections anticipate a net immigration of 182,000, of which 132,000 are economically active persons, and increased female activity which will bring another 120,000 women onto the labour market. Clearly, there are some labour reserves in the group of self-employed, both amongst men and women, where proportionately more than twice as many people are employed as in Britain, for example. But agriculture and the secondary sector have already been drained of much of their surplus, while the service sector is most difficult to squeeze economically and electorally. Today only 4.5% of Belgium's labour force is employed in agriculture and the level will have fallen to 3.6%

[1] Werner's projections are based on OECD (1970) and the population projections of the EEC used in this chapter.

Table 7-I: Some indicators of the socio-demographic development of the population of *Belgium*.

		1950 (1947) Both	1950 (1947) Male	1950 (1947) Female	1960 (1961) Both	1960 (1961) Male	1960 (1961) Female	1969 Both	1969 Male	1969 Female	1980 Both	1980 Male	1980 Female
POPULATION (end of year)	1,000	8,654	4,257	4,397	9,178	4,498	4,680	9,660	4,730	4,930	10,151[a]	4,982	5,112
0-14		21.0%	21.6%	20.4%	23.7%	24.6%	22.8%	23.6%	24.7%	22.6%	-	23.6%	21.3%
15-64		67.9%	68.3%	67.5%	64.3%	65.1%	63.6%	63.0%	64.1%	62.0%	-	64.9%	62.5%
65+		11.1%	10.1%	12.1%	12.0%	10.3%	13.6%	13.3%	11.2%	15.4%	-	11.5%	15.7%
Birth rate (live b.) per 1,000		16.5	-	-	16.9	-	-	14.6	-	-	-	-	-
Death rate (all ages) per 1,000		12.0	-	-	12.3	-	-	12.4	-	-	-	-	-
Life expectancy (at age 0) years		-	62.0	67.3	-	67.7	73.5	-	-	-	-	-	-
CIVIL EMPL. (excl. unempl.)	1,000	3,412	2,398	1,014	3,447	2,390	1,057	3,683	2,483	1,200	4,123[b]	2,710	1,161
Activity rate (8 as % of 1)		39.4	56.3	23.1	37.6	53.1	22.6	38.1	52.5	24.3	40.6	54.4	22.6
Unemployed (as % of 8)		(2.7%)	(3.0%)	(2.0%)	3.7%	4.1%	2.9%	2.7%	2.5%	2.9%			
SELF-EMPL. (as % of 8)		(23.0%)	(24.4%)	(18.5%)	19.5%	19.3%	(18.5%)	16.5%	19.6%[d]	14.9%[d]			
In prim. sec.	1,000	(230.9)	(212.3)	(18.5)	174	(150.1)	(20.4)	130	124.4[d]	13.5[d]			
In second. sec.	1,000	(217.3)	(195.0)	(22.3)	159	(134.3)	(10.4)[f]	147	143.0[d]	9.6[d]			
In tert. sec.	1,000	(321.5)	(213.5)	(106.0)	337	(206.4)[f]	(141.9)[f]	331	216.1[d]	125.6[d]			
FAMILY WORK. (as % of 8)		(6.7%)	(5.3%)	(11.1%)	6.7%	(3.0%)	(9.3%)	4.9%	1.9%[d]	12.2%[d]			
In prim. sec.	1,000	(131.7)	(92.0)	(39.7)	103	(37.6)	(19.7)	47	21.9[d]	35.3[d]			
In second. sec.	1,000	(28.3)	(21.9)	(6.3)	47	(16.0)[f]	(4.8)[f]	46	10.8[d]	11.9[d]			
In tert. sec.	1,000	(63.2)	(20.2)	(43.1)	81	(22.8)[f]	(62.2)[f]	87	13.2[d]	74.4[d]			
WAGE & SAL. EARN. (as % of 8)		(70.4%)	(70.4%)	(70.4%)	73.8%	76.8%	(71.4%)	78.6%	79.8%	76.1%			
In prim. sec.	1,000	(60.2)	(57.4)	(2.9)	23	(24.8)	(1.3)	14	13	1			
In second. sec.	1,000	(1,452.3)	(1,162.8)	(289.4)	1,405	(1,165.3)[f]	(274.8)[f]	1,460	1,165	294			
In tert. sec.	1,000	(044.6)	(572.3)	(272.3)	1,117	(704.7)[f]	(373.8)[f]	1,421	803	619			
PRIMARY SEC. (as % of 8)		(12.6%)	(14.2%)	(7.6%)	8.7%	(8.6%)	(4.5%)	5.2%	0.7%[d,e]	0.1%[d,e]			
SECOND. SEC. (as % of 8)		(50.7%)	(54.2%)	(39.6%)	46.8%	(53.4%)[f]	(31.9%)[f]	44.9%	58.8%[d,e]	32.2%[d,e]			
TERTIARY SEC. (as % of 8)		(36.7%)	(31.6%)	(52.8%)	44.5%	(38.0%)[f]	(63.6%)[f]	49.9%	40.5%[d,e]	67.8%[d,e]			

Note: Footnotes to this table appear at foot of following page.

five years hence (Marsh, 1971, p. 102). So the net immigration of 132,000 foreign workers does not seem unrealistic if economic growth is to be maintained and the rapid increase of the tertiary sector not checked (especially the number of female family workers).

(b) FRANCE

France's development is Belgium's development writ large. A slow natural increase of the resident population, sustained to a large extent by first- and second-generation immigrants, is accompanied by a relative decline in indigenous entrants to the labour market and needs to be supplemented by the immigration of foreign workers. In France's case, the trend towards longer schooling and earlier retirements reduces the potential labour supply by about 1,650,000 people in 1980 and the expected increase in female participation cannot begin to make good these losses (see Table 7–2). The aggregate effect of the socio-demographic changes is to take 1,315,000 persons off the labour market in 1980 who would be there under current conditions. If one assumes a labour force participation rate of 66% for the anticipated net gain of 1,260,000 immigrants, one arrives at an additional supply of about 830,000 workers. France's planners obviously expect that more of their unemployed will be absorbed in the future than previously, when between 200,000 and 300,000 workers could not find jobs under full employment conditions; or they expect that technological advances will reduce labour demand; or they may budget for lower growth rates of the economy. Internally it is well known that there are pockets of labour surplus which could make the import of foreign workers superfluous to some extent. The service sector in general and the retail trade in particular are overmanned, and in

---

- = Not available.
a = The 'Both' sexes figure is adjusted for decrease in birth rate (−155,000) and for migratory gain (+182,000). Difference = +27,000. Male and female figures = natural development.
b = The 'Both' sexes figure is adjusted for increased female activity rates (+120,000) and migratory gain (+132,000). Difference = +252,000. Male and female figures = constant participation rates.
c = Agriculture, etc., only. Mining is included in secondary sector (as is construction, electricity, gas, and water).
d = EEC (sample survey, spring 1969).
e = Distribution of wage and salary earners only.
f = Including activities not adequately described.
Source: Statistisches Amt . . . (1970, 1971); *Year Book of Labour Statistics*.

Table 7-2:   Some indicators of the socio-demographic development of the population of *France*.

	1958 (1954)			1965 (1962)			1969			1975			1980		
	Both	Male	Female	Both	Male	Female	Both	Male	Female	Both	Male	Female	Both	Male	Female
POPULATION (end of year) 1,000	45,015	21,809	23,206	49,150	24,022	25,128	50,522	24,641	25,881	52,643[a]	25,396	26,512	54,796[a]	26,299	27,237
0-14	25.9%	27.3%	24.7%	25.3%	26.4%	24.3%	24.8%	25.9%	23.8%	–	25.3%	23.3%	–	24.7%	22.8%
15-64	62.5%	63.8%	51.2%	62.5%	64.3%	60.9%	62.3%	64.0%	60.7%	–	63.8%	60.7%	–	63.9%	60.9%
65+	11.6%	8.9%	14.1%	12.1%	9.3%	14.8%	12.8%	10.0%	15.5%	–	10.9%	16.1%	–	11.4%	16.3%
Birth rate (live b.) per 1,000	18.1			17.7			16.7								
Death rate (all ages) per 1,000	11.0			11.5			12.2								
Life expectancy (at age 0) years		65.0[b]	–[b] 71.2[b]		67.2[c]	73.8[c]		68.0[d]	75.5[d]						
CIVIL EMPL. (excl. unempl.) 1,000	18,823	(12,660.9)	(6,506.2)	19,560	(12,457.2)	(6,489.2)	20,154	12,663[g]	7,371[g]	21,668[e]	14,547	8,152	22,334[e]	15,206	8,437
Activity rate (8 as % of 1)	41.8	(58.1)	(28.0)	39.8	(51.9)	(25.8)	39.9	(51.4)[g]	(28.5)[g]	41.2	57.3	30.7	40.8	57.8	31.0
Unemployed (as % of 8)	1.0%	(1.5%)	(2.2%)	1.4%	(0.9%)	(0.8%)	1.7%	1.5[g]	2.1[g]						
SELF-EMPL. & FAM. WORK. (as % of 8)	31.5%	(31.4%)	(40.7%)	25.9%	26.7%	(31.5%)	23.1%	22.2[g]	24.0[g]						
In prim. sec. 1,000	3,432	(2,368.1)	(1,647.7)	2,731	(1,864.8)	(1,166.6)	2,385	1,326.4[g]	859.8[g]						
In second. sec. 1,000	830	(725.9)	(204.0)	742	(602.8)	(142.2)	718	629.0[g]	171.6[g]						
In tert. sec. 1,000	1,681	(884.3)[i]	(759.2)[i]	1,590	(855.9)	(734.3)	1,550	861.8[g]	236.9[g]						
WAGE & SAL. EARN. (as % of 8)	68.4%	(68.6%)	(59.3%)	74.1%	(73.3%)	(68.5%)	76.9%	77.8[g]	76.0[g]						
In prim. sec. 1,000	1,023	(1,019.8)	(177.1)	749	(768.7)	(106.4)	626	455.4[g]	79.4[g]						
In sec. sec. 1,000	6,516	(4,447.2)	(1,463.7)	7,262	(5,106.4)	(1,585.5)	7,450	5,434.2[g]	1,755.8[g]						
In tert. sec. 1,000	5,311	(3,215.5)[i]	(2,218.5)[i]	6,486	(3,268.6)	(2,754.2)	7,425	3,956.2[g]	3,766.9[g]						
PRIMARY SEC. [f] (as % of 8)	23.7%	(26.8%)	(28.0%)	17.8%	(21.1%)	(19.6%)	14.9%	4.6[h],[g]	1.4[h],[g]						
SECOND. SEC. (as % of 3)	39.0%	(40.9%)	(25.6%)	40.9%	(45.6%)	(26.5%)	40.5%	55.2[h],[g]	31.3[h],[g]						
TERTIARY SEC. (as % of 8)	37.3%	(32.4%)[i]	(46.3%)[i]	41.3%	(33.1%)	(53.8%)	44.5%	40.2[h],[g]	67.2[h],[g]						

a = The 'Both' sexes figures are adjusted for migratory gain (+735,000 in 1975 and +1,260,000 in 1980). Male and female figures = natural development.   b = 1952-6.   c = 1960.   d = 1968.

e = The 'Both' sexes figures are adjusted for longer schooling (−815,000 in 1975 [−502,000 males and −313,000 females] and −977,000 in 1980 [−592,000 males and −385,000 females]) and changes in labour force participation rates (+209,000 in 1975 [−53,000 males and +262,000 females] and +338,000 in 1980 [−92,000 males and +430,000 females]), as well as for a decrease in the pensionable age (−425,000 in 1975 [−295,000 males and −130,000 females] and −670,000 in 1980 [−454,000 males and −216,000 females]). Difference = −1,031,000 in 1975 and −1,315,000 in 1980. Male and female figures = constant participation rates.

f = See note c of Table 7-1.   g = EEC sample survey, spring 1969.

h = Distribution of wage and salary earners only.   i = Including activities not adequately described.

Source: Statistisches Amt . . . (1970, 1971); *Year Book of Labour Statistics*.

1971 over 13% of the total active population drew their livelihood from the land. It is also well known that both retail traders and farmers are a potent political force in France who determinedly resist governmental attempts to give the screw of economic pressure another turn. It seems that the restructuring of the French economy depends on the death rate among farmers. The average French farmer is in his fifties, and for a generation now his children have been leaving the land to find work in small towns and in the Paris region. Five years from now the agricultural labour force is expected to have fallen to 10.5% (Marsh, 1971, p. 102), and by the end of the seventies it may be down to 6%. The corresponding increase in the industrial or tertiary labour force will almost certainly not be fed by farmers, for most of them will withdraw from the labour market completely. Consequently foreign workers will continue to have to make good the losses resulting from longer schooling, earlier retirements, and lack of industrial and geographical mobility on the part of French retail traders and farmers.

(c) GERMANY

In economic terms, Germany has a very unfavourable age composition, especially its female population. This is compounded by a drop in the birth rate below reproduction level since 1969 (a development which is also visible for Sweden and Denmark, for example; see *Le Monde*, 31 Aug. 1971, p. 11). There are annually 200,000 births fewer than there used to be. This is itself a reflection of the baby *baisse* in 1951–3 following the post-war baby boom. The lower number of marriages and births has been preceded by a lower number of new entrants to the labour market. Moreover, the decreased number of new entrants had stayed longer at school and in greater proportions than previous generations.[2] Persons also tend to retire earlier as compared with ten or fifteen years ago,

---

[2] For the male population, the labour force participation rate has decreased during the period 1960–8 by 4.5% p.a. for the 14–19 year olds, by 0.6% p.a. for the 20–24 year olds, and by 0.3% for the 25–29 year olds. Compared with 1960, 'the corresponding reduction in the number of economically active males amounts to 155,000 in 1970, 545,000 in 1975, and 960,000 in 1980'. For the female population, schooling decreased the labour force participation rate only for the 14–19 age bracket. 'The corresponding reduction in economically active females would seem to amount to 115,000 in 1970, about 400,000 in 1975 and 670,000 in 1980' (Statistisches Amt . . . , 1971, p. 18). During the period 1970–80, longer schooling will therefore reduce the German labour supply by about 1,360,000 workers!

Table 7-3: Some indicators of the socio-demographic development of the population of the *Federal Republic of Germany.*

	1950[a] Both	Male	Female	1960 (1961) Both	Male	Female	1969 Both	Male	Female	1975 Both	Male	Female[d]	1980[d] Both	Male	Female[d]
POPULATION (end of year) 1,000	50,336	23,405	26,931	55,785	26,174	29,611	61,195	29,180	32,015	63,142	29,174	31,851	64,402	29,629	31,979
0-14	23.6%	25.7%	21.7%	21.9%	23.8%	20.3%	23.2%	24.9%	21.6%	23.5%	23.2%	20.2%	22.6%	21.7%	19.1%
15-64	67.2%	55.4%	68.7%	67.4%	57.1%	67.8%	63.8%	54.6%	63.1%	62.6%	65.3%	63.0%	63.2%	66.8%	63.1%
65+	9.3%	8.9%	9.6%	10.6%	9.1%	12.0%	13.0%	10.5%	15.2%	13.9%	11.5%	16.7%	14.0%	11.5%	17.8%
Birth rate (live b.) per 1,000	16.2	—	—	17.4	—	—	14.8	—	—	—	—	—	—	—	—
Death rate (all ages) per 1,000	10.5	—	—	11.6	—	—	12.2	—	—	—	—	—	—	—	—
Life expectancy (at age 0) years	—	64.6	68.5	—	66.7	71.9	—	67.6[a]	73.6[a]	—	—	—	—	—	—
CIVIL EMPL. (excl. unempl.)1,000	21,153	13,587	7,566	25,954	16,149	9,805	26,337	16,796	9,551	27,152	17,343	9,297	27,838	17,924	9,544
Activity rate (8 as % of 1)	42.0	59.2	28.1	46.5	61.7	33.1	43.0	57.5	29.8	43.0	59.4	29.2	43.2	60.5	29.8
Unemployed (as % of 8)				1.0%	1.1%	0.9%	0.7%	0.7%	0.6%	0.8%			0.8%		
SELF-EMPL. (as % of 8)	14.0%	18.0%	7.6%	12.7%	(14.9%)	(7.3%)	11.1%	14.0%[g]	6.3%[g]	16.1%[c]			14.2%[c]		
in prim. sec.[b] 1,000	1,252.4	1,037.7	214.7	1,159	(914.4)	(227.5)	854	636.9[g]	100.1[g]						
in second. sec. 1,000	939.3[f]	789.5[f]	149.8[f]	808	(678.5)[f]	(108.9)[f]	700	613.6[g]	57.2[g]						
in tert. sec. 1,000	1,066.6[f]	825.1[f]	241.5[f]	1,317	(917.3)[f]	(391.3)[f]	1,373	894.6[g]	327.3[g]						
FAMILY WORK. (as % of 8)	14.4%	4.5%	32.0%	10.1%	(2.8%)	(22.0%)	7.5%	1.3%[g]	16.9%[g]						
in prim. sec. 1,000	2,732.7	536.1	2,196.6	1,931	(378.9)	(1,611.6)	1,380	167.6[g]	913.9[g]						
in second. sec. 1,000	164.8[f]	59.7[f]	105.1[f]	248	(39.5)[f]	(185.2)[f]	163	10.3[g]	114.8[g]						
in tert. sec. 1,000	286.8[f]	46.5[f]	240.3[f]	453	(53.1)[f]	(369.4)[f]	432	27.7[g]	294.0[g]						
WAGE & SAL. EARN. (as % of 8)	70.8%	76.7%	60.4%	77.2%	(82.3%)	(70.7%)	81.4%	84.3%	76.3%	83.9%			85.8%		
in prim. sec. 1,000	1,128.6	742.5	386.1	533	(332.0)	(122.4)	299	215	84						
in sec. sec. 1,000	6,363.9[f]	6,612.8[f]	1,751.1[f]	11,462	(9,013.5)[f]	(3,036.0)[f]	12,073	9,155	2,918						
in tert. sec. 1,000	6,138.8[f]	3,475.6[f]	2,563.2[f]	8,043	(4,562.3)[f]	(3,859.4)[f]	9,063	4,781	4,282						
PRIMARY SEC.[b] (as % of 8)	23.2%	16.4%	35.2%	14.0%	(9.6%)	(19.8%)	9.6%	1.6%[g,h]	1.2%[g,h]	7.4%			6.0%		
SECOND. SEC. (as % of 8)	42.9%[f]	52.8%[f]	25.2%[f]	48.2%	(57.6%)[f]	(33.5%)[f]	49.1%	63.3%[g,h]	43.5%[g,h]	48.7%			48.3%		
TERTIARY SEC. (as % of 8)	33.5%[f]	30.8%[f]	39.6%[f]	37.8%	(32.7%)[f]	(46.7%)[f]	41.3%	35.2%[g,h]	55.3%[g,h]	43.9%			45.7%		

especially the men. On the other hand, there is a noticeable increase in the participation of married women.[3] Together, this has led to a stagnation of the native German labour supply in the early sixties and an annual reduction of about 100,000 since the mid-sixties which will continue until the mid-seventies. It is only after 1975 that the native German labour force will start to increase again with an improvement in the age structure.

However, these projections may be overtaken by recent political developments which are likely to reduce the labour supply even further. The educational reforms under consideration would withhold another 1.2 million pupils and students from the labour market by 1985 and education would swallow up one-third of all employees in the public sector compared with the present one-fifth. It is for these and financial reasons that the reform proposals have been scaled down by 25% (*Der Spiegel*, 12 April 1971, p. 23). The other major reform, the introduction of the age limit for pensions at sixty instead of sixty-five, had to be turned on the same grounds into a flexible pensionable age which permits workers to retire from sixty-three onwards if they so desire. It is expected to reduce the German supply by up to 150,000. But not only do the numbers of German workers decrease: those who are employed are likely to

[3] See the detailed projections by Klauder and Kühlewind (1970), who found that married women were the only female group with a significant increase in labour force participation rates. This kept the over-all female rates constant with an insignificant tendency to increase.

---

a = 1966–8.
b = See note c of Table 7–1.
c = Self employed plus unpaid family workers.
d = Whereas the 'Both' sexes figures are based on the last available projections (*BMWI*, 1970), the 'Male' and 'Female' figures are taken from earlier estimates (Statistisches Amt . . . , 1971) and refer to the natural development (rows 1–4) and constant participation rates (row 8). Adjustments for changes in labour force participation (longer schooling, earlier retirement, and increased female activity) bring the 1975 'Both' sexes figure on civil employment to 26,356,000 and the 1980 figure to 26,972,000; to these must be added the likely migratory gain (see Statistisches Amt . . . , 1971, p. 22).
e = All 1950 figures in this and all the following rows exclude Berlin (West) and the Saar.
f = Including activities not adequately described.
g = EEC sample survey, spring 1969.
h = Distribution of wage and salary earners only.
Source: Statistisches Amt . . . (1970, 1971); *BMWI* (1970); *Year Book of Labour Statistics*.

work fewer hours by 1980 and have longer holidays, which means that man-hours will decrease further. A significantly decreased labour input will thus have to provide the goods and services for a significantly increased proportion of dependent people, and of course these goods and services will have to increase in volume and standard in the coming years. Apart from the demographic development (which would increase the burden on the shrinking active population even at a constant supply of goods and services), the political and social reforms aiming at a greater supply of public services can only be financed through high growth of the economy. Growth potential would be wasted, however, if a given capital stock could not be used fully when the indigenous labour force decreased. The import of foreign workers therefore becomes a precondition for maintaining high real growth.

This sketch of the German situation indicates the reasons underlying the net immigration of 1.1 million foreign workers during the period 1960–9 and the expected further increase of exactly the same magnitude for the following sixteen years (*BMWI*, 1970, p. 16; the average number of employed foreigners in 1969 was 1,366,000). The central estimate for the average number of employed foreigners was put one year ago at 2,088,000 for 1975, 2,282,000 for 1980, and 2,460,000 for 1985 (*BMWI*, 1970, p. 16). At the seasonal peak in the autumn of 1971, the projected level for 1980 had already been reached—and this did not signal the end of the labour import.

Internal labour movements from sectors of low productivity to those of high productivity are not foreseen to be markedly different from those of the sixties and will therefore not result in a greater reduction of the need for foreign manpower. In static economic models, the actual or potential labour surplus in agriculture, retail services, and mining, for example, has often been seen as obviating the need for employing foreigners. But today Germany employs only about one-third of its 1958 labour force in mining, i.e. 400,000 less; the rapid establishment of supermarkets during the sixties has forced over 50,000 retailers to close down; and agriculture has shed over 1 million, mainly elderly workers—yet, even if two-thirds of these have gone into more productive sectors instead of retiring or finding marginal employment, they have obviously not been of sufficient numbers to reduce the need for foreign workers at the work benches of industry. The expected further decrease of the agricultural labour force by 1 million during the seventies to a level of 4% is not nearly enough to fill the gaps created by extended schooling.

(d) ITALY

In Italy, too, the number of active persons is growing more slowly than the population as a whole (see Table 7–4). This is primarily due to increased compulsory schooling and a withdrawal of married women from the labour market following their move from the countryside—the South in particular—to the towns, particularly those in the North, a movement which is continuing unabated. Longer schooling and decreased female participation have given Italy one of the lowest activity rates of developed countries; and in aggregate terms Italy must for long have been considered a developed country. The same holds true for the demographic scene. Since the early fifties, Italy's birth rate has been at the same level as that of other Western European countries and the mean number of children per marriage has been around 2.5. The North and the Centre have exhibited Europe's lowest birth rates at below reproduction levels and have only during the last years recovered some dynamism. The relatively high fertility levels in the South, on the other hand, have come down fast recently. Considering the group of potential future migrants, i.e. the 15–24 year olds in the six southern regions and in the rest of Italy, one finds that this group grew annually by 2% in the South during the period 1961–71 and fell at an annual rate of 0.8% in the rest of the country, giving an over-all annual rate of increase of 0.4%. The projected annual development for the period 1971–81 is +0.8% for the South and +0.7% for the rest (Livi-Bacci, 1971, p. 43).

Hand in hand with a reduction of the previous demographic pressure went the absorption of Italy's manpower surplus both through the home economy and the unhindered migrations into most Western European countries. Not only has the industrial triangle of Genoa—Milan—Turin attracted millions of Southerners since the War, but the need to emigrate from the South has decreased with the slow but steady establishment of industrial nuclei. Greater opportunities in the South have without doubt helped to check out-migrations (Rogers, 1970). They have also changed the composition of those who notify their interest in migrating abroad. The Italian authorities estimated that of the 300,000 or so who in 1965 were available for employment in EEC countries, about one-third

Table 7-4: Some indicators of the socio-demographic development of the population of *Italy*.

		1951 Both	1951 Male	1951 Female	1961 Both	1961 Male	1961 Female	1969 Both	1969 Male	1969 Female	1975 Both	1975 Male	1975 Female	1980[b] Both	1980[b] Male	1980[b] Female
1 POPULATION (end of year)	1,000	47,159	22,961	24,198	50,524	24,784	25,840	52,329[a]	25,535	26,800	56,485	27,681	28,804	58,409	28,631	29,778
2 0-14		26.3%	27.6%	25.1%	24.5%	25.6%	23.5%	25.3%	26.4%	24.2%	24.9%	26.0%	23.9%	24.7%	25.8%	23.7%
3 15-64		65.4%	64.7%	66.1%	66.0%	66.2%	65.8%	65.0%	65.0%	65.1%	63.3%	63.9%	62.7%	62.8%	63.5%	62.1%
4 65+		8.3%	7.7%	8.8%	9.5%	8.2%	10.6%	9.7%	8.6%	10.7%	11.8%	10.1%	13.4%	12.5%	10.8%	14.2%
5 Birth rate (live b.) per 1,000		18.4	-	-	18.4	-	-	17.3	-	-	-	-	-	-	-	-
6 Death rate (all ages) per 1,000		10.3	-	-	9.3	-	-	9.9	-	-	-	-	-	-	-	-
7 Life expectancy (at age 0) year			63.7[c]	67.2[c]		67.2[c]	72.3[c]		-	-	-	-	-	-	71[c]	75[c]
8 CIVIL EMPL. (excl. unempl.) 1,000		19,577.3	14,663.4	4,913.9	19,592.1	14,727.9	4,864.1	18,673	13,600	5,073	20,933	15,480	5,453	21,514	15,920	5,594
9 Activity rate (8 as % 1)		41.5	63.9	20.3	38.7	59.4	18.8	35.7	53.3	18.9	37.1	55.9	18.9	36.8	55.6	18.8
10 Unemployed (as % of 8)		8.8%	-	-	3.5%	-	-	4.8%	4.6%[f]	5.2%						
11 SELF-EMPL. (as % of 8)		23.5%	27.4%	11.8%	21.1%	23.9%	12.5%	23.8%	26.6%[f]	15.8%[f]						
12 In prim. sec.	1,000	2,572.0	2,352.2	219.8	1,957.9	1,766.4	191.5	1,653	1,465.9[f]	204.4[f]						
13 In second.sec.	1,000	812.6	695.9	116.7	810.1	693.4	116.6	1,832	898.8[f]	196.2[f]						
14 In tert. sec.	1,000	1,220.6	976.8	243.8	1,366.4	1,064.1	302.3	1,666	1,234.5[f]	369.4[f]						
15 FAMILY WORK (as % of 8)		17.4%	14.5%	26.0%	10.5%	8.0%	18.0%	8.9%	4.7%[f]	19.2%[f]						
16 In prim. sec.	1,000	3,001.8	1,844.4	1,157.4	1,623.6	917.6	706.0	1,030	386.9[f]	593.1[f]						
17 In second.sec.	1,000	146.0	126.0	20.0	142.1	108.0	34.1	157	87.2[f]	61.7[f]						
18 In tert. sec.	1,000	258.3	159.7	98.5	292.1	156.2	135.9	481	157.9[f]	282.5[f]						
19 WAGE & SAL. EARN. (as % of 8)		59.1%	58.0%	62.2%	68.4%	68.0%	69.4%	67.2%	68.4%	64.1%[f]						
20 In prim. sec.	1,000	2,687.3	2,031.1	656.2	2,111.5	1,510.2	601.3	1,339	945	394						
21 In second.sec.	1,000	5,331.1	4,091.1	1,240.0	7,011.3	5,640.9	1,370.4	6,759	5,379	1,380						
22 In tert. sec.	1,000	3,547.5	2,386.2	1,161.3	4,277.1	2,871.1	1,406.0	4,456	2,976	1,480						
23 PRIMARY SEC. (as % of 8)		42.2%	42.5%	41.4%	29.1%	28.5%	30.8%	21.5%	10.2%[f,g]	12.1%[f,g]						
24 SECOND. SEC. (as % of 8)		32.1%	33.5%	28.0%	40.6%	43.7%	31.3%	43.1%	57.8%[f,g]	42.4%[f,g]						
25 TERTIARY SEC. (as % of 8)		25.7%	24.0%	30.6%	30.3%	27.8%	37.9%	35.4%	32.0%	45.5%[f,g]						

a = "All figures in the first four rows of 1969 relate to the beginning of 1969.

b = "Figures relate to natural development and include migratory movements, but not changes in labour force participation.

c = Professor M. Livi-Bacci, private communication.

e = See note c of Table 7-1.

f = EEG sample survey, spring 1969.

g = Distribution of wage and salary earners only.

Source: Statistisches Amt . . . (1970, 1971); *Year Book of Labour Statistics*.

were skilled and semi-skilled workers, one-third experienced (mostly unskilled) workers, and one-third completely unskilled workers. In 1971, their over-all number had fallen to 80,000; the proportion of skilled and semi-skilled workers was at 20%, while unskilled workers made up 55% of the total (Kommission ..., 1966a, 1971a; also Böhning, 1970a, p. 11). The situation in Italy's agriculture is currently fifteen years behind that of Germany and seven to eight years behind that of France in terms of the proportion and surplus of manpower. In 1971, about 3.4 million workers, or 18% of Italy's labour force, were working on the land. Of the farmers, 1,200,000 were over the age of fifty-five, and 80% of these had no successors waiting to take over the farms (*The Times*, 3 April 1971). By 1980, Italy's agricultural work-force is likely to be in the region of 2 millions, which would mean that Italy would be only about ten years behind Germany and five years behind France.

However, the slow-down of the Italian economy has obviously retarded the absorption of surplus manpower and increased the volume of hidden unemployment. The fact that during the years 1969 and 1970 the number of Italian new entrants in Community countries was considerably higher than the number of those who had notified their desire to emigrate, points in the same direction. 'A recent estimate in the CENSIS report to the National Economic Council put the number of "hidden unemployed" at between 2.5 million and 3 million' (CEC, 1971, p. 20). Together with the 900,000 officially registered unemployed, they constitute an intra-European migration potential of perhaps 400,000 workers.[4] According to official projections, which seemed to disregard this possible foreign drain, Italy will still have the same manpower surplus of 4 millions in 1980 (Europäische Gemeinschaften, 1970, p. 51; also Danieli, 1971). In other words, although the peak of Italian emigration may have been passed ten years ago, new Italian emigrants will be with us for some years to come. Intense labour demand in other Community countries could set in motion the majority of the 400,000 potential emigrants in a very short time. Afterwards the level of migratory exchanges between Italy and the receiving countries would approach that of developed countries, that is, it would be very small in net terms in relation to the population of the sending countries.

[4] On the arbitrary but plausible assumption that 10% of them might go abroad, as 10% of Italy's present labour force has gone to other European countries.

Table 7–5: Some indicators of the socio-demographic development of the population of the *Netherlands*.

		1950 (1947)			1960			1968 (1969)			1980		
		Both	Male	Female	Both	Male	Female	Both	Male	Female	Both	Male	Female
FOPULATION (end of year)	1,000	10,201	5,084	5,117	11,556	5,754	5,802	12,958	6,465	6,493	14,462[a]	7,579	7,678
C-14		29.4%	30.2%	28.6%	30.0%	30.9%	29.1%	(27.4%)	(28.1%)	(26.7%)	–	31.1%	29.3%
15-64		62.8%	62.3%	63.3%	61.0%	60.6%	61.3%	(62.5%)	(63.0%)	(62.0%)	–	60.0%	58.6%
65+		7.8%	7.5%	8.1%	9.1%	8.5%	9.6%	(10.1%)	(9.0%)	(11.3%)	–	8.9%	12.1%
Birth rate (live b) per 1,000		22.7			20.8			(19.2)			–		
Death rate (all ages) per 1,000		7.5			7.6			(8.4)			–		
Life expectancy (at age 0)			70.6	72.9		71.4[b]	74.8[b]		71.1[c]	75.9[c]	–		
CIVIL EMPL. (excl. unempl.)	1,000	(3,610.6)	(2,685.9)	(924.7)	4,168.6	3,240.5	928.1	4,270.6[e]	3,276.0	994.5	5,430[f]	4,096	1,268
Activity rate (8 as % of 1)		(19.9%)	–	–	36.1	56.3	16.0	33.4	51.3	15.5	37.5	54.0	16.5
Unemployed (as % of 8)		–	–	–	1.2%	1.4%	0.6%	2.0%	2.2%	1.2%			
SELF-EMPL. (as % of 8)		(19.9%)	(24.2%)	(7.4%)	15.4%	18.3%	5.4%	14.1%	17.1%	4.5%			
in prim. sec.	1,000	(251.9)	(238.1)	(13.8)	224.4	218.9	5.5	193.4	190.4	–			
in second.sec.	1,000	(167.1)	(154.5)	(12.6)	133.3	126.7	6.6	114.6	110.5	4.1			
in tert. sec.	1,000	(300.8)[d]	(258.5)[d]	(42.3)[d]	286.1[d]	247.8[d]	38.4[d]	295.6	258.2	37.4			
FAMILY WORK. (as % of 8)		(11.2%)	(6.2%)	(25.7%)	4.7%	3.2%	10.1%	3.7%	1.3%	11.3%			
in prim. sec.	1,000	(253.4)	(111.4)	(142.0)	92.5	61.8	30.7	58.2	26.6	31.6			
in second. sec.	1,000	(29.7)	(25.7)	(4.0)	21.3	18.8	2.5	16.8	4.5	12.3			
in tert. sec.	1,000	(120.4)[d]	(28.8)[d]	(91.6)[d]	83.9[d]	23.3[d]	60.6[d]	81.2	12.4	68.8			
WAGE & SAL. EARN. (as % of 8)		(68.9%)	(69.6%)	(66.9%)	79.8%	78.5%	84.5%	82.1%	81.5%	84.0%			
in prim. sec.	1,000	(242.2)	(229.0)	(13.1)	129.8	125.5	4.4	93.5	86.8	6.7			
in second. sec.	1,000	(1,091.1)	(947.2)	(143.9)	1,603.2	1,400.9	202.3	1,602.4	1,384.0	218.4			
in tert. sec.	1,000	(1,154.0)[d]	(692.6)[d]	(461.4)[d]	1,594.1[d]	1,016.9[d]	577.2[d]	1,810.0	1,200.0	610.0			
PRIMARY SEC. (as % of 8)		(20.7%)	(21.5%)	(18.3%)	10.7%	12.5%	4.4%	8.1%	3.2%[g]	0.8%[g]			
SECOND.SEC. (as % of 8)		(35.7%)[d]	(42.0%)[d]	(17.4%)[d]	42.2%[d]	47.7%[d]	22.8%[d]	40.6%[d]	51.8%[g]	26.2%[g]			
TERTIARY SEC. (as % of 8)		(43.6%)[d]	(35.5%)[d]	(64.4%)[d]	47.1%[d]	39.7%[d]	72.9%[d]	51.2%[d]	44.9%[g]	73.0%[g]			

(e) THE NETHERLANDS

The Dutch birth rate is still higher than the Italian and is expected to remain relatively high. The Dutch economy can expect a fairly large supply of new indigenous workers (Werner, 1971). The peculiar characteristic of the Netherlands is that this supply will consist predominantly of men. The employment of women has been very much discouraged by Dutch society and only recently have there been any signs that this is changing. However, the low over-all activity rate in the region of 16% will not change drastically in the coming decade as higher economic activity by adult women is largely offset by lower economic activity of adolescents due to longer schooling. Internally there are no large pockets of labour surplus. Past economic performance would suggest a small migratory gain of 87,000 non-Dutch workers, plus dependants which the Dutch calculations have not taken into account.

(f) GREAT BRITAIN

The population of Britain (see Table 7–6) is expected to increase by about 0.5% p.a. during the seventies. The proportion of economically inactive persons will also increase during this period to a dependency ratio of 677 per 1,000 of the population of working age (Thompson, 1970, especially p. 28).[5] According to the memorandum of the Department of Employment and Productivity to the Select Committee on Science and Technology (1971, p. 71), the total growth in the working population up to 1981 may be 830,000, almost the whole of which will occur after 1977. During the preceding years, the low birth rates of the early fifties and the raising

[5] 1969 = 655 per 1,000.

---

a = The 'Both' sexes figure is adjusted for the recent decrease in the birth rate (−882,000) and for migratory gain (+87,000). Difference = −795,000. Male and female figures = natural development.

b = 1956–60.

c = 1961–5.

d = Including activities not adequately described.

e = Figures for 1968 in this and all the following rows are taken from the EEC sample survey of spring 1968.

f = The 'Both' sexes figure is adjusted for longer schooling (−230,000), increase in female activity (+242,000), decrease in pensionable age (−33,000), and migratory gain (+87,000). Difference = +66,000. Male and female figures = constant participation rates.

g = Distribution of wage and salary earners only.

i = See note c of Table 7–1.

Source: Statistisches Amt . . . (1970, 1971); *Year Book of Labour Statistics*.

Table 7-6: Some indicators of the socio-demographic development of the population of *Great Britain*.

	1951			1961			1970			1981		
	Both	Male	Female	Both	Male	Female	Both	Male	Female	Both	Male	Female
POPULATION (de facto) 1,000	50,287	24,163	26,124	51,350	24,833	26,517	54,187	26,328	27,859	57,248[a]	28,000[a]	29,248[a]
0-14	22.6%	24.1%	21.3%	23.2%	24.6%	21.9%	23.9%	25.2%	22.6%	23.9%	25.0%	22.9%
15-64/59	63.8%	66.1%	61.2%	62.0%	66.0%	58.3%	60.2%	64.7%	55.9%	59.6%	64.0%	55.5%
60/65+	13.6%	9.3%	17.5%	14.8%	9.4%	19.8%	15.9%	10.1%	21.5%	16.5%	11.0%	21.6%
Birth rate (live b.) per 1,000	15.8[b]			17.8[b]			16.7%[c]					
Death rate (all ages) per 1,000	12.5[b]	13.4[b]	11.8[b]	12.0	12.6[d]	11.4[b]	11.9[c]	12.5[c]	11.3[c]			
Life expectancy (at age 0) years		66.2[b]	71.2		68.1	74.0[d]		68.7[e]	74.9[e]			
CIVIL EMPL. (excl. unempl.)1,000	22,214	14,859	7,355	23,925	15,662	8,243	24,148			26,338	16,956	9,432
Activity rate (8 as % of 1)	44.2	61.5	28.2	46.6	63.1	31.1	44.6			46.1	60.6	32.2
Unemployed (wholly, as % of 8)	0.8%	0.8%	0.8%	1.0%	1.2%	0.8%	2.3%	(475)[i]	(80)[i]			
SELF-EMPL. (as % of 8)	7.6%	9.1%	4.5%	7.7%	9.2%	4.4%	7.2%					
FAMILY WORK. (as % of 8)	0.2%	0.1%	0.6%	0.8%	0.5%	1.3%	-					
WAGE & SAL. EARN. (as % of 8)	92.1%	90.8%	94.9%	91.6%	90.2%	94.3%	92.8%[h]	(13,832)[h,j]	(8,573)[h,j]			
PRIMARY SEC. f (as % of 8)	5.2%	6.9%	1.7%	3.7%	4.8%	1.3%	1.7%[k]					
SECOND. SEC. (as % of 8)	50.6%	55.8%	39.3%	47.5%	53.3%	35.5%	48.4%[k]					
TERTIARY SEC. (as % of 8)	44.2%[g]	37.4%[g]	59.0%[g]	48.8%[g]	41.8%[g]	63.2%[g]	49.9%[k]					

a = The UK projection in *Social Trends* was reduced by an estimated 815,000 males and 840,000 females for Northern Ireland.
b = Base: UK.   d = England and Wales 1960-2.   e = England and Wales 1967-9.
c = 1969.
f = See note c for Table 7-1.   g = Including activities not adequately described.   h = Including family workers.
i = Absolute figures in thousands.   j = Distribution of wage and salary earners.
Source: *Annual Abstract of Statistics; Social Trends* (1970); *Year Book of Labour Statistics*; 1961 Census: Great Britain, Summary Tables; *Monthly Digest of Statistics*.

of the school-leaving age after 1972 will actually reduce the supply of indigenous labour. Of course, in Britain this is unlikely to lead to an immediate inflow of foreign workers because the demand for labour is low and the level of unemployment high.[6] The expected recovery in economic activity may lead to the absorption of 300,000 to 400,000 of the unemployed, but it is more than probable that the 'shake out' by industry has left the country with 300,000 to 400,000 more unemployed for some years to come than would have been the case under comparable conditions of economic activity during the fifties or early sixties. It must also be borne in mind that the system of unemployment registration and the low level of economic activity have endowed Britain with a considerable amount of hidden unemployment. As much as one-third of the available labour supply —or half as much again as the registered unemployed—may be assumed to consist of hidden unemployed (Standing, 1971).

Britain's coloured population is still increasing disproportionately with respect to the total population. Although the birth rate is approaching that of the white population (Simpson, 1970; *Race Today*, various issues), the absolute number of coloured births is out of proportion because the coloured Commonwealth population is, of course, concentrated in the child-bearing ages. Deaths are consequently rare. Net immigration, too, still contributes to the increase of coloured British. A projection by the Runnymede Trust (1970) based on 1.5 million coloured immigrants in 1969 and assuming a rise in the number of births from 53,000 in that year (deaths: 3,000) to 62,000 in 1975 (deaths: 4,900) and 70,000 in 1980 (deaths: 6,400) plus an annual net immigration of 25,000— a very generous assumption—arrives at a figure of 2 million coloured British in 1975 and 2,430,000 in 1980. An increasing proportion of this number will have been born in these islands, certainly well over 30% by the year 1980, and will therefore be citizens of the UK and Colonies.

This survey of the socio-demographic background of the main countries of the enlarged EEC has shown that judging from past trends there are likely to be major labour shortages in Germany,

---

[6] This view has now been given legal backing, as it were, by Mr. R. Carr's statement in the House of Commons: 'the Government have decided to cease, as from 1st January, 1972, issuing work permits in industry and commerce for unskilled and semi-skilled alien men for all countries other than the European Economic Community, Norway and Denmark' (HC Deb., 11 Nov. 1971, col. 201).

E

particularly, and in France, and absolutely and relatively smaller shortages in Belgium and the Netherlands. Italy, and to a lesser extent Britain, will find themselves with a small labour surplus, especially amongst semi-skilled and unskilled workers. Agriculture has ceased to be the main supplier of labour surplus in the European Community and its place has been taken by associated or non-associated developing countries. Six and a half million people left the agricultural sector of the EEC between 1958 and 1970, i.e. 40% of the labour force on the land. Between 1971 and 1976, another 1.3 millions are expected to leave agriculture, and after 1976 one may expect an acceleration in the rate of departures so that by 1980 the proportion of the population of the Six employed in agriculture will in all probability be in the region of 6%. As in 1971 over 31% of the agricultural labour force of 9.6 millions was over the age of sixty (67% over the age of forty), and as in 1976, 36% of the labour force of 8.3 millions will be over sixty (71% over forty), one can clearly discount the agricultural sector as a major source of labour supply for the present member countries even under radically changed agricultural and training policies (CEC, 1971, pp. 16 ff.; Statistisches Amt . . . , 1971, pp. 132*–3*; and Marsh, 1971, p. 102).

On the basis of the 1968-based projection of this chapter, a labour shortage of over 2.1 million workers is expected for the Six by 1980. This figure must be related to a realistic emigration potential of about 400,000 workers in Italy. Since 1968 the exceptional boom conditions in Germany, and in France as well, have resulted in a net immigration of around 1 million. However, this figure cannot simply be deducted from the former 2.1 millions because, at least in the case of Germany, the likely level of employment of foreigners in 1980 must be considerably higher than the 2.3 millions projected in 1970, a figure already reached at the time of writing. My own estimate is that the number of employed foreigners will be in the region of 2.8 to 2.9 millions by 1980. Thus, one may assume a reduction of about 500,000 in the 1968-based projection due to developments since that time, which means that between now and 1980 there is likely to be a net immigration into the present members of the Community of around 1.6 million workers.

8

The Economic Prospects: Britain and Germany

A continuation of the pattern of economic development of the last ten to fifteen years could potentially induce a significant proportion of British workers to move to the places of intense labour shortage on the Continent. The potential becomes a likelihood if one considers that non-idiosyncratic labour movements between industrialized countries are determined primarily by the difference in wage levels (Böhning, 1970d)[1] and that the wage levels in terms of both money wages and real wages are certain to be higher in some continental countries than here; the German and Dutch gross wages are already above the British level. Italy, Belgium, and the Netherlands as well as the smaller members of the enlarged Community may be neglected in the following analysis because in absolute and relative terms their demand for foreign labour is small both in relation to their own and to the British labour market. Even a significant wage pull in the Low Countries, requiring another 87,000 foreign workers by 1980, could only attract a comparatively small number of Britons.

Despite the fact that it heads the EEC league of GNP per capita, France does not seem to be a particularly attractive proposition for British manual or white-collar workers. Direct money wages

---

[1] The 'brain drain' is the best exemplification of this hypothesis. Labour movements from developing to industrialized countries with a work permit system, on the other hand, are primarily determined by the demand for labour in the latter: wage differentials play only a supplementary role.

are considerably lower than here[2]—largely due to the fact that direct wages paid by the French employer constitute a smaller proportion of the worker's income than elsewhere, whereas he receives fringe benefits (like social security payments and family allowances) on a greater scale than in Germany or the Benelux countries. The total labour costs for EEC employers have a far greater degree of similarity than do the wage packets they hand out to their employees (Wedel, 1970, Part II; Cox, 1963; *Common Market and the Common Man*, 1971; Swann, 1970, pp. 125 ff.; and Beever, 1969, p. 23). But labour movements between developed countries, although they involve large proportions of semi-skilled and highly skilled personnel, are determined rather more by money wages than by real wages. Information on money wages is easier to come by and therefore dominates the potential migrant's mind. Information on real wages and living standards is more fragmentary and selective; and the only reliable method of comparing consumer purchasing power (i.e. the cross-country shopping basket method) is practical only for an experienced statistician and still leaves him with two answers in two different currencies (European Coal ..., 1957). A migrant worker can really find out only after his migration what the real wages are in the receiving country—and more often than not he finds that real wages are rather lower than expected and that he will have to stay and work longer in order to achieve what he set out to do. If, then, France's wage structure remains unchanged during the seventies, as seems certain, the large demand for foreign workers will not attract significantly more Britons than in the past. Moreover, France does not appear to be particularly interested in British workers as it has traditional sources of labour supply in the Iberian peninsula and in North and Central Africa.

This leaves us with a comparison between Britain and Germany, the country where the absolute demand for foreign workers is as high as in France and where money wages, if not real wages, are higher than in any other EEC country. Will the British and German economies grow at a similar differential rate in the next decade as

---

2 As exchange rates do not correspond at all closely to domestic purchasing power, GNP per capita is not a reliable substitute measurement for living standards or wage levels. Moreover, the GNP yardstick does not take account of the composition of output; the USSR and the UK have the same GNP per capita level but the consumer goods endowment in the latter is incomparably higher than in the former.

during the past ten to fifteen years? Will the already noticeable wage gap widen further in Germany's favour and thereby provide the necessary pull for labour movements from here to Germany? Will Britain's entry into the EEC affect the growth of the British economy and/or British wages? Will not technological development during the following years either depress the demand for labour or change its character so that there is little room for the employment of foreigners in post-industrial Germany?

To start with the British economy: its output per employed person (productivity) has grown at an annual average rate of 2.4% during the period 1955–68. (These and the subsequent figures according to OECD, 1970, pp. 35 ff.) The total increase of 38.4% is more than half derived from the growth in industrial productivity (20.1%) and only about one-eighth derives from growth in employment (5%). There is some evidence that the low rate of productivity increase accelerated a little during the sixties, but 'it should also be noted that, in order to produce significant differences in cumulated growth over periods as short, relatively, as five or ten years, changes in trend rates of growth of productivity would have to be of an intensity which has not been observed hitherto' (OECD, 1970, p. 83). The OECD (1970, pp. 77–8) estimated that during the period 1970–80 Britain's productivity would reach an annual average rate of 2.9%, thus climbing by 37% in ten years. If anything, this pre-EEC entry projection may be revised upwards for three reasons. Firstly, the Conservative Government's tax reforms ought to raise the investment ratio of British industry. Secondly, the Industrial Relations Act ought to have beneficial effects in the medium and long term. Thirdly, the 'shake out' by industry could have the same favourable results in Britain as it had in Germany during the 1966–7 recession, where it paved the way for a relatively fast rise in productivity (Kasper and Schmidt, 1971). A prerequisite of such a development is, however, that more efficient use of labour goes hand in hand with the modernization of the capital stock, especially in the field of infrastructure and factory building, and there are little signs as yet that this has happened on a sufficient scale.

In the somewhat delicate state of the British economy at the moment it is difficult to anticipate with certainty the impact of entry into the Common Market. It is clear, however, that the effect of the EEC's agricultural policy will be adverse in terms of real income or consumption and that the expected gains from industrial competition, restructuring, and higher investment will take time to materialize and outweigh the costs of the agricultural policy. Williamson's (1971, p. 45) 'central guess' put the industrial benefits at 'something in the region of $\frac{1}{2}$ per cent from each of the three extra sources distinguished (economies of scale, competition, investment), giving a total of $1\frac{1}{2}$ per cent on GNP by the end of the transition (1978), or 0.3 per cent on the growth rate' (also Miller, 1971). Layton's (1971, p. 71) examination of the prospects of major growth industries (vehicles and suppliers, chemicals, aerospace and heavy electrical equipment, computers) led him to predict, conservatively, a productivity rise of 5% by 1980. 'An improvement of this order could mean that Britain's economy, by 1980, might have grown by some 42 per cent compared with the 37 per cent predicted by the OECD.' Such an increase would correspond to an average annual rate of growth in productivity of 3.3% compared with the OECD's 2.9%.[3] By analogy, one may revise the projected trend rate of the Gross Domestic Product (GDP) (1970–80 = 3.2%) upwards by three or four percentage points to a level of, perhaps, 3.5% for the seventies as a whole.

Germany's productivity grew at an average annual rate of 4.4% during the period 1956–68. As in Britain's case, the increase was more than half derived from the growth in industrial productivity (44%) and one-eighth derived from the growth in employment (10.1%), but of course the total increase stood much higher at 84.8% (OECD, 1970, pp. 35 ff.). There is no evidence of any slowing down in the underlying rate of increase in productivity. On the contrary, the rate climbed from 4.3% to 4.7% from the first half to the second half of the sixties. Both the OECD's (1970, p. 77) own estimate and that of the planners in Bonn (*BMWI*, 1970, p. 20) put the annual average rate of growth, at constant prices, at 4.5% for the seventies.

At present the German economy is on a downswing, but it is not yet clear whether this will lead to a recession during 1972, or a recovery before the end of that year. An export-led recovery on the 1967–8 pattern is unlikely to occur on the same scale after the

3 As Layton himself puts the annual improvement in productivity for the economy as a whole at 'between 1 and 2 per cent' it seems that he expects a much higher level of productivity growth towards the end of the transitional period and little immediate improvement.

1969 revaluation, the floating of the Deutsche Mark since April 1971, and the August import surcharge in the United States. Exports will clearly rise at a lower rate than in the past, even with a recovery of the US and the world economy and the abolition of the import surcharge. Mr. Nixon's protective measures may cost Germany between 100,000 and 200,000 jobs and depress the growth of the GNP by a few percentage points.

The underlying strength of the German economy is jeopardized more by the new militancy on the shop-floor than by the vagaries of the business cycle. 'Stagflation' has been unknown so far in post-war Germany, because the trade unions brought their members to accept a reduction in wage-drift and a stagnation in wage rates when the economy cooled down, and even a drop in real wages when the country was hit by the 1967 recession. During the wage bargaining of 1967 the unions set their sights low and dates of expiry generally two years ahead. The subsequent exceptional boom increased employers' profits quickly and greatly and led to a series of wild-cat strikes in 1969 when the trade union leadership seemed to be satisfied with less than their shop-floor members. In 1969 and 1970 the employers willingly paid out from their full pockets (OECD, 1971, pp. 12–13). In the autumn of 1971, the structure of wage bargaining led to the situation where a wage round was due at the time when profits had dropped sharply and while inflation had reached the unprecedented level of 5 to 6%. Stirrings on the shop-floor and the shock of 1969 have put the union leadership in the unenviable position of having to ask for greater wage rises than their economic expertise would permit them to do. The outcome of this wage round is still uncertain. If it shows up the 1969 situation as a temporary aberration, the growth of the German economy will be back at the level of the sixties by mid-1973 at the latest, when the present government faces an election. If not, then Germany could well enter a period of lower growth.

The enlargement of the Common Market may not be much less beneficial to Germany's industry than to Britain's. Germany's home market will increase by about one-third (UK, Denmark, Norway, and Ireland), while Britain's increase amounts to less than 50% (assuming the EFTA area to be Britain's home market and disregarding the preferential access to associated members). Moreover, Germany does not incur new agricultural costs and transfer payments. But how will British and German wage levels compare in the future? Table 8–1 gives the development of money wages for blue- and white-collar workers in the two countries and projected future levels at varying revaluation premiums. It shows a tremendous wage gap in favour of Germany during the seventies, which reverses the situation of the fifties. Male manual workers had earned about the same amount of money in terms of £p in 1962–3, but the British worker had to work six hours more per week for his wages than his German colleague. Both had the same hourly earnings in 1961 (32p). German female manual workers overtook their British counterparts at about the same time and with a rate of increase (8.7% in terms of DM) which was not only considerably higher than the British rate (6.4)%) but also higher than the growth rate for German males. The German male white-collar worker, on the other hand, did not catch up with his British colleague before 1969.

The money wage gap widened in favour of Germany because wages rose between 1 and 2% faster in Germany than in Britain and because of the two revaluations of the DM (March 1961 and October 1969) and the devaluation of the pound in November 1967.

---

a = All manufacturing industries; mining and quarrying; construction; gas, electricity, and water; transport and communication; certain miscellaneous services; and public administration—during October of each year.
b = 21 years and over, excluding men ordinarily employed as part-time workers.
c = 18 years and over, working full time.
d = 1948 Standard Industrial Classification (rest: 1958 SIC).
e = April 1970 (Basis C).
f = Administrative, technical, and clerical employees in manufacturing; mining and quarrying; construction; and gas, electricity, and water; monthly paid and weekly paid combined on weekly basis; during October of each year.
g = Full-time and part-time.
h = All manufacturing industries; mining and quarrying; construction; and gas, electricity, and water; average in each year.
i = Working full time.
j = Current rates of exchange.
k = Sales and technical staff in industry and trade, working full time.
l = Assuming an average annual growth of 7.5%.
m = Assuming an average annual growth of 8%.
n = Assuming a devaluation of £p against DM of 10%.
o = Assuming a devaluation of £p against DM of 15%.
p = Assuming a devaluation of £p against DM of 27.5%.
Source: *Gazette*; *Statistisches Jahrbuch für die Bundesrepublik Deutschland*.

Table 8-1: Average gross weekly earnings and hours of work of manual workers in industrial activities, and average gross weekly earnings of white-collar workers in non-agricultural activities, in the *United Kingdom* and the *Federal Republic of Germany*, by sex, 1958-1970.

	United Kingdom						Federal Republic of Germany									
	Manual workers [a]				White-collar [f]		Manual workers [h]						White-collar workers			
	Male [b]	Hours [b,c]	Female [c]	Hours [c]	Male	Female [g]	Male		Hours	Female		Hours	Male		Female [k]	
	£p		£p		£p	£p	£p	DM		£p	DM		£p	DM	£p	DM
1958	12.84 [d]	47.7 [d]	6.70 [d]	41.2	-	-	9.91	116	42.2	5.81	68	39.1	12.59	147	7.31	86
1959	13.56	48.5	7.04	41.6	18.06	7.60	10.42	122	41.9	6.23	73	38.9	13.16	154	7.63	89
1960	14.54	48.0	7.42	40.5	19.18	7.97	11.44	134	42.7	7.00	82	39.5	14.25	167	8.26	97
1961	15.34	47.4	7.73	39.7	20.15	8.40	13.23	147	41.5	8.19	91	38.0	16.37	182	9.57	106
1962	15.86	47.0	8.04	39.4	21.08	8.79	14.49	161	41.4	9.09	101	38.3	17.76	197	10.53	117
1963	16.75	47.6	8.41	39.7	22.11	9.14	15.48	172	40.9	9.72	108	38.3	16.83	210	11.38	126
1964	18.11	47.7	8.96	39.4	23.58	9.73	16.74	186	42.0	10.35	115	37.6	20.13	224	12.00	133
1965	19.59	47.0	9.60	38.7	25.45	10.46	18.45	205	41.0	11.52	128	38.0	21.91	243	13.19	147
1966	20.31	46.0	10.07	38.1	26.75	11.13	19.44	216	40.8	12.33	137	37.2	23.55	261	14.33	159
1967	21.38	46.2	10.56	38.2	27.93	11.74	19.35	215	40.3	12.42	138	37.2	24.40	271	14.95	166
1968	23.00	46.4	11.30	38.3	29.90	12.47	23.71	228	39.9	15.18	146	36.4	29.62	285	18.05	174
1969	24.82	46.5	12.11	38.1	32.18	13.42	26.62	256	40.4	16.95	163	36.7	32.54	313	19.78	190
1970	28.05	45.7	13.99 [g]	37.3	36.25	15.51	33.46	292	40.1	20.97	183	35.9	40.17	351	24.60	215
—skilled	27.90 [e]		13.40 [e]				35.64	311		22.92	200					
—semi	26.00 [e]		13.40 [e]				31.97	279		21.32	186					
—unsk.	22.60 [e]		12.70 [e]				28.53	249		20.40	178					
rate of change	+6.8%	-0.4%	+6.4%	-0.7%	+6.6%	+6.7%	+10.9%	+8.1%	-0.4%	+11.5%	+8.7%	-0.7%	+10.3%	+7.6%	+10.8%	+8.0%
1975	40.30 [l]		20.10 [l]		52.00 [l]	22.30 [l]	54.60 [n]	429 [m]		34.20 [n]	269 [m]		65.60 [o]	516 [m]	40.20 [o]	316 [m]
1975							57.80 [o]			36.30 [o]			69.50 [o]		42.60 [o]	
1980	57.80 [l]		28.80 [l]		74.70 [l]	32.00 [l]	84.90 [p]	630 [m]		53.20 [o]	395 [m]		102.20 [p]	758 [m]	62.50 [p]	464 [m]
1980							100.00 [p]			62.70 [p]			119.70 [p]		73.30 [p]	

These changes in the exchange rate increased the money value of the DM towards £p by over 27%. The evaluation of the attraction of German wages must be conducted in terms of £p because this is the way potential British migrants visualize their earnings. It is necessary, therefore, to consider further revaluations. By late 1971 the DM had floated upwards by over 12% against the dollar and by over 6% against the pound. The Washington settlement of the currency crisis did in fact create a smaller gap between £p and DM than was generally expected. This was due to some skilful bargaining on the German side and the inflexible British position with respect to an unchanged gold parity of the pound in conjunction with the fairly substantial American devaluation. The new central rate differential between £p and DM is 4.6%. The actual differential could grow to 9% within the newly established wider bands. More important, however, is the fact that the DM was *de facto* devalued by 2.2% compared with its pre-Washington ('clean') floating rate towards Germany's trading partners in the OECD. The £p actually underwent a slight revaluation compared with its ('dirty') floating rate and faces, in particular, stronger American competition. In my opinion, Washington has left the £p potentially overvalued and the DM potentially undervalued. The lowest revaluation premium given in Table 8–1 is therefore 10% for 1975. There have already been widespread discussions of a devaluation of the pound prior to entry into the EEC to make this enterprise economically successful.[4] Furthermore, it must be assumed that the projected differential growth of productivity in the Common Market countries and in Britain—which amounts to at least 1% as far as Britain and Germany are concerned—is bound to lead to exchange rate pressures when seen in conjunction with Britain's higher level of inflation (and notwithstanding the current discussion about exchange rates in the EEC). I have therefore given alternative revaluation premiums in Table 8–1 for 1975 and 1980, the highest of which is equal to the change between 1961 and 1969.

The small differences in the trend rates for blue-collar and white-collar money wages have been neglected in the projection, and the domestic growth rates have been increased by almost 1% to 7.5% for Britain, and decreased slightly to 8% in the case of

---

[4] Kaldor (1971, p. 71), for example, put the required devaluation at 10 to 15%, Williamson's (1971, p. 20) model presupposes 'any necessary change in the exchange rate'.

Germany, to take account of the growth prospects of the economies described earlier. Britain's growth of GDP and productivity was said to average out almost 1% higher (3.5% instead of 2.7% and 3.3% instead of 2.4%, respectively) than growth rates for the last ten or fifteen years. Germany's growth rates are assumed to be consonant with the past trend values (GDP 4.6%, productivity 4.5%), which presupposes that detrimental effects from more militant wage bargaining are cancelled out by the beneficial effects deriving from Britain's entry into the EEC. This comparison is possibly biased against Germany inasmuch as changes in money wages usually vary to a smaller degree than changes in productivity, and also because it seems that Germany's economy will settle at a higher plateau of inflation than in the past (2.6%), thereby pushing up money wages.

At any rate, it is certain that for the hitherto underrepresented group of British migrants, i.e. male manual workers, the wage gap may be in the region of £15 per week by the middle of the decade and £30 to £40 per week by 1980. Their wives, too, might earn a similar differential if they went to Germany. A few hours of overtime at the lower level of hours of work in Germany could easily mean that there a British wage-earner could earn twice as much as he could do at home in terms of £p. I have at different times and with different methods arrived at essentially the same figures (one can, for example, weight a trend rate in favour of more recent periods or assume that productivity growth plus inflation growth circumscribe the growth of money wages) and the fact that they are if anything biased against Germany should inspire confidence in the calculations. I have also taken the calculation further to consider real wages and predictably found a still larger differential there (see Table 8-2). The comparison of real wages is much facilitated by the fact that money wages in Britain and Germany were about the same in 1962 and that the price indices in both countries are based on that year. The only major uncertainty about the size of the wage differential derives from the extent of the revaluation premium.

But, one may ask, will not Britain's entry into the Common Market have a direct effect on British wage levels quite apart from the assumed growth effect on industry? Traditionally it has been held that in a customs union with free movement of labour the

Table 8-2: Real hourly earnings of male manual workers in the *United Kingdom* and the *Federal Republic of Germany*, 1958–1970.

	UK	Germany	
	£p	£p	DM
1958	0.29	0.25	2.97
1959	0.30	0.27	3.11
1960	0.32	0.28	3.31
1961	0.33	0.33	3.63
1962	0.33	0.35	3.89
1963	0.34	0.37	4.09
1964	0.36	0.38	4.20
1965	0.37	0.41	4.59
1966	0.38	0.43	4.69
1967	0.39	0.42	4.67
1968	0.40	0.51	4.92
1969	0.40	0.55	5.31
1970	0.44	0.67	5.89
rate of change	3.6%	8.8%	5.9%
1975	0.52^a	0.93^n	7.34^b
1975		0.99^o	
1980	0.62^a	1.23^o	9.15^b
1980		1.46^p	

Gross weekly earnings were converted into hourly earnings and these were deflated by the general index of retail prices in the case of the UK (1962 = 100, average annual rate of increase = 3.9%) and by the consumer price index for a four-person employee household where the head of household is the sole bread-winner with a medium-range income in the case of Germany (1962 = 100, average annual rate of increase = 2.6%).

a = Assuming an average annual growth of 3.5% (inflation 4%).
b = Assuming an average annual growth of 4.5% (inflation 3.5%).
n,o,p = See Table 8-1.
Source: See Table 8-1.

differences in wage levels would narrow[5] rather than widen. This view, however, attaches too much significance to one single factor to the detriment of other probably more important factors like, for example, the competitive situation. Trend rates in wage levels

[5] For the EEC, see Yannopoulos (1969). His evidence is less than sufficient, to say the least. Firstly, he compares two single years in quick succession when the different economies were at different stages of the business cycle. Secondly, he compares total wage costs which (as indicated above, p. 116) are certainly much more in line than money or real wages. The fact is that real wages in the two countries with the highest levels at the inception of the Common Market (Germany and the Netherlands) have grown fastest, but in Belgium and France (and Italy), which had a comparable starting-point at a lower level, real wages have grown more slowly at differential rates. Okun (1968) found that migration actually widened income levels.

between countries are as rigid as wage differentials within countries. Moreover, inter-industrial wage levels tend to resemble each other between countries (Lampert, 1969, p. 386; *Gazette*, Sept. 1968, p. 732). It seems to me that an equalization effect has in the past not existed with respect to money or real wages and will probably not occur in the seventies either, certainly as regards money wages.

More likely sources of influence on British money wage levels are the costly agricultural policy of the EEC, the introduction of the Value Added Tax (VAT), and the proposed reform of Britain's pension system which would bring it more into line with those in the Common Market countries by demanding a larger contribution from the employer than from the employee (*Common Market and the Common Man*, 1971, p. 20; also Wedel, 1970, pp. 595 ff.). To prevent a rise in their total wage costs, employers would probably reduce the growth of money wages or increase their prices. The regressivity of VAT compared with Britain's Purchase Tax will decrease the after-tax income of the lower income groups (Dosser, 1971); in other words, it will hit the bulk of the clerical and manual workers who form the biggest pool of potential migrants. The workers' likely response is a demand for higher wages to compensate for the reduction in real wages. The same reaction seems certain as regards the adverse effects of the agricultural policy on account of both higher food prices and transfer payments. One does not have to agree with Kaldor's pessimistic conclusions to see that directly or indirectly the Common Agricultural Policy will eat into the real income of, particularly, the lower income groups. One may concur with Josling's (1971) alternative calculations and yet dismiss them as irrelevant, for when it comes to future wage negotiations it does not matter so much what does happen but what one believes is happening—everybody believes that food prices and other prices will increase solely on account of our entry into the EEC. Naturally, this must lead to wage pressure, to higher money wages, to increases in total wage costs, possibly to higher prices, to a worsening of industry's competitiveness, and to a devaluation....

A summary evaluation of the three main effects of accession to the EEC on British wages would appear to suggest more upward pressure on money wages and more downward pressure on real wages for at least the transitional period. This would justify the higher rate of increase assumed in Table 8–1 (for example, 7.5% as opposed to the 1958–70 average of 6.8% for male manual

workers), which is of the same differential as the projected productivity increase. It would also justify holding the growth of real
wages in Table 8–2 at its trend rate (3.5% as opposed to the
1958–70 average of 3.6%).

Finally, are we facing significant changes in the pattern of demand for labour which would either obviate the need for foreign
workers altogether or make the employment of target workers impossible without a prior extended period of special vocational training? The first problem is that of technological change and its labour-
saving character. Practically all kinds of technological change are
labour saving (Friedrichs, 1969). The saving of labour input experienced by the German economy during the sixties has been in the
region of 6 to 9% per annum. The socio-demographic projections
of the previous chapter assume a continuation of the speed of inno-
vation and application of technology. There is no evidence to
suggest that the speed of technological change will increase
dramatically during the seventies—labour productivity was seen to
remain at a fairly constant level (Dinter, 1969). Certainly, the industrial work-force seems to have reached or surpassed its highest
share of the total in post-industrial countries while within the industrial work-force there is a significant shift from blue-collar to white-
collar employment. In labour-importing countries, however, this
shift has been carried almost exclusively by the indigenous labour
force (see Chapter 4, especially Table 4–2). Within the blue-collar
sector there are now fairly stable proportions of unskilled and semi-
skilled workers, i.e. the group most suitable for the employment
of newly entering foreign workers.[6] Moreover, because higher final
demand and increased competition call for greatest productivity and
quickest amortization of equipment, the patterns of blue-collar work
are changing towards more continuous or semi-continuous working,
which means more high-frequency repetitive jobs and shift-work
(CEC, 1971, pp. 36, 39). Thus, the potential for the employment of
foreigners in the manufacturing industry and post-industrial societies
is far from exhausted and may even become greater as new technology is introduced. The potential in the service sector may be
assumed to be fairly stable; but this sector is actually increasing in

[6] In 1951, 17% of the male manual workers in Germany were unskilled and
25% semi-skilled; in 1962 the proportions had changed to 12% and 32%,
respectively, and exactly the same proportions obtained in 1968 (calculated
according to Lampert, 1969, p. 427; and Statistisches Amt . . . , 1969a).

relative if not absolute numbers, so that here there will be no fall-off of demand for foreign workers. Lastly, one should not presume that there is an inflexible one-way relationship between new technology and the type of labour demand. The history of the self-feeding process of labour immigration in post-war Europe showed that employers often adapted their pattern of demand to the type of labour available, i.e. to the foreigner with unknown skills and little understanding of the host language.

PART THREE

BRITAIN'S ACCESSION TO THE EEC SYSTEM OF FREEDOM OF MOVEMENT AND THE FUTURE OF LABOUR MIGRATION ACROSS THE CHANNEL

9

The Problem of UK Nationality

The Conservative Government of 1970 accepted the EEC's policy of free movement, like its predecessors, but asked for transitional safeguards for Northern Ireland (HC Deb., 20 May 1971, col. 342; and *The United Kingdom and the European Community*, para. 143–4). These seem to have been granted. The safeguarding of Employment (Northern Ireland) Act 1947, which prevents labour movements into Northern Ireland, will continue to be in force until 1978. (The Republic of Ireland also asked for and was granted a five-year transition period in which its labour market would not be open to other EEC nationals.) The Channel Islands and the Isle of Man are offered free trade in agricultural and industrial goods and exemptions from other Common Market rules (*The Times*, 10 Nov. 1971), despite the fact that they are, in the words of Article 227(4) of the Treaty, 'European territories for whose external relations a Member State is responsible' and should therefore be subject to all Treaty provisions. This means that, although the common travel area established by the Immigration Act 1971 between these islands and the UK will be maintained, workers from continental EEC countries cannot claim the right of free entry for purposes of work. The whole of England, Wales, and Scotland, however, will be encompassed by the free movement system as from 1 January 1973, assuming this to be the date of Britain's entry into the EEC.

But who on the British side will be entitled to move to other Common Market countries? The question arises because of the involved nature of the British nationality law. Article 1 of Regulation 1612/68 states unequivocally that '*any national* of a Member State, *irrespective* of his place of residence' is entitled to freedom of movement within the Community. It is of course the prerogative of member countries to determine who bears their nationality or citizenship, and on the Continent the entitlement is usually certified by an identity card or passport. Britain, of course, is different. A passport does not define a UK national because there are in the law of this country no UK nationals. There are only 'citizens of the UK and Colonies' and these comprise both British born and bred citizens of the *United Kingdom* and the indigenous population in dependent territories, i.e. citizens of the *Colonies,* whose passports are issued by a colonial government. The latter do not possess the right to enter the UK freely unless they have 'at any time been settled in the United Kingdom and Islands and had at that time (and while such a citizen) been ordinarily resident there for the last five years or more' (clause 2 [1] [c] of the Immigration Act 1971). Furthermore, any citizen of the UK and Colonies also has the status of a 'British subject', and as, according to the British Nationality Act 1948, the expressions 'British subject' and 'Commonwealth citizen' have the same meaning and do entail full civil rights in the United Kingdom, it would be appropriate to consider *all British subjects resident in the UK free of immigration controls* as UK nationals (not, of course, *any* British subject who is a Commonwealth citizen of an independent Commonwealth country '*irrespective* of his place of residence' since Britain terminated their right of free entry into the UK through the Commonwealth Immigrants Act 1962). If politically they were considered worthy of the paraphernalia of British citizenship, why should they, or at least those who are free of immigration controls, economically not be considered worthy of the right to sell their labour freely throughout the EEC area if and when Britain joined the Common Market? The point here is, of course, that the Commonwealth citizens of independent Commonwealth countries referred to are predominantly coloured, and it would certainly not please the anti-immigration lobby in this country to have economic, social, and legal rights extended to the Black British which would put them on a par with white British, nor would it please the racialist elements in Community countries to see Black British grasping the opportunity of going to work on the Continent.[1] The saga does not end here, because all Commonwealth citizens resident in the UK prior to the Immigration Act 1971 have the automatic right to register as citizens of the UK and Colonies after five years' residence in these islands. The Commonwealth Immigrants Act 1968 further complicated the picture by denying the right of free entry into Britain to citizens of the UK and Colonies who could not point to British descent, i.e. in particular, the so-called East African Asians whose passports are issued by the British Government through its High Commissions in East Africa (henceforth 'UK passport-holders'). One can readily see how confused national and international policy-makers in the Common Market must have been when considering the problem of UK nationality.

The reaction in Community circles was to look for a valid criterion for establishing UK nationality and to evaluate the numbers any definition would involve. Mr. Harold Wilson had pointed to a restrictive solution in 1967 by referring to registration for Commonwealth citizens and to a five-year qualifying period for citizens of the UK and Colonies subject to immigration control (HC Deb., 8 May 1967, col. 1086–7). When the negotiations got under way again in 1969/70, the Commission still seemed unsure what this solution involved and, naturally, it fell back on the age-old reciprocity principle. That is, it appeared to accept the registration criteria for Commonwealth citizens[2] but only for those who as citizens of the UK and Colonies would forfeit or surrender their original citizenship (Böhning, 1970a, p. 14; and 1970b, p. 402). Although dual nationality was not completely ruled out under the law of various Common Market countries, it was certainly the exception rather than the rule,[3] and more importantly, naturaliza-

---

[1] Right-wing pressure in the Dutch Cabinet led the Dutch to claim that only people born in member countries should be able to move freely to work in other EEC countries—a notion clearly irreconcilable with EEC legislation. According to the *Daily Mirror* of 10 December 1971, a Dutch Foreign Ministry spokesman said: 'We think they [Commonwealth citizens] would come here because of our good social services. Besides, many Dutch people speak English, and we are not far away from Britain.' See also the *Guardian* (16 December 1971).

[2] By referring without comment to Mr. Wilson's statement in its 'Opinion concerning the application for membership from the United Kingdom, Ireland, Denmark and Norway' (COM(69)1000, Annex, 6 Oct. 1969, p. 46).

[3] Whereas in 1970 dual nationality was permitted by the following non-white Commonwealth countries: Barbados, Cyprus, Gambia, Guyana, Jamaica,

tion on the Continent was conditional while registration in Britain was automatic. Theoretically, any British government could reverse its attitude towards Commonwealth immigration and large-scale automatic registration could then put the EEC at the mercy of British immigration politics. Increasing acquaintance with the jungle of British immigration law—and until very late in the negotiations no national government seemed to be fully aware of the problems involved and the Commission appeared to be the sole negotiator— led officials in Brussels to toy with different criteria, for example, the civil rights criterion. This was an obvious solution prior to the residence and employment controls proposed by the Immigration Bill as it corresponded closest to the consequences of continental naturalization. The Bill itself completely baffled the Eurocrats and led them to ask the British Government whom *they* considered a national of the UK. It was only on the last day of November 1971 that Mr. G. Rippon officially handed over a definition which ran as follows:

Citizens of the United Kingdom and Colonies or British subjects not possessing that citizenship or the citizenship of any other Commonwealth country or territory, who, in either case, have the right of abode in the United Kingdom, and are therefore exempt from United Kingdom immigration control.

As the Opposition was quick to point out, this definition had no legal standing in any of the immigration or nationality laws, to which Mr. Rippon retorted that this definition is 'the view we take for the purpose of accession to this Treaty' and that it was on 'the authority of the Government in relation to ... the problems which arise on the free movement of labour'. On UK passport-holders, Mr. Rippon told the House of Commons that they should qualify for free movement in the EEC after five years' ordinary residence in the UK (HC Deb., 1 Dec. 1961, col. 446, 455, 450).

The British position, then, is an extremely restrictive one. Firstly, citizens of the UK and *Colonies* without the right of abode (Immigration Act 1971, clause 2 [1] [c]; and above p. 131), and this means almost all of them, will not enjoy the right to move freely through-

Malaysia, Nigeria, and Sierra Leone, which meant that almost half of all Commonwealth citizens who had registered during the sixties could or did possess dual nationality.

out the EEC. All British dependent territories are offered association under Part IV of the Treaty or similar relationships in the
case of Hong Kong and Gibraltar (*The United Kingdom and the
European Community*, para. 118). The presumption of Article 135 in
Part IV is that freedom of movement shall not extend to populations in
associated territories unless the Council of Ministers unanimously
agrees to the contrary (see above p. 12, especially note 2). Secondly,
UK passport-holders will need to qualify for inclusion in the EEC's
free movement system by undergoing the residence qualification for
patriality. Thirdly, Commonwealth citizens resident in this country
are not covered by free movement simply because they are free of
immigration controls or have stayed here continuously for five years
or more: they have to be registered as citizens of the UK and
Colonies.

Mr. Rippon's definition is congruent with the patriality principle
of the Immigration Act 1971, except that it does not cover citizens
of independent Commonwealth countries who have the right of
abode but not citizenship of the UK and Colonies (clauses 2 [1] [d]
and 2 [2] of the Act). The Government's position is perfectly
understandable and corresponds to EEC usage for populations under
colonial or semi-colonial rule. Its attitude towards UK passport-
holders can easily be rationalized but leaves one with the bitter
impression that but for the Immigration Act 1971 it would have
been illegitimate to impose a residence qualification for eligibility
as UK nationals. Under the old Commonwealth Immigrants Act
1968 no such yardstick was available, and prior to that Act the
'irrespective of his place of residence' provision of Regulation
1612/68 would therefore have applied. What is most disappointing,
however, is the Government's position on Commonwealth immigrants admitted into this country for settlement free of controls,
or who will still be so admitted under the Immigration Act, but
who are not yet eligible for registration or who for one reason or
another are not availing themselves of this opportunity: and this
applies to the great majority of Black British. The Government
first assured them, and then put into statutory form, that their pre-
Immigration Act rights would not be affected by the Act (clause
1[2]); it made them for all practical purposes indistinguishable
from patrials by safeguarding their right of settlement, of unrestricted residence and employment, of unhindered return after
temporary absence, and, of course, their right to vote and stand in

elections—only to go back on its assurance when deciding who should not be a UK national for purposes of free movement if and when Britain joins the Community.

This retrograde step must be considered short-sighted for at least two reasons. Firstly, it seemed that the Commission would have been prepared to accept as UK nationals the whole Commonwealth immigrant population not subject to immigration controls (Böhning, 1971b, pp. 9–10) if Britain had asked them to do so. There were faultless criteria for such a definition and the Community would not have been on very sure ground in questioning seriously the right of a prospective member state to define its own nationality (as long as such a definition does not exclude nationals from the rights and obligations of membership to which they are entitled by Community law). Therefore, neither the Council of Ministers nor the Commission can or will fight the battle of the Black British for them. One might have expected serious resistance from Brussels to an all-encompassing definition if Britain had not, in 1962, terminated the right of uncontrolled entry for coloured Commonwealth citizens; or at least an attempt to confine this problem to the 'institutional ties' provision of the EEC legislation (see above pp. 11–12, 14, 18). But the statutory termination of the right to free entry in 1962 and the subsequent introduction of what is now a comprehensive work permit procedure do not even make this necessary.

Secondly, one cannot help wondering why the Government today seeks to exclude the majority of coloured immigrants from the benefits and privileges of free movement when sooner or later the majority of them will become eligible due to the simple process of demographic growth. Consider only the transitional period 1973–8. (The following figures and calculations are based on data from the Runnymede Trust, 1970, and Home Office, *Statistics of Persons acquiring Citizenship*. . . .) On 1 January 1973 the coloured population of this country will number about 1,870,000. At current trends at least 175,000 coloured people will have registered in the UK before 1973 as citizens of the UK and Colonies and thereby become patrials (an even larger number will have registered outside these islands but they may be ignored for present purposes). Since the beginning of the coloured immigration there may be assumed to have been around 500,000 coloured births in this country, i.e. births of citizens of the UK and Colonies with patrial status. On the other side, at most 25,000 people with patrial status may be assumed to have died or re-emigrated (in which case they will have been included in the net migration figures) in the meantime. This would result in 650,000 patrials out of 1,870,000 coloured people, i.e. over one-third. Admittedly, the great majority of the coloured children will not have reached working age by 1973, but those who are not already with us as the much discussed problem of second-generation school-leavers also inflate the figure of the total coloured population. On 1 January 1978 the coloured population will have risen to perhaps 2,300,000. At present trends a further 150,000 people will have registered in this country, assuming that they maintain their low degree of registration. There will also be another 300,000 coloured births, and presumably 50,000 coloured patrials will have died (or be included in the net migration figures as re-emigrated), leaving 1,100,000 coloured patrials, i.e. 48% of all coloured immigrants. Perhaps just under half of these will be of working age, which means that approximately one in three of the coloured working population will already be entitled to move freely to other EEC countries when Britain is a full member of the Community, and sometime during the eighties more than half of Britain's coloured workers will have the status of Community workers. Surely, one did not have to introduce discrimination in the field of employment in 1971 between practically indistinguishable groups of coloured people when there was no need for such an action and when one can foresee its progressive inapplicability.

10

Legislative Problems of Britain's Entry

During the passage of the Immigration Bill the problem of accommodating the Common Market legislation on free movement was pressed on a number of occasions by the Opposition. The Home Secretary professed not to be perturbed by EEC regulations and directives and claimed that he was able to deal with them by way of administrative action without having to amend his Bill. 'As far as I am advised', he said, 'nothing one can see in accepting the principles of the Treaty of Rome would involve an amendment of the Bill. It would involve some amendment of the rules under the Bill' (HC Deb., 20 May 1971, pp. 1136–7; see also 16 June 1971, col. 581–2, 772). Mr. Maudling's advice was certainly wrong. It is a well-known fact that Community regulations have the quality of law and supersede national law where the two are in contradiction, and that the regulations are not subject to alteration by national decision-making processes (see above p. 19). The proper way to incorporate Community regulations is either to amend contradictory legislation point by point or to insert a general exemption clause[1] and, in addition, to publish the regulations in the form of acts or statutory instruments. The intenton of relegating Community provisions conflicting with British law to the immigration rules can at best only be described as uninformed and un-European.

The immigration rules are an exception even in British law. On

---

[1] Clause 1(4) of the Immigration Act is not a sufficient exemption clause ('subject or not to conditions') as it refers to the rules and practice of administration, not to the principles of legislation.

F

the face of it they belong to the realm of delegated legislation where Parliament has delegated its law-making power to Ministers subject to its affirmative approval or, in minor cases, to negative annulment. In the sphere of immigration law, the first point to make is that 'at present the immigration rules are subject to no Parliamentary control at all. Parliament has not exercised control over the immigration rules under any previous Administration' (Lord Windlesham, in HL Deb., 12 Oct. 1971, col. 319; see also Lord Gardiner, col. 323 ff.: 'There is no other case that I know of in English law in which a Minister can make rules and regulations which have the force of law without submitting them to the ordinary Parliamentary approval'). The present Government tried to maintain this position in its Bill, but in the course of the debates in the House of Commons the Home Secretary agreed that the immigration rules should be made subject to the negative annulment procedure in either House of Parliament (Immigration Act 1971, clause 3[2]). However, the Home Secretary did not actually propose to put the rules before Parliament but only his 'statement of the rules'. Lord Windlesham claimed that the 'statement of the rules' is identical with the rules (HL Deb., 12 Oct. 1971, col. 321)—but there is no way of knowing. The fact is that, in Lord Windlesham's own words:

> immigration rules are not statutory instruments. The draftsman has deliberately avoided using words such as 'laying the rules before Parliament' because these words are associated with Parliamentary control of statutory instruments. The rules are not statutory instruments but rules of guidance for immigration officers issued by the Secretary of State.

In other words, the Home Secretary has kept his rule-making power; he makes the law but not in the form of law and not couched in the legal language of statutory instruments; he gives notice to Parliament of his intentions by way of a statement; if Parliament disapproves of this statement the Home Secretary may or may not change his rules and/or his statement about them—one cannot tell. The points at issue here in relation to the EEC legislation are, firstly, whether the Home Secretary can as hitherto make any immigration rules he likes, incorporating or not part or the whole of the free movement regulations; secondly, whether a 'statement' of no legal consequence is sufficient to give effect to Common Market law; and thirdly, whether any such rules and regulations, or statements of them, could be subjected to Parliamentary control. The answer in all three cases is, no.

Firstly, the Home Secretary is bound by the EEC regulations (and by the principles and aims of EEC directives). He has no choice but to enact them, to enact them in full, and not to uphold any contrary legislation. Secondly, administrative guidelines to immigration officers notified to Parliament by a statement are of insufficient legal standing to conform with EEC principles (as the French already had to concede to the Commission: they originally put the Common Market legislation on free movement in administrative circulars, the Commission objected, and in January 1970 it appeared in the form of a *décret* in the *Journal Officiel*). EEC law is comparable to British acts and statutory instruments. In addition to publication in the *Official Journal of the Community* (Article 191 of the Treaty), it requires publication at domestic level—not in order to come into force but, and in this the Commission is on unassailable ground, because you cannot give people rights without informing them of these rights and without making them enforceable in the courts. Thirdly, supposing for the sake of argument that free movement regulations could be published in Britain as immigration rules, this does not mean that they could also be subjected to a negative resolution by either House of Parliament. EEC regulations are as immune towards parliamentary encroachment as they are towards governmental interference.

Which parts of the British immigration law do not comply with EEC requirements? (See also Böhning and Stephen, 1971a; Stephen, 1971b; Böhning, 1971b, p. 9; and Chapter 2 above.)[2] First of all, the whole of the work permit procedure[3] will become inapplicable. This does not mean that Community citizens become patrials, but like patrials they have the *right* to enter this country freely in their search for work and contrary British legislation is null and void. Employment or occupational or regional restrictions may not be imposed upon them (see clauses 1 [4] and 3 [1] [c] of the Immigration Act 1971; see also Home Office, Feb. 1971, para.

---

2 In this section only the broad areas of contradiction will be indicated where the principles of legislation and administration are incompatible; supplementary provisions need not be enumerated in full.

3 Deriving from the Aliens Restriction (Amendment) Act 1919 and the Aliens Order 1953 (see Aliens: Instructions to Immigration Officers, Cmnd. 4296) as well as the Immigration Act 1971 (see Home Office, Feb. 1971 and March 1971).

24–5; and March 1971, para. 19–20); the five-year residence permit becomes a mere formality; but registration with the police (or possibly the Department of Employment) may be maintained. The entry of dependants as defined by Article 10 of Regulation 1612/68 becomes a right, too, and not an administrative discretion (see Home Office, Feb. 1971, para. 35; also above pp. 16–17). Both workers and dependants will be able to enter Britain not 'by permission' (clause 1 [2] of the Immigration Act 1971) but by virtue of the superior Common Market law. Furthermore, whereas clause 3(2) of the Race Relations Act 1968 permits discrimination in the field of employment if, as in the case of aliens, it is based on immigration controls introduced by statutory provision, Regulation 1612/68 makes any such discrimination unlawful as far as Community workers are concerned.

The deportation procedure also becomes partly inapplicable for EEC nationals. The Immigration Act makes a non-patrial liable to deportation if the Home Secretary 'deems his deportation to be conducive to the public good' (clause 3 [5][b]), or if 'he is convicted of an offence for which he is punishable with imprisonment and on his conviction is recommended for deportation by a court' (clause 3 [6]). The Act later specifies the phrase 'conducive to the public good' as 'being in the interests of national security or of the relations between the United Kingdom and any other country, or . . . other reasons of a political nature' (clauses 14 [3] and 15 [3]). The Government thus gave itself virtually limitless powers to subsume anything or anybody it considers undesirable under this vague provision. Directive 64/221, on the other hand, implies that *ordre public* can only be invoked on serious non-economic political grounds and it would therefore seem to relate only to the first two specifications of conducive grounds, that is, not to *any* 'reasons of a political nature'. *Ordre public* as used in the Treaty, and the regulations and directives made under it, is an autonomous concept of Community law and is therefore not identical with any similar concept in the municipal law of member countries—the latter has to adapt to the former, not vice versa. At the very least, the denial of the right of appeal in cases involving conducive grounds will be illegal for Community citizens because the Community law does not exempt this sphere from the appeals procedure (clauses 13 [5], 14 [3], and 15 [3] of the Immigration Act; Articles 8 and 9 of Directive 64/221; and also above pp. 20–1). As far as deportation for conviction of an indictable offence is concerned, the Community's legislation states unequivocally that such grounds are insufficient on their own (Article 3 [2] of Directive 64/221). Consequently, clauses 3 (6) and 6 (1) of the Immigration Act and subsidiary provisions will become inoperative for Frenchmen, Germans, etc. —and for the Irish.

Furthermore, the provisions establishing liability to deportation for uninvolved members of a family—reminiscent of the kith and kin ideology of Nazi law—will be expressly abolished by superior Community law for Community citizens in cases where the measures against the principal deportee were taken on grounds of public policy or public security (clause 3 [5] [c] of the Immigration Act; para. 46–51 of *Revised Draft Immigration Rules*, Cmnd. 4792; Article 3 [1] of Directive 64/221 and also p. 20 above). The deportation of an EEC national on the grounds that he is 'receiving treatment for mental illness as an in-patient' (clause 90 of the Mental Health Act 1959; clause 82 of the Mental Health [Scotland] Act 1960; and clause 30 [1] of the Immigration Act) will be unlawful if this illness occurred 'after the initial residence permit has been issued' (Article 4 [2] of Directive 64/221). A question mark would also seem to be hanging over the hostage provision of the Immigration Act (clause 3 [7]).

Finally, a number of unrelated and dispersed provisions are incompatible with EEC requirements. The unrepealed sections of the Aliens Restriction (Amendment) Act 1919, where they relate to the field of employment, will have to give way to Community law. The stipulation that a person must return to his own country if he wants to appeal against a refusal of leave to enter the UK, 'unless he was refused leave at a port of entry and at a time when he held a current entry clearance or was a person named in a current work permit' (clause 13 [3] of the Immigration Act), also does not meet EEC standards (see Article 7 in conjunction with Article 8 of Directive 64/221), even disregarding the fact that Community citizens do not require an entry clearance or work permit but only their identity card or passport (Article 3 of Directive 68/360). And last but not least, the administrative discretion over giving indefinite leave to remain in the UK will be superseded by a legal right for EEC nationals in the cases defined by Regulation 1251/70 (see above pp. 22–3) and will become enforceable in the courts.

II

The Size and Direction of Cross-Channel Migratory Exchanges

The preceding sections showed that there is likely to be a continuing strong demand for foreign workers on the Continent, especially in France and Germany. At the same time the French income struc-ture shows little sign of changing towards higher money wages and lower extra-wage components[1] and the wage gap between Britain and Germany shows every sign of increasing in absolute terms for both money and real wages. This opens up the likelihood, if not certainty, of a significant migration of British workers to Germany. Such a development would have been almost unimaginable at the time of the creation of the Common Market, unless one was under the false impression that freedom of movement would in itself lead to greatly increased migrations. The then Parliamentary Under-Secretary at the Home Office, Dame Patricia Hornsby-Smith, said in October 1957 that 'Britain is an attractive country with its welfare service and full employment, and if the gates were opened at least a quarter of a million Europeans would come in' (in Roche, 1969, p. 194). Mr. H. Wilson saw the situation more soberly in his speech of 8 May 1967 when he explained the Government's belief that there is not likely to be 'any large net increase in the number of EEC nationals coming here to work. There may be a greater interchange with our nationals going to the Community to work and more

[1] The French have just secured their partial exemption from the family allowance provisions of the new EEC regime on social security for migrant workers (see above pp. 23–4), which confirms their will to uphold these and other fringe benefits.

Community nationals coming here, but the net inflow is not likely to be much greater than it is now' (HC Deb., 8 May 1967, col. 1085). Mr. R. Carr seemed to echo this view recently, although somewhat more guardedly: '... we believe that there is not likely to be a mass migration of labour on any scale that we could possibly find objectionable' (HC Deb., 25 Oct. 1971, col. 1369). His decision a fortnight later not to issue any further work permits to unskilled or semi-skilled non-EEC nationals except (on a decreasing scale) in the hotel and catering industry may be interpreted in many ways, but it certainly does not mean that the Employment Minister anticipates a replacement of workers from third countries by Community workers, i.e. significantly increased immigration of unskilled or semi-skilled EEC nationals (HC Deb., 11 Nov. 1971, col. 201-2; and p.113, note 6).[2]

Writing at the turn of the decade, Beever (1969, pp. 46–7), Castles (1970, p. 15), and Böhning (1970a, pp. 9–12, 15; and 1970b, pp. 401–2), did not expect dramatically increased cross-Channel migrations either. At that time I was certainly deceived by the beginning of an explosion in money wages in Britain and the slow pace of wage growth in Germany during the years 1966—8 deriving from the traditionally 'responsible' attitude of the trade unions. During that period the annual rate of growth for male manual earnings was 5.5% in Britain and 3.6% in Germany, and gross weekly earnings were at a comparable level (see Table 8–1 above). It seemed that the money wage gap would not widen unduly in the foreseeable future. However, the wage projections of autumn 1971 have certainly played a role in reversing my judgement about the size of the outflow of British workers (Böhning, 1971c, p. 23).

Contrariwise, the new projections confirmed the expectation that the inflow of continental EEC nationals would not increase significantly after Britain's accession to the free movement system. To put it bluntly, migrant workers are not attracted by high unemploy-

[2] The accompanying statement by the Department of Employment made clear that these measures were designed to provide jobs for British workers; see the *Guardian* (12 November 1971). What is not clear, however, is whether 'alien men' refers only to male workers or whether it refers in the abstract to men and women. Applications of skilled and highly skilled workers and applications outside industry and commerce (and hotel and catering) will presumably still be granted, e.g. for agricultural workers and hairdressers. Commonwealth vouchers remain unaffected.

ment and low wages. There are 'no queues in Italy for British jobs', as a *Times* (4 May 1971) headline proclaimed, and there are no queues in other Common Market countries either (see above pp. 48–52, 84–5, 107–9). This does not rule out the possibility that marginally more Germans, Frenchmen, Italians, and so on, may enter this country after 1973 than would be the case at present trends and under the present procedure. There are always a few who for highly personal reasons move about and take up an opportunity which might previously not have been open to them. There is also the possibility that with the now definite future introduction of freedom of movement between Turkey and the Community (see above pp. 90–1) an appreciable number of Turks will come to Britain towards the end of the seventies or later, especially if the hoped-for dynamic effects of entry into the EEC should materialize. The number of Turkish new entrants has already increased tenfold since 1958, reaching a total of 850 last year (see Table 3–8). But one should not forget the basic fact that labour migration, particularly on the international plane, is a two-sided affair with intervening opportunities. Surplus labour does not move seemingly predestined to areas with a high standard of living. The potential labour supply requires and must match a specific demand in order to lead to actual movements. The Turkish potential is best employable in unskilled and semi-skilled manual work, that is, exactly those positions where the British labour supply is abundant and the demand for labour lacking (as Mr. Carr's statement emphasized). Moreover, the intervening opportunities in the form of Germany and France will keep back some of the Turks setting out to look for work in Britain. The 'cheap labour' argument does not hold true either. Cheap labour does not simply find employment through being able—or forced—to accept low wages, and it might well refuse such wages if, as in the case of the Turks, it is familiar with German wage levels. In present-day Britain cheap labour can only be employed if trade unions or shop stewards permit employers to make individual exceptions and/or if the 'no less favourable wage' stipulation is not enforced by the labour market authorities. Lowwage sectors such as nursing, municipal services, the hotel and catering industry, or agriculture do not pay low wages because they employ foreigners (some sectors do not employ them in significant numbers) but rather they do so for socio-historical reasons which have nothing to do with the availability of foreign workers.[3]

Only the number of French workers immigrating into the UK has tended to rise recently among EEC nationals. Numbers from the Benelux countries have remained virtually unchanged and those from Germany and Italy have fallen (see Table 3-8). The German and Italian trend will presumably level off very soon irrespective of Britain joining the Common Market. Except in the French case, it is quite obvious that present-day EEC immigration streams are not primarily economic migration streams but are to a large extent taking place for idiosyncratic reasons: that is, they contain a higher proportion of people who migrate for reasons of a personal nature or because they want to learn English for professional purposes; they also contain a larger proportion of highly skilled managers and salesmen, who are sent abroad by their parent companies, as compared with large-scale migrations into Germany or Switzerland. Mr. Carr's measures will further raise the proportion of alien white-collar immigrants and it is actually in the composition rather than the numbers that one might foresee a change in Britain's immigration stream if and when it joins the Community. Stephen (1971a, p. 130) has maintained that one effect of Britain's accession to the free movement system would be 'an increase in the number of executive and professional people travelling between Britain and the Continental countries to gain experience and practise languages'.[4] I would concur with this judgement but would qualify it in so far as I see the increase, especially as far as the inflow into Britain is concerned, to be small and without significant effect on the over-all number of immigrating Community workers, and I would also assume that any white-collar increase is more likely to derive from a general EEC effect (trade) rather than from a specific free move-

---

3 One may question the values of a society which attaches so little standing, in terms of income and status, to some of its most important functions that the indigenous population avoids them wherever it can; one may also question the blatant contradiction between social priority and actual social status in the case of, for example, nurses, on the one hand, and secretaries, on the other; but one cannot deny the fact that the very system which has the economic relationship between supply and demand as its basic premise also produces the non-economic distortions in occupational wage differentials which make the relationship between scarcity of labour and wage levels at best a tenuous one.

4 Hollingsworth (1971) concluded that Britain will lose more managers and professional workers than it will gain after entry, which is a continuation of present trends.

ment effect. In summary, I would expect that throughout the seventies the number of Benelux, German, and Italian new entrants will be roughly the same as they are today. Danes, Norwegians, and the Irish would not come in greater numbers either simply because they and Britain are part of the enlarged Community. The number of French new entrants is difficult to predict but I would assume that the upward trend will soon flatten off. In all cases, however, the composition of the immigration streams will change slowly but noticeably as the proportion of white-collar workers rises relative to manual workers and slightly faster than would be the case if Britain stayed outside the EEC.

The same faster increase in the number and proportion of white-collar workers would presumably take place in the case of British out-migrants to all other countries of the enlarged Community except Germany. Here, too, this is more likely to be attributable to a general EEC effect than to free movement effects. The over-all number of British out-migrants may increase marginally if one assumes that the number of blue-collar workers remains stable. Increases of blue-collar emigrations are unlikely to be significant in terms of the British labour market in the case of France (because of low money wages and despite the strong demand for foreign labour), Italy (because of its low wage level and not yet extensive demand for foreigners), Belgium (because of its relatively low money wages, not very attractive image, and its comparatively small demand for foreigners), the Netherlands (because its numerically low demand for foreigners is unlikely to act as a significant pull despite competitive wages), or in the case of Luxembourg, Denmark, Norway, or Ireland (where the labour markets are too small to exert significant effects). It is only in the case of Germany that a *strong* demand for foreign labour in a *large* labour market and a *marked* wage pull occur together.

However, are these considerations not based on cold statistics and do they not fail to take into account widely held images, traditions, cultural and language barriers? Britain's working class and lower middle class still believe to a large extent that they have the highest standard of living in Europe, and when they travel to the Continent they find the higher real income of Germans and Frenchmen, whom they see living in large blocks of flats with, if anything, fewer rooms and amenities than in British houses, difficult to believe; there are more cars about, true, but fewer TVs and telephones; and so on. Yet, the impressionistic standard of living argument remains at the surface, not because it is necessarily selective,[5] but because it fails to take into account that target workers from highly industrialized countries are motivated by wage differentials—primarily money wage differentials—rather than elusive differentials of living standards, and that they are usually quite well informed about the former but know little about the latter.

The traditional argument[6] sees emigration as too invariable a phenomenon and it does not appreciate fully that the variations in what one might call intra-Anglo-Saxon migration are very much determined by the economic conditions in the receiving countries. Within the fairly steady out-migration recorded by the International Passenger Survey, great fluctuations take place in the size of the streams to various countries. Canada and the United States, for example, absorbed (net) seven times as many citizens of the UK and Colonies as South Africa in 1966–7, but in 1969–70 South Africa absorbed as many as the two countries taken together (*Registrar General's Quarterly Return for England and Wales*). This points to the fact that, although there are long-established migration chains, for the British migration streams there is also a strong element of target worker migration and certain destinations are interchangeable. Consequently, those emigrants who do not move in an established familial or locational chain could easily be diverted by the new opportunities on the Continent, especially if more extensive travelling and better information make people more familiar with the European scene. I am not denying the force of history and tradition but I have no doubt that a significant proportion of the British migration pool, perhaps 10 to 20%, is potentially attractable by the prospering areas of Europe and that the vicinity of the Continent will make the idea of polyannual target migration (as opposed to emigration) more widespread than it has been in the

---

[5] One could point to longer holidays and greater travelling on the Continent, or to the much higher number of doctors per 1,000 inhabitants. See Central Statistical Office (1970, 1971); *The Common Market and the Common Man* (1971); and for Germany, *Bericht der Bundesregierung und Materialien zur Lage der Nation 1971* (1971).

[6] Put succinctly by Hollingsworth (1972): '. . . very many people have relatives in remote parts of the world, and emigration seems more like going to a distant part of the same country than the international movement it really is. A common language and very similar legal systems also diminish both the psychological difficulty of emigrating and the sense of having to make an irretrievable break with one's homeland,'

past, especially amongst unskilled and semi-skilled workers who have hitherto been underrepresented in British out-migration streams.

Culture and language are definite barriers to international migration but, again, one should not overrate their importance, even in the case of the British working class and lower middle class who are popularly portrayed as incapable and unwilling to learn a foreign language. Semi-literate Turkish farmers or Yugoslav bricklayers are objectively in a worse position and subjectively as little inclined to learn German or French as any factory hand in Dagenham or Manchester. Yet, they migrate in thousands: not always because they are forced by circumstances at home but because of the irresistible wage pull in Central Europe.[7] And there are already thousands of Britons working on the Continent for whom the cultural and language barriers did not pose an absolute deterrent: 18,000 were employed in Germany in the autumn of 1971; 3,000 in the Netherlands and 3,000 in Denmark in 1970; and so on.

In the German case a specific hurdle may be thought to lie in the deep-seated resentments stemming from the War, both on the German and the British side. Fifteen to twenty years after the War the British garrisons in Germany were still very much isolated socially. During the sixties the 'economic miracle' led to a somewhat superior-pitying attitude on the German side, which replaced the war-time aversions, and to a hurt-pride attitude on the British side, neither of which was very conducive to friendly neighbourly relations. However, the war-time aversions are largely confined to the older generations in Britain and as most potential migrants are part of the post-war generation, there should be no greater hurdles to a British migration to Germany than in other cases of migrations to ethnically different countries.

Shop-floor militancy has been mentioned as a reason for limiting the large-scale employment of British workers in Germany (*Der Spiegel*, No. 3, 1971; *Daily Telegraph Magazine*, 26 Nov. 1971). I do not think that German employers will see this as a major hurdle to the engagement of Britons. Every foreign nationality has had its particular adjustment problems when it first came to Germany. Those who cannot or will not adapt will never be able to take home the big wage packets they have been hoping for and they might soon

---

[7] Yugoslav skilled workers are an instructive case here; see Baucic (1971). For Turks, see Abadan (1966), p. 107.

find themselves in a situation where an unsuccessful return home is the only way open to them. On the other hand, one must not think that every British worker is a potential troublemaker in the German context. The first results of a pilot study on British workers in Germany, which I have been undertaking, repeatedly contain references to dissatisfaction with strikes, demarcation, etc., on the side of British migrants. The desire for a higher standard of living and job security and for untroubled labour relations often go together. Furthermore, German employers are potentially more interested in skilled or semi-skilled British workers used to the living and working conditions of a highly industrialized and urbanized society than in Southern Italians or Turks. It appears that in early 1971 German employers desperately short of skilled manual workers pressed the German labour market authorities to get in touch with their British partners. (See e.g. *Daily Telegraph* of 28 January 1971, and the *Sun* of 19 May 1971. Both papers quoted a figure of 200,000 German jobs for British workers, which was the estimate of the Under-Secretary of State at the Ministry of Labour in Bonn.) The two sides finally stopped short of a recruitment agreement on the German-Mediterranean pattern, but drew up a model contract of employment similar to the one incorporated in those agreements and arranged to circulate German vacancies in British labour exchanges. (See *The Times* of 19 May, 14 and 19 June, 11 September, 26 November 1971; and Department of Employment, 1971.) The model contract of employment contains, on German insistence, a stipulation which gives German employers a legal device against job demarcation: 'The employer undertakes to employ the employee as ... (job description) which will include such *related duties as are normal.*'

My own guesstimate is that, if the German economy maintains its growth rate of the sixties (see Chapter 8), one may expect an annual flow of British workers to Germany in the region of 10,000 men and women. If the economy should again overheat on the 1969 scale, this level may rise to 20,000 in a peak year. At return rates similar to those of Mediterranean workers, the size of the British work-force in Germany may be around 100,000 at the turn of the decade and could possibly have reached the 150,000 mark.

What is the likely composition of this stream? First of all, it will not consist simply of unemployed unskilled workers. Skilled workers will be amongst the first to leave the production lines of Britain to earn higher wages in Germany. According to my hypothesis of the four stages of maturing migrations (see Chapter 4), the better qualified and informed workers from the most highly developed parts of the country—the South-East, the Midlands, Yorkshire, and Lancashire—are likely to be overrepresented initially. Yugoslavia has seen its skilled personnel drained away to the fleshpots of Germany, while being stuck with a quarter of a million unskilled and semi-skilled workers. The same could happen here. Since the British migration stream to Germany has definitely lost its idiosyncratic character from the end of the sixties, the number of unskilled new entrants in manufacturing occupations has not increased disproportionately, whereas skilled or semi-skilled workers in engineering occupations increased considerably (see Table 11–1). Half the British new entrants have gone into service occupations, where they are overrepresented in trade, money, and insurance affairs as well as in public and private service occupations.[8] This holds true for both men and women. In Germany there are, for example, large numbers of British teachers of English (*Der Spiegel*, No. 23, 1971). Contrary to what one might expect, the British Army of the Rhine is not a big employer of British labour. Twenty-eight thousand out of the 30,000 civilians working in support of BAOR are local workers. The still large proportion of art occupations revealed by Table 11–1 presumably includes many entertainers for the British Forces. In the future, the typical industrial occupations (metal goods, electricity, food, etc.) will certainly further increase their share of the in-migration relative to art occupations.

As far as the colour composition of the migration is concerned, I have little doubt that Black Britons will be underrepresented— whether or not all those free of controls are finally covered by the free movement system or only those with patrial status. In the latter case the underrepresentation will be even more marked than in the former. It seems that the Black British are currently undergoing a period of stabilization rather than renewed mobility. Certainly, there are adventurous elements amongst the West Indian population in particular. There is of course also the general dissatisfaction of the coloured population with their status and prospects and those of their children. But at the same time the coloured population has put down roots, and it is unlikely that it will want

---

[8] According to the data on sector of employment (not reproduced here).

Table 11–1: Newly entering citizens of the UK and Colonies by occupation of engagement, in the *Federal Republic of Germany*, 1968–1970, in percentages.

	Agri-culture	Metal, electricity (engineering)	Textile, food and beverages	Unskilled manufacturing occupations	Con-struction	Trans-port	Hotel and restaurant	Art	Other (service)
1968	0.7	7.2	3.3	4.1	1.5	1.3	3.9	29.8	48.1
1969	0.6	14.4	3.4	4.7	1.4	1.7	3.0	20.7	49.7
1970	0.5	18.4	3.4	3.7	2.2	1.6	3.3	14.1	52.6

Source: *Erfahrungsbericht 1968, 1969, 1970* (1969, 1970, 1971).

to uproot itself again on a significant scale to leave a cultural context it has become accustomed to, to face the uncertainties of an entirely new and unknown cultural and political context where there are no sufficiently large and homogeneous ethnic communities to serve as a shell for the adjustment process (for Germany, see above p. 39). In the comparable case of French or Dutch West Indians, no significant on-migration to other EEC countries has been observed. It is not unlikely that a few Indian entrepreneurs or male Pakistani groups unadapted to the British situation might try their luck in Germany, but in neither case is it likely to result in an immediate large increase of the practically non-existent migration of Commonwealth citizens from Britain to Germany.

The future, then, looks different from the general expectation five or ten years ago. Instead of increased immigration of European workers, one must expect increased emigration of British workers. Instead of increased low-skilled working-class migration, one can foresee a greater participation of highly skilled middle-class migrants. In place of the assumed effects of an 'open door' policy, one finds that freedom of movement *enables* workers to take up opportunities while it does not—within the economic, social, and demographic framework of the EEC—*cause* an increase in migratory exhanges as such. The predicted large-scale British emigration to Germany also looks more likely to originate in a diversion of British emigration streams away from the Commonwealth rather than in an autonomous increase of migrations to the Continent. As far as the British side is concerned, one can only deplore the lack of understanding of the legal and political nature of the European Community, particularly as regards the notion of supremacy of Community law. One can foresee long and bitter political disputes about British compliance with Community decisions dressed up in theological arguments about the sovereignty of Parliament, common law, etc. But one has to acknowledge that ten or twelve years ago the notion of supremacy of Community law was laughed at by continental politicians and that it took years to filter through from the academic level via the Court of Justice in Luxembourg to the national courts of the Six and to become accepted by them and the politicians. As far as the continental members of the EEC are concerned, one cannot but congratulate them on the achievements in the sphere of intra-Community migrations. But one must at the same time sound a warning bell that all is not well when the Dutch Government prevents the West Indian section of its own citizens from participating in the EEC's free movement system and seeks to exclude the coloured section of the British population from it with arguments which, to British ears, have a familiar ring about them and are not based on a cool evaluation of the facts.

Appendix
UK Nationality, Freedom of Movement, and the Treaty of Brussels

When this book went to press, the Treaty of Accession was signed in Brussels and published shortly afterwards in Britain.[1] The 'Final Act', which was also signed on 22 January 1972 and forms part of the documents relating to the accession of the new member states, has two documents annexed to it which are directly related to the matter discussed in this book and which require a few comments.

The first of these is a 'Joint Declaration on the Free Movement of Workers' by the old and new member states and the President of the Council of the European Communities. It reads:

The enlargement of the Community could give rise to certain difficulties for the social situation in one or more Member States as regards the application of the provisions relating to the free movement of workers. The Member States declare that they reserve the right, should difficulties of that nature arise, to bring the matter before the institutions of the Community in order to obtain a solution to this problem in accordance with the provisions of the Treaties establishing the European Communities and the provisions adopted in application thereof.

The second is a 'Declaration by the Government of the United Kingdom of Great Britain and Northern Ireland on the Definition of the Term "Nationals" ' and reads:

At the time of the signature of the Treaty of Accession, the Government of the United Kingdom ... make the following Declaration: 'As to

---

[1] The full title runs as follows: 'Treaty concerning the Accession of the Kingdom of Denmark, Ireland, the Kingdom of Norway and the United Kingdom of Great Britain and Northern Ireland to the European Economic Community and the European Atomic Energy Community (with Final Act), Brussels, 22 January 1972' (London, HMSO, 1972) (Cmnd. 4862–1 and 4862–11).

the United Kingdom..., the terms "nationals", "nationals of Member States" or "nationals of Member States and overseas countries and territories" wherever used in the Treaty establishing the European Economic Community... or in any of the Community acts deriving from those Treaties, are to be understood to refer to:

  (a) persons who are citizens of the United Kingdom and Colonies or British subjects not possessing that citizenship or the citizenship of any other Commonwealth country or territory, who, in either case, have the right of abode in the United Kingdom and are therefore exempt from United Kingdom immigration control;

  (b) persons who are citizens of the United Kingdom and Colonies by birth or by registration or naturalisation in Gibraltar, or whose father was so born, registered or naturalised.'

To look at the nationality question first, one recognizes under point (a) Mr. G. Rippon's statement of November 1971 (cf. above p. 133 et seq.). Point (b), however, is new. Gibraltar—in British law a self-governing colony—is according to Community law a 'European territory for whose external relations a Member State is responsible' (Article 227[4] of the Treaty of Rome). All provisions of the Treaty of Rome therefore apply to Gibraltar. But Article 28 of the Treaty of Accession of 22 January 1972 exempts Gibraltar from some of the Community provisions though not from the free movement regime. As the patriality definition of the Immigration Act 1971 (or its truncated form under point (a) above) does not cover Gibraltarians of UK citizenship who have not been ordinarily resident in the UK for the last five years, it was obviously appropriate to specify that they also possess the right to free movement. Thus we have patrial British subjects with[2] and without[3] the right to free movement in the EEC and non-patrial British subjects with[4] and without[5] that right. And we have coloured citizens of the UK and Colonies who are legally settled in the UK without the right to freedom of movement[6] and white citizens of the UK and Colonies who have never settled in this country but possess this right.[7] The insidious distinctions are wholly consistent with an immigration policy which rightly bears the trade mark racialist.

2 Point (a) of Mr. Rippon's definition.
3 Commonwealth citizens under Articles 2 (1)(d) and 2 (2) of the Immigration Act 1971, e.g. Australians who renounced their citizenship of the UK and Colonies.
4 Gibraltarians of the definition under (b) above.
5 The majority of coloured Commonwealth citizens settled in this country.
6 UK passport-holders from East Africa who have not yet been in this country for five years.
7 Gibraltarians of the definition under (b) above.

The charge of racialism must also be levelled at the Joint Declaration. It is known that the Dutch Government purported that Black Britons 'would take advantage of' the free movement provisions and go to the Netherlands in great numbers, and these contentions were believed to be shared by the Germans (see above p. 132, especially note 1; and *The Times* of 15 Jan. 1972). This political pressure was finally formalized in this incredibly vague Joint Declaration which, although not visibly applicable to Black Britons, is in reality only directed against them—for no other reason than their colour and regardless of the fact that the majority of Black UK nationals will have been born and educated in the UK and will have worked and voted there.

Leaving aside the question of nationality, it must be questioned whether the Joint Declaration is commensurate with the Treaty of Rome and its derivative legislation. First of all, the Treaty of Accession is subordinate to the constitutive Treaty of Rome and its derivative legislation unless the 'Act concerning the Conditions of Accession and the Adjustments to the Treaties', which forms the main body of the Treaty of Accession, specifies otherwise.[8] The Annexes, Protocols, and Letters appended to this Act are an integral part of it (see Article 158)—but not the Joint Declaration or the unilateral declaration by HM Government on nationality. The latter two are annexed to the 'Final Act' (see Cmnd. 4862-I, pp. 111–14), which is not an integral part of the Act itself. The latter contains all the permanent adjustments to the Treaty of Rome and its derivative legislation (Articles 10 to 28 of the Act) as well as the transitional measures for the period of adaptation (Articles 31 to 138).[9] There is no section on the freedom of movement for workers as such. Consequently, the free movement system as described in this book remains in force unaltered. The Joint Declaration, of course, does not speak of permanent or transitional adjustments. So what status and effect has it? Does it comply with the existing free movement regime?

[8] Article 2 of the said Act states: 'From the date of accession, the provisions of the original Treaties and the acts adopted by the institutions of the Communities shall be binding on the new Member States and shall apply in those states under the conditions laid down in those Treaties and in this Act.' See also Articles 3, 4, 6, 149, and 152 of the Act.

[9] Article 133, for example, refers to the Annex which provides for the transitional exemption of Northern Ireland from the free movement system (see Cmnd. 4862-II, p. 154).

In my opinion the Joint Declaration infringes the free movement
system by opening up the possibility of taking completely discre-
tionary measures without reference to any criteria by which the
legitimacy of invoking such measures can be judged. *Free movement* is limited by the Treaty of Rome on the specific grounds of
public policy, public security, or public health (see Article 48,
above p. 4). The *vacancy clearance* system, though not the right
to free movement, may be temporarily suspended on the explicit
and circumscribed grounds of Article 20(1) of Regulation 1612/68
(see above pp. 17–18 for text), i.e. *when living standards and employment in a region or an occupation are seriously endangered*. The
reference to *certain difficulties for the social situation* in the Joint
Declaration seeks to add new, entirely vague, and arbitrary criteria
to the explicit provision currently in force in an unauthorized
manner. This means that measures taken under the Joint Declaration must be considered illegal and invalid—and may be challenged
through the Court of Justice in Luxembourg.

Moreover, the institutional procedure for a move with a view to
suspending the workings of the common labour market is left in the
dark. It seems that *any* member state, whether concerned or not,
could bring the matter 'before the institutions of the Community'.
It is not said, however, *which* institution is to be the addressee of
such a move—the Council, the Commission, the Court of Justice?
The further reference to obtaining 'a solution in accordance with
the provisions of the Treaties establishing the European Communities and the provisions adopted in application thereof' is not entirely
clear either. It could mean that a decision by whichever institution
takes that decision must be on the lines of Article 20 of Regulation
1612/68, that is, temporary and relating to the vacancy clearance
system only. Or it could refer to the institutional procedure contained in that article, that is, a decision by the Commission with
provision for an appeal to the Council. In that case, however, the
reference to 'the Treaties' would seem to be superfluous; for the
Treaty of Rome foresees no such procedure in Articles 48 and 49 and
carries only a general *economic* safeguard clause (Article 226) which
became inapplicable with the end of the transitional period in
1970; and the Treaty in Brussels carries no more than a general
safeguard clause (Article 135 of the Act) restricted to the *economic*
(not the social) situation for *new* member countries for the *transitional* period only. Prima facie it appears, then, that the reference is

either to the field of suspension or the institutional procedure (or both) established in Article 20 of Regulation 1612/68 and that it enlarges the area ('social situation') in which suspensions can be requested. The original provisions obviously did not meet the Dutch-German objections to an assumed influx of coloured citizens of the UK. The Joint Declaration gives the Netherlands and Germany and every other member country the assurance that measures could be taken, at least until challenged in Court, which are not authorized by the present free movement regime. One cannot help feeling, however, that this deliberately vague document hides a more specific agreement reached during the entry negotiations and read into the minutes of a meeting, which is kept secret for fear of contradicting too openly the existing system.

In effect, the Joint Declaration may never be invoked and its legality may therefore never be tested. The definition of a UK national in the Declaration by the British Government, on the other hand, might very well not survive the first year of Britain's membership of the EEC. Article 173(2) of the Treaty of Rome would seem to be applicable here, in the substance of the case if not in the letter of the law.[10] This provides for a personal complaint procedure to the Court of Justice in Luxembourg. It is usually to be instituted within two months of the publication of the measure being challenged, but this must surely be taken to mean two months after the Treaty of Accession enters into force on, presumably, 1 January 1973. However, the expiry of this two months' period would not mean that the British nationality definition is immune from legal scrutiny for ever. After 1 January 1973 any British subject resident in the UK free of controls but not defined as a UK national setting out to a continental member country in the search for work and finding himself refused work and residence on the grounds that he is not a national of a member country, could challenge such a decision in the local courts. Depending somewhat on the way the case is processed, the local court in question may request a ruling on the definition of UK nationality from the Court of Justice (see Article 177 of the Treaty of Rome; also Lagrange, 1971, pp. 313–24).

10 'Any natural or legal person may . . . institute proceedings against a decision addressed to that person or against a decision which, although in the form of a regulation or a decision directed to another person, is of direct and individual concern to the former.'

The possibility of challenging the nationality definition arises because, even though the term national, etc., is used repeatedly in Community law, it is not conclusively defined by Community law. Consequently, the Court of Justice is likely to see it as lying within its competence to adjudicate on the notion of nationality.[11] If it declares the case admissible, the chances of having Mr. Rippon's definition quashed would appear at least even. One could point to the fact that it is inconsistent and discriminatory that British subjects admitted for settlement in the UK free of residence or employment controls, who are as British subjects also in possession of British political rights (voting in local and general elections, standing in elections and for jury, etc.), should have infringed their economic right of selling their labour throughout what in future will be Britain's home labour market, i.e. the whole of the enlarged EEC. Generally, the progression is from inferior economic rights to superior political rights, and once political allegiance is established economic rights cannot rightfully be denied. This is certainly the practice of the continental member countries of the EEC (except for Dutch citizens from the West Indies)[12] and it would seem that the definition of UK nationality introduces an element of discrimination which runs counter to the most fundamental tenet of the Treaty of Rome.

[11] More specifically, one could argue along the lines of the Hoekstra Case (see Brinkhorst and Schermers, 1969, pp. 232 ff.), where the Court of Justice held that 'Articles 48 to 51 of the Treaty, in providing for the free movement of "workers", thereby lend this concept (of "worker") a Community meaning; were the meaning of this term to depend on national law, each member state would then be able to modify the concept of "migrant worker" and to arbitrarily exclude certain groups of persons from the protection of the Treaty; furthermore, nothing in the Treaty Articles 48 to 51 indicates that those provisions left the definition of the word "worker" to the provisions of national law'.

[12] The exclusion of the Dutch West Indians could be challenged on the same lines, and implicitly Article 42(3) of Regulation 1612/68 as well.

Bibliography

ABADAN, N. (1966)   'Studie über die Lage und die Probleme der türkischen Gastarbeiter in der Bundesrepublik Deutschland', in Europäische Schriften des Bildungswerks Europäische Politik, *Arbeitsplatz Europa*, Heft II. Cologne, pp. 102–24.

AGUIRRE, J. M., ed. (1968)   *Umfrage*, 2nd ed. Freiburg, Referat zur Spanierbetreuung beim Deutschen Caritasverband.

ALLEFRESDE, M. (1971)   'The Finnish immigration to Sweden and its consequences'. Paris. (Report to the OECD Manpower and Social Affairs Directorate.)

ALTARELLI, A. (1969)   *Die soziale Lage der innerhalb der Gemeinschaft zu—und abwandernden Arbeitnehmer und ihrer Familienangehörigen: Zusammenfassender Bericht über die verschiedenen Probleme, die aus der Sicht des Herkunftlandes geprüft wurden.* Brussels, Kommission der Europäischen Gemeinschaften. (14.846/V/69-D.)

AMERSFOORT, J. M. M. van (1968)   *Surinamers in de lage landen.* 's-Gravenhage, Staatsuitgeverij.

Amtliche nachrichten (various)   Nuremberg, Bundesanstalt für Arbeit.

Annuaire statistique de la France (various)   Paris, Institut National de la Statistique et des Études Économiques.

DER ASSOZIATIONSRAT (n.d.)   *Assoziation EWG—Türkei: Zusatzprotokoll, Finanzprotokoll, EGKS-Abkommen, Schlussakte, unterzeichnet am 23 November 1970 in Brüssel.* Brüssel.

BAGLEY, C. (1971a)   'Immigrant minorities in the Netherlands: integration and assimilation'. *International migration review*, Vol. 5, No. 1, pp. 18–35.

—— (1971b)   'Immigration and social policy in the Netherlands'. *New community*, Vol. 1, No. 1, pp. 25–8.

BARR, J. (1964)   'Napoli, Bedfordshire'. *New society*, 2 April 1964, pp. 7–10.

BAUCIC, I. (1971)   'The effects of emigration from Yugoslavia and the problems of returning emigrant workers'. Paris. (Report to the OECD Manpower and Social Affairs Directorate.)

BEEVER, R. C. (1969)   *Trade unions and free labour movement in the EEC*. London, Chatham House/PEP.

Bericht der Bundesregierung und Materialien zur Lage der Nation 1971 (1971)   Bundesminister für innerdeutsche Beziehungen, Bonn.

BERICHT DER STUDIENKOMMISSION FÜR DAS PROBLEM DER AUSLÄNDISCHEN ARBEITSKRÄFTE (1964)   *Das Problem der ausländischen Arbeitskräfte*. Bern, Bundesamt für Industrie, Gewerbe und Arbeit.

BLANDY, R. (1968)   ' "Brain-drains" in an integrating Europe'. *Contemporary education review*, Vol. 12, No. 2, pp. 180–93.

BMWI (1970)   Vorabdruck aus 'Die wirtschaftliche Lage in der Bundesrepublik Deutschland'. *Vierteljahresbericht*, III. Bonn.

BÖHNING, W. R. (1970a)   'Problems and prospects of labour migration upon Britain's entry into the EEC'. *Migration today*, No. 15, Autumn 1970, pp. 5–15.

——— (1970b)   'Britain, the EEC, and the free movement of labour'. *Race today*, Vol. 2, No. 11, pp. 400–2.

——— (1970c)   'Foreign workers in post-war Germany'. *The new atlantis*, Vol. 2, No. 1, pp. 12–38.

——— (1970d)   'The differential strength of demand and wage factors in intra-European labour mobility: with special reference to West Germany, 1957–1968'. *International migration*, Vol. VIII, No. 4, pp. 193–202.

——— (1971b)   'Britain, the EEC and labour migration'. *New community*, Vol. 1, No. 1, pp. 7–10.

——— (1971c)   'Immigrant workers in West Germany'. *New community*, Vol. 1, No. 1. pp. 21–4.

——— (1971d)   'The social and occupational apprenticeship of Mediterranean migrant workers in West Germany', in LIVI-BACCI, M., ed., *The demographic and social pattern of emigration from the southern European countries*. Firenze, Dipartimento Statistico Matematica.

——— and STEPHEN, DAVID (1971a)   *The EEC and the migration of workers: the EEC's system of free movement of labour and the implication of United Kingdom entry*. London, Runnymede Trust.

BOUSCAREN, A. T. (1969)   *European economic community migrations*. The Hague, Nijhoff.

BRINKHORST, L. J., and SCHERMERS, H. G. (1969)   *Juridical remedies in the European communities: a case book*. London, Stevens.

BROWN, E. D. (1963)   'Labour law and social security: harmonisation or co-existence?'. *Current legal problems*, Vol. 16, pp. 178–96.

BROWN, J. (1970)   *The un-melting pot: an English town and its immigrants*. London, Macmillan.

Bulletin of the European communities (various)   Commission of the European Communities, Brussels.

Bundesarbeitsblatt (various)   Bundesminister für Arbeit und Sozial-ordnung, Bonn.

CAMPBELL, A. (1971)   *Common Market law.* London and New York, Longmans and Oceana. (Supplement 2/71.)

CASTLES, S. (1970)   'Immigration and the Common Market'. *Venture,* Vol. 22, No. 6, pp. 11–16.

—— and CASTLES, G. (1971)   'Immigrant workers and class structure in France'. *Race,* Vol. XII, No. 3, pp. 329–35.

CENTRAAL BUREAU VOOR DE STATISTIEK, ed. (various) *Sociale maandstatistiek.* 's-Gravenhage.

CENTRAL STATISTICAL OFFICE, ed. (1970)   *Social trends,* No. 1. London, H.M.S.O.

—— (1971)   *Social trends,* No. 2. London, H.M.S.O.

—— (various)   *Annual abstract of statistics.* London, H.M.S.O.

—— (various)   *The Registrar General's quarterly return for England and Wales.* London, H.M.S.O.

CHADWICK-JONES, J. K. (1964)   'The acceptance and socialization of immigrant workers in the steel industry'. *Sociological review,* Vol. 12, No. 2, pp. 169–83.

COHEN, B. G., and JENNER, P. J. (1968)   'The employment of immigrants: a case study within the wool industry'. *Race,* Vol. X, No. 1, pp. 41–56.

COMMISSION OF THE EUROPEAN COMMUNITIES (1971) *Preliminary guidelines for a social policy program in the Community,* Supplement 2/71. Annex to the *Bulletin of the European Communities,* No. 4.

The Common Market and the common man: social policy and working and living conditions in the European Community (1971)   3rd ed. Brussels.

COX, R. W. (1963)   'Social and labour policy in the European Economic Community'. *Journal of industrial relations,* Vol. 1, No. 1, pp. 5–22.

DAHLBERG, K. A. (1968)   'The EEC Commission and the politics of the free movement of labour'. *Journal of Common Market studies,* Vol. 6, No. 4, pp. 310–33.

DANIELI, L. (1971)   'Labour scarcities and labour redundancies in Europe by 1980: an experimental study', in LIVI-BACCI, M., ed., *The demographic and social pattern of emigration from the southern European countries.* Firenze Dipartimento Statistico Matematica.

DANIELSON, R. (1970)   'Foreign workers in Norway'. *Migration news,* Vol. 19, No. 1, pp. 13–16.

DAVISON, R. B. (1963)   'Immigration and unemployment in the United Kingdom, 1955–1962'. *British journal of industrial relations,* Vol. 1, No. 1, pp. 43–61.

DELERM, R. (1964)   'La population noire en France'. *Population*, Vol. 19, No. 3, pp. 515–28.

DELGADO, J. M. (1966)   *Anpassungsprobleme der spanischen Gastarbeiter in Deutschland: Eine sozialpsychologische Untersuchung.* Ph.D. thesis for University of Cologne.

DÉPARTEMENT FÉDÉRAL DE L'ÉCONOMIE PUBLIQUE, ed. (various)   *La vie économique.* Bern, Département Fédéral de l'Économie Publique.

DEPARTMENT OF EMPLOYMENT (1971)   *The Employment of British workers in Germany.* London, H.M.S.O.

DEPARTMENT OF HEALTH AND SOCIAL SECURITY (1970) *Unemployment benefit.* London, H.M.S.O. (Leaflet NI12.)

DEUTSCHER STÄDTETAG (1964)   'Eingliederung ausländischer Arbeitskräfte—Rundfrage'. Cologne. (Abt. 4/44-49/pl R997.)

—— (1971)   *Hinweise zur Hilfe für ausländische Arbeitnehmer,* Sozialpolitische Schriften des Deutschen Städtetages, Nr. 6. Cologne.

DINTER, H.-J. (1969)   'Zum Tempo von Strukturwandlungen'. *Mitteilungen* (Institut für Arbeitsmarkt und Berufsforschung), Nr. 6, pp. 447–55.

DOSSER, D. (1971)   'Taxation', in PINDER, J. ed., *The economics of Europe: what the Common Market means for Britain.* London, C. Knight, pp. 185–211.

DOUBLET, J. (1965).   'Migrations in Europe'. *International social science journal,* Vol. XVII, pp. 284–96.

EIDGENÖSSISCHES STATISTISCHES AMT, ed. (various) *Statistisches Jahrbuch der Schweiz.* Basle, Birkhäuser.

EINZIG, P. (1971)   *The case against joining the Common Market.* London, etc., Macmillan.

Erfahrungsbericht: Ausländische Arbeitnehmer (various).   (Supplement to *Amtliche Nachrichten.*)

EUROPÄISCHE GEMEINSCHAFTEN (1970)   *Konferenz über Arbeitsmarktfragen, Entwurf eines Protokolls.* Brüssel. (1287/70 [CONFSOC 37].)

EUROPEAN COAL AND STEEL COMMUNITY (1957)   *Real incomes of workers in the Community.* Luxembourg.

FEATHER, V. (1971)   'Labour and Social Security'. *Into Europe: practical implications for British industry and commerce of joining the Common Market.* London, London Chamber of Commerce, pp. 53–7.

FELDSTEIN, H. S. (1967).   'A study of transaction and political integration: transnational labour flow within the European Economic Community'. *Journal of Common Market studies,* Vol. VI, No. 1, pp. 24–55.

FRIEDRICHS, G. (1969)   'Technischer Wandel und seine Auswirkungen auf Beschäftigung und Lohn', in ARNDT, H., ed., *Lohnpolitik und Einkommensverteilung.* Berlin, Duncker and Humblot, pp. 616–712.

GALLUP (1969) *Gallup political index*. London. (Report No. 116.)

HAAN, E. de (1969) *Die soziale Lage der innerhalb der Gemeinschaft zu- und abwandernden Arbeitnehmer und ihrer Familien: Zusammenfassender Bericht zum Thema Familienzusammenführung*. Brussels, Kommission der Europäischen Gemeinschaften. (14.996/V/69.)

HAGMANN, H.-M. (1971) 'Les pays d'immigration', in LIVI-BACCI, M., and HAGMANN, H.-M., eds., *Report on the demographic and social pattern of migrants in Europe, especially with regard to international migrations*. Strasbourg, Council of Europe. (CDE[71]T.IV.)

HEIDE, H. ter (1971) 'Labour migration from the Mediterranean area to the Benelux countries'. Strasbourg, Council of Europe (CDE[71]T.IV.)

HENTSCHEL, R. *et al.* (1968) 'Die Integration der ausländischen Arbeitnehmer in Köln, Tabellenband'. Cologne. (Mimeographed.)

HOGEBRINK, L. J. (1970) 'Opposition to government policy on migrant workers in the Netherlands'. *Migration today*, No. 15, Autumn 1970, pp. 16–24.

HOLLENBERG, W. A. (1965) 'Der Familienwohnungsbedarf ausländischer Arbeitnehmer'. *Bundesbaublatt*, Vol. 15, No. 5, pp. 218–22.

HOLLINGSWORTH, T. H. (1972) 'Emigration from the United Kingdom and the Republic of Ireland', in LIVI-BACCI, M., ed., *The demographic and social pattern of emigration from the southern European countries*. Firenze, Dipartimento Statistico Matematico.

HOME OFFICE (February 1971) *Immigration bill, draft immigration rules: control of entry*. London, H.M.S.O. (Cmnd. 4606.)

—— (March 1971) *Immigration bill, draft rules: control after entry*. London, H.M.S.O. (Cmnd. 4610.)

—— (July 1971) *The United Kingdom and the European communities*. London, H.M.S.O. (Cmnd. 4715.)

—— (various) *Commonwealth immigrants act, 1962: statistics*. London, H.M.S.O.

—— (various) *Statistics of persons acquiring citizenship of the United Kingdom and colonies*. London, H.M.S.O.

—— (various) *Statistics of persons entering and leaving the United Kingdom*. London, H.M.S.O.

HOUSE OF COMMONS/HOUSE OF LORDS (various) *Parliamentary Debates: Official Reports*. London, H.M.S.O.

INTERNATIONAL LABOUR ORGANISATION (various) *Year book of labour statistics*. Geneva.

JONES, J., and SMITH, A. (1970) *The economic impact of Commonwealth immigration*. London, Cambridge University Press, for National Institute of Economic and Social Research.

JOSLING, T. (1971) 'The agricultural burden: a reappraisal', in PINDER, J., ed., *The economics of Europe: what the Common Market means for Britain*. London, C. Knight, pp. 72–93.

Journal officiel des communautés Européennes (various).

KALDOR, N. (1971)　'The dynamic effects of the Common Market', in EVANS, D., ed., *Destiny or delusion: Britain and the Common Market*. London, Gollancz, pp. 59–91.

KARADIA, C. (1971)　'Cold comfort for Norway's Pakistanis'. *Race today*, Vol. 3, No. 10, pp. 344–5.

KASPER, W., and SCHMIDT, K. D. (1971)　'West German business cycles in the sixties'. *The times* (London and Cambridge Economic Bulletin), 21 July 1971, p. 19.

KLAUDER, W., and KÜHLEWIND, G. (1970)　'Projektion des Angebots an inländischen Arbeitskräften in der Bundesrepublik Deutschland für die Jahre 1973, 1975 und 1980'. *Mitteilungen aus der Arbeitsmarkt—und Berufsforschung*, Vol. 3, No. 1, pp. 10–32.

KOMMISSION, EUROPÄISCHE WIRTSHAFTSGEMEINSCHAFT (n.d.)　*Abkommen zur Gründung einer Assoziation zwischen der Europäischen Wirtschaftsgemeinschaft und Griechenland und Anhänge*. Brussels.

—— (n.d.)　*Abkommen zur Gründung einer Assoziation zwischen der Europäischen Wirtschaftsgemeinschaft und der Türkei und Anhänge*. Brussels.

KOMMISSION ... (1966a, 1967a, 1968a, 1969a, 1970a, 1971a)　*Die Freizügigkeit der Arbeitskräfte und die Arbeitsmärkte in der EWG— 1966; 1967; 1968; 1969; 1970; 1971*. Brussels.

KOMMISSION DER EUROPÄISCHEN GEMEINSCHAFTEN (1970b)　*Vergleichende Darstellung der Systeme der Sozialen Sicherheit in den Mitgliedstaaten der Europäischen Gemeinschaften: 1. Allgemeine Systeme*. 6th ed. Brussels.

LAGRANGE, M. (1971)　'The European court of justice and national courts: the theory of the acte clair: a bone of contention or a source of unity?'. *Common Market law review*, Vol. 8, No. 3, pp. 313–24.

LAMPERT, H. (1969)　'Bestimmungspründe und Lenkungsfunktion branchenmässiger und regionaler Lohnunterschiede', in ARNDT, H., ed., *Lohnpolitik und Einkommensverteilung*. Berlin, Duncker and Humblot, pp. 377–443.

LAYTON, C. (1971)　'The benefits of scale for industry', in PINDER, J., ed., *The economics of Europe: what the Common Market means for Britain*. London, C. Knight, pp. 46–71.

LIVI-BACCI, M. (1971)　'The countries of emigration', in LIVI-BACCI, M., and HAGMANN, H.-M., eds., *Report on the demographic and social pattern of migrants in Europe, especially with regard to international migrations*. Strasbourg, Council of Europe. (CDE[71]T.IV.)

LUTZ, V. (1963)　'Foreign workers and domestic wage levels, with an illustration from the Swiss case'. *Banca nazionale del lavoro quarterly review*, Vol. XVI, No. 64, pp. 3–68.

LYON-CAEN, G. (1967)—'La réserve de l'ordre public en matière de liberté d'établissement et de libre circulation'. *Revue trimestrielle de droit européene*, Vol. 2, No. 4, pp. 693–705.

MARPLAN, ed. (1970) 'Gastarbeiter in Deutschland: Ergebnisse zu Fragen der sozialen Situation'. Frankfurt/Main. (Mimeographed.)

MARSH, J. (1971) 'The changing structure of agriculture in the EEC', in PINDER, J., ed., *The economics of Europe: what the Common Market means for Britain*. London, C. Knight, pp. 94–116.

MAYER, K. B. (1965) 'Post-war migration to Switzerland'. *International migration*, Vol. 3, No. 3, pp. 122–37.

—— (1971) 'Foreign workers in Switzerland and Austria'. Strasbourg, Council of Europe. (CDE[71]T.IV.)

McDONALD, J. R. (1965) 'The repatriation of French Algerians'. *International migration*, Vol. 3, No. 3, pp. 146–57.

—— (1969) 'Labor immigration in France, 1946–1965'. *Annals of the association of American geographers*, Vol. 59, No. 1, pp. 116–34.

MEADE, J. E. (1970) *U K., Commonwealth and Common Market: a reappraisal*. London, Institute of Economic Affairs.

MEHRLÄNDER, U. (1969) *Beschäftigung ausländischer Arbeitnehmer in der Bundesrepublik Deutschland unter spezieller Berücksichtigung von Nordrhein-Westfalen*. Cologne and Opladen, Westdeutscher Verlag.

MERX, V. (1967) 'Ausländische Arbeitskräfte im Deutschen Reich und in der Bundesrepublik: Eine Gegenüberstellung'. *Wirtschaftspolitische chronik*, No. 1. pp. 65–91.

MILLER, M. H. (1971) 'Estimates of the static balance-of-payments and welfare costs compared', in PINDER, J., ed., *The economics of Europe: what the Common Market means for Britain*. London, C. Knight, pp. 117–51.

MINISTRY OF LABOUR/DEPARTMENT OF EMPLOYMENT AND PRODUCTIVITY/DEPARTMENT OF EMPLOYMENT (various) *Gazette*. London, H.M.S.O.

OECD (1970) *The growth of output, 1960–1980: retrospect, prospect and problems of policy*. Paris, OECD.

—— (1971) *Germany*. Paris, OECD. (Economic Surveys.)

OKUN, B. (1968) 'Interstate population migration and state income inequality: a simultaneous equation approach'. *Economic development and cultural change*, Vol. 16, No. 2, pp. 297–313.

PATTERSON, S. (1968) *Immigrants in industry*. London, Oxford University Press, for Institute of Race Relations.

PEACH, C. (1965) 'West Indian migration to Britain: the economic factors'. *Race*, Vol. 7, No. 1, pp. 31–46.

PRESLE, A. de la (1971) 'Immigrant and minority groups in France'. *New community*, Vol. 1, No. 1, pp. 16–20.

RAISON, T., and TAYLOR, H. (1966) 'Britain into Europe: do we want to join?'. *New society*, 23 June 1966, pp. 6–9.

Rapport annuel 1970 de l'inspecteur générale des affaires sociales (1971) Paris.

REINANS, S. (1971) 'Immigrants in Sweden'. Strasbourg, Council of Europe. (CDE[71]T.IV.)

ROCHCAU, G. (1968) 'The free movement of European workers and its limits'. *Migration news*, Vol. 17, No. 2, pp. 11–14.

ROCHE, T. W. E. (1969) *The key in the lock: a history of immigration control in England from 1066 to the present day*. London, Murray.

ROGERS, A. (1970) 'Migration and industrial development: the southern Italian experience'. *Economic geography*, Vol. 46, No. 2, pp. 111–35.

ROSE, A. M. (1969) *Migrants in Europe: problems of acceptance and adjustment*. Minneapolis, University of Minnesota Press.

Runnymede Trust (1970) 'The size of the coloured population in 1985'. London, Runnymede Trust. (Mimeographed.)

——(1971) *Immigration and settlement 1963–1970*. London, Runnymede Trust.

SAFILIOS-ROTHSCHILD, C. (1971) 'The relationship between fertility and women's social and economic condition in Greece', paper presented to the Second European Demographic Conference, Strasbourg.

SELECT COMMITTEE ON SCIENCE AND TECHNOLOGY (1971) *Population of the United Kingdom*. London, H.M.S.O.

SIMPSON, R. E. D. (1970) 'Birthrates: a five-year comparative study'. *Race today*, Vol. 2, No. 8, pp. 256–65.

Stafbureau statistiek (1971) Ministry of Culture, Recreation and Social Work. (Statistisch Cahier No. 11.)

STANDING, G. (1971) 'Hidden workless'. *New society*, 14 October 1971, pp. 6–9.

Statistiques du travail et de la sécurité sociale (various). Paris, Ministère du Travail et de la Sécurité Sociale.

STATISTISCHES AMT DER EUROPÄISCHEN GEMEIN-SCHAFTEN (1969) *Sozialstatistik: Jahrbuch 1968*. Luxemburg.

—— (1969a) *Sozialstatistik: Struktur und Verteilung der Löhne 1966 —Deutschland (B.R.)*. Luxemburg.

—— (1971) *Sozialstatistik 4–1970: Bevölkerung und Erwerbsbevölkerung 1970–1980*. Luxemburg.

STATISTISCHES BUNDESAMT (1966) *Bevölkerung und Kultur: Volks-und Berufszählung vom 6. Juni 1961, Heft 7, Ausländer*. Stuttgart and Mainz, Kohlhammer.

—— (various) *Statistisches Jahrbuch für die Bundesrepublik Deutschland*. Stuttgart and Mainz, Kohlhammer.

STEPHEN, D. (1970) *Immigration and race relations*. London, Fabian Society. (Fabian Research Series, 291.)

—— (1971a) 'The social consequences', in EVANS, D., ed., *Destiny or delusion: Britain and the Common Market*. London, Gollancz, pp. 122–38.

—— (1971b) 'Immigration: the challenge of the Common Market'. *Race today*, Vol. 3, No. 8, p. 254.

SWANN, D. (1970)   The economics of the Common Market. Harmondsworth, Penguin.

SWEDISH INSTITUTE (1970)   Immigration and immigration policy in Sweden. Stockholm, Swedish Institute. (Fact Sheets on Sweden.)

TANNAHILL, J. A. (1958)   European volunteer workers in Britain. Manchester, University of Manchester Press.

THOMPSON, J. (1970)   'The growth of population to the end of the century'. Social trends, No. 1, pp. 21–32.

TIMUR, S. (1971)   'Socio-economic determinants of differential fertility in Turkey', paper presented to the Second European Population Conference, Strasbourg.

The United Kingdom and the European Community (July 1971) London, H.M.S.O. (Cmnd. 4715.)

WEDEL J. (1970)   'Social security and economic integration—I : freedom of movement and the social protection of migrants; II : their interaction with special regard to social cost'. International labour review, Vol. 102, Nos. 5 and 6, pp. 455–74 and 591–614, respectively.

WENGER, J. de (1969)   Die soziale Lage der innerhalb der Gemeinschaft zu-und abwandernden Arbeitnehmer und ihrer Familienangehörigen: Die Anpassungsprobleme innerhalb der Gemeinschaft zu- und abwandernder Arbeitnehmer und ihrer Familienangehörigen. Brussels, Kommission der Europäischen Gemeinschaften. (21.711/V/69-D.)

WERNER, H. (1971)   'Angebot und Nachfrage an Arbeitskräften in den EWG-Ländern bis 1980'. Erlangen, Institut für Arbeitsmarkt—und Berufsforschung. (Mimeographed.)

WILLIAMSON, J. (1971)   'Trade and economic growth', in PINDER, J., ed., The economics of Europe: what the Common Market means for Britain. London, C. Knight, pp. 19–45.

YANNOPOULOS, G. N. (1969)   'Economic integration and labour movements', in DENTON, G. R., ed., Economic integration in Europe. London, Weidenfeld & Nicolson, pp. 220–45.

BIBLIOGRAPHY